Robert (Bob) Cleworth MPhil has compiled five books, one on Australian War Graves and Missing Australians, in addition to three publications on the work of RAAF Catalina Operations in World War II. He was, for a number of years, Secretary of the Catalina Association of New South Wales.

John Suter Linton has worked extensively in the print and electronic media as a journalist, feature writer, researcher, scriptwriter, editor and producer. He is also the author of six true-crime novels.

ROBERT CLEWORTH and JOHN SUTER LINTON

RAAF BLACK CATS

The secret history of the covert Catalina mine-laying operations to cripple Japan's war machine

ALLEN&UNWIN
SYDNEY • MELBOURNE • AUCKLAND • LONDON

First published in 2019

Allen & Unwin
83 Alexander Street
Crows Nest NSW 2065
Australia
Phone: (61 2) 8425 0100
Email: info@allenandunwin.com
Web: www.allenandunwin.com

A catalogue record for this book is available from the National Library of Australia

ISBN 978 1 76063 306 6

Maps by MAPgraphics
Index by Puddingburn
Set in 11.5/17 pt Minion by Midland Typesetters, Australia
Printed and bound in Australia by Pegasus Media & Logistics

15 14

MIX
Paper | Supporting responsible forestry
FSC® C008194

The paper in this book is FSC® certified. FSC® promotes environmentally responsible, socially beneficial and economically viable management of the world's forests.

EU Authorised Representative: Easy Access System Europe, Mustamäe tee 50, 10621 Tallinn, Estonia, gpsr.requests@easproject.com

CONTENTS

'[T]he slow frail RAAF Catalinas, designed for anti-submarine patrols, assumed the mantle of Australia's very long-range bombing and mine laying force. They were the first to bomb Japanese installations after the downward thrust to New Guinea; they were the first to mine Japanese occupied ports, from the Netherlands East Indies to the China Coast; they were first in and last out in the evacuation of our prisoners-of-war on the cessation of hostilities . . . Mention World War II air power to the current generation and its thoughts may turn to the heroic Spitfires and Lancasters. Mention of the word Catalina in this context, even coupled with the details of the tragic loss of well over 300 of their aircrew, may draw only an uncomprehending stare.'

The late Sir Richard Kingsland AO, CBE, DFC,
former RAAF Commanding Officer of 11 Squadron

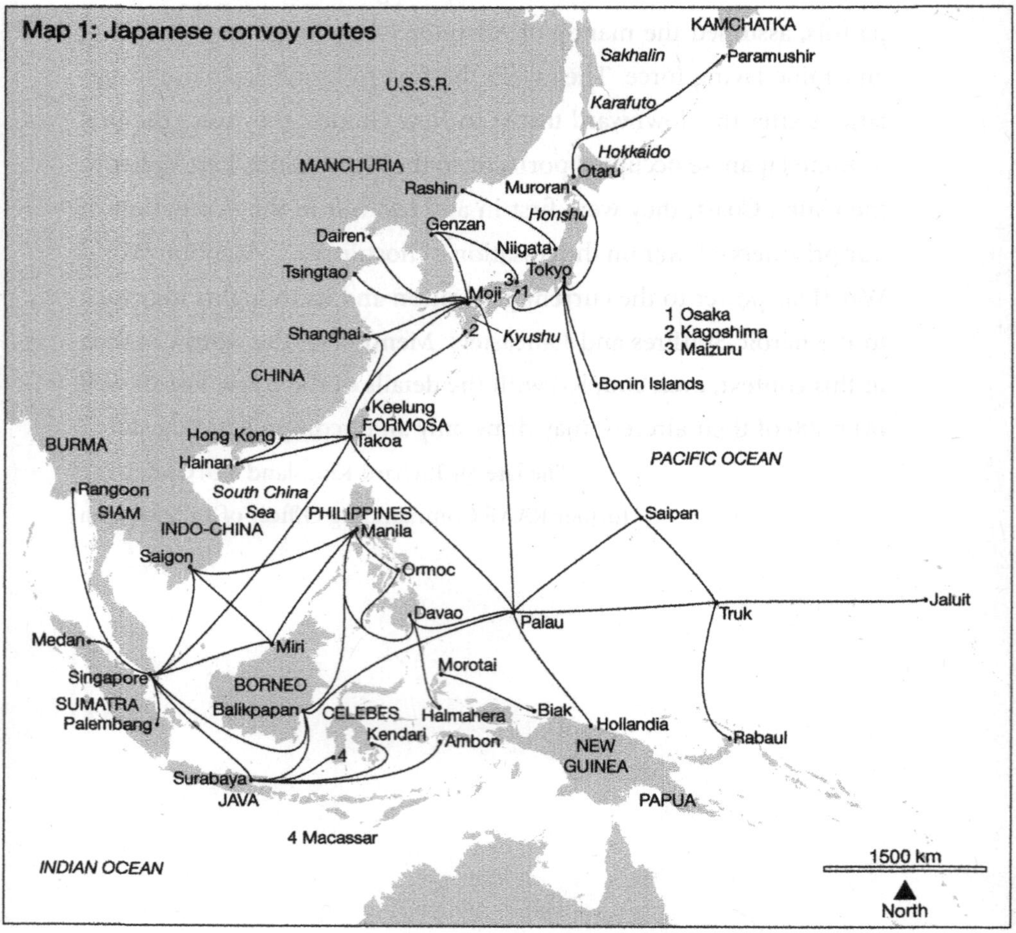
Map 1: Japanese convoy routes
KAMCHATKA
Sakhalin
Paramushir
U.S.S.R.
Karafuto
Hokkaido
MANCHURIA
Otaru
Rashin
Muroran
Honshu
Genzan
Dairen
Niigata
Tsingtao
Tokyo
Moji
1 Osaka
2 Kagoshima
3 Maizuru
Shanghai
Kyushu
CHINA
Bonin Islands
Keelung
FORMOSA
Hong Kong
Takoa
BURMA
Hainan
PACIFIC OCEAN
Rangoon
South China Sea
SIAM
PHILIPPINES
Manila
Saipan
INDO-CHINA
Saigon
Ormoc
Davao
Palau
Truk
Jaluit
Medan
Miri
Morotai
Singapore
BORNEO
SUMATRA
Balikpapan
CELEBES
Halmahera
Biak
Palembang
Hollandia
Kendari
Ambon
Rabaul
NEW GUINEA
Surabaya
JAVA
PAPUA
4 Macassar
INDIAN OCEAN
1500 km
North

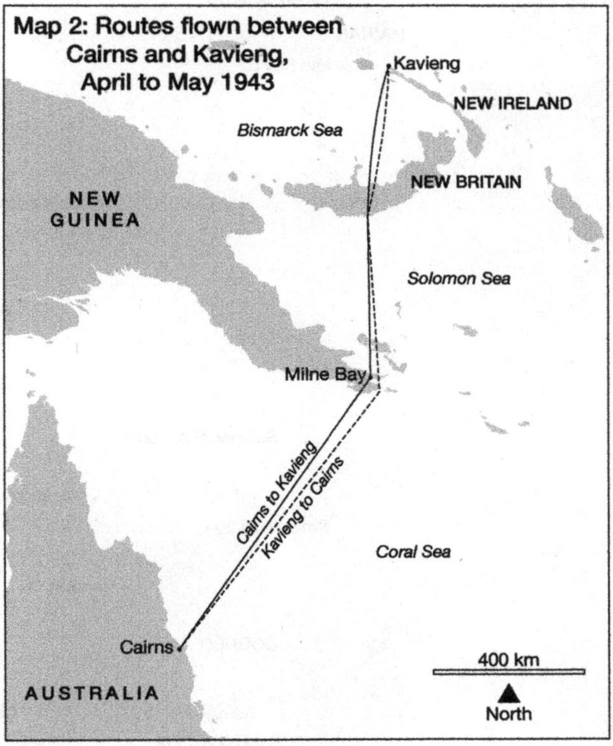
Map 2: Routes flown between
Cairns and Kavieng,
April to May 1943
Kavieng
NEW IRELAND
Bismarck Sea
NEW BRITAIN
NEW
GUINEA
Solomon Sea
Milne Bay
Cairns to Kavieng
Kavieng to Cairns
Coral Sea
Cairns
400 km
AUSTRALIA
North

Wenzhou 8
CHINA
Amoy 114
FORMOSA
Swatow 31
Makung 10
Takao 18
Hong Kong 152
Hainan Strait 131
HAINAN
Yulinkan Bay 52
THAILAND
Manila Bay 54
PHILIPPINES
Balabac Strait 60
Sandakan 12
MALAYA
Brunei Bay 20
Tarakan 30
Banka Strait 28
Lembeh Strait 4
BORNEO
Kau Bay 62
SUMATRA
Samarinda 12
CELEBES
Vesuvius Bay 8
Balikpapan 118
Bangka Strait 117
Kendari 44
Laut Strait 209
Parepare 14
Wowoni Strait 24
Cape Selatan 28
Tioro Strait 76
Macassar 142
Buton Strait 42
Tana Keke Strait 43
Baubau 4
JAVA
Surabaya 399
Malosoro 15
Laikang Bay 8
Cape Bulu Bulu 12
Pomalaa 51
Kolaka 12
Pasuruan 8
Probolinggo 8
Bima 8
Panarukan 10
Waingapu 4

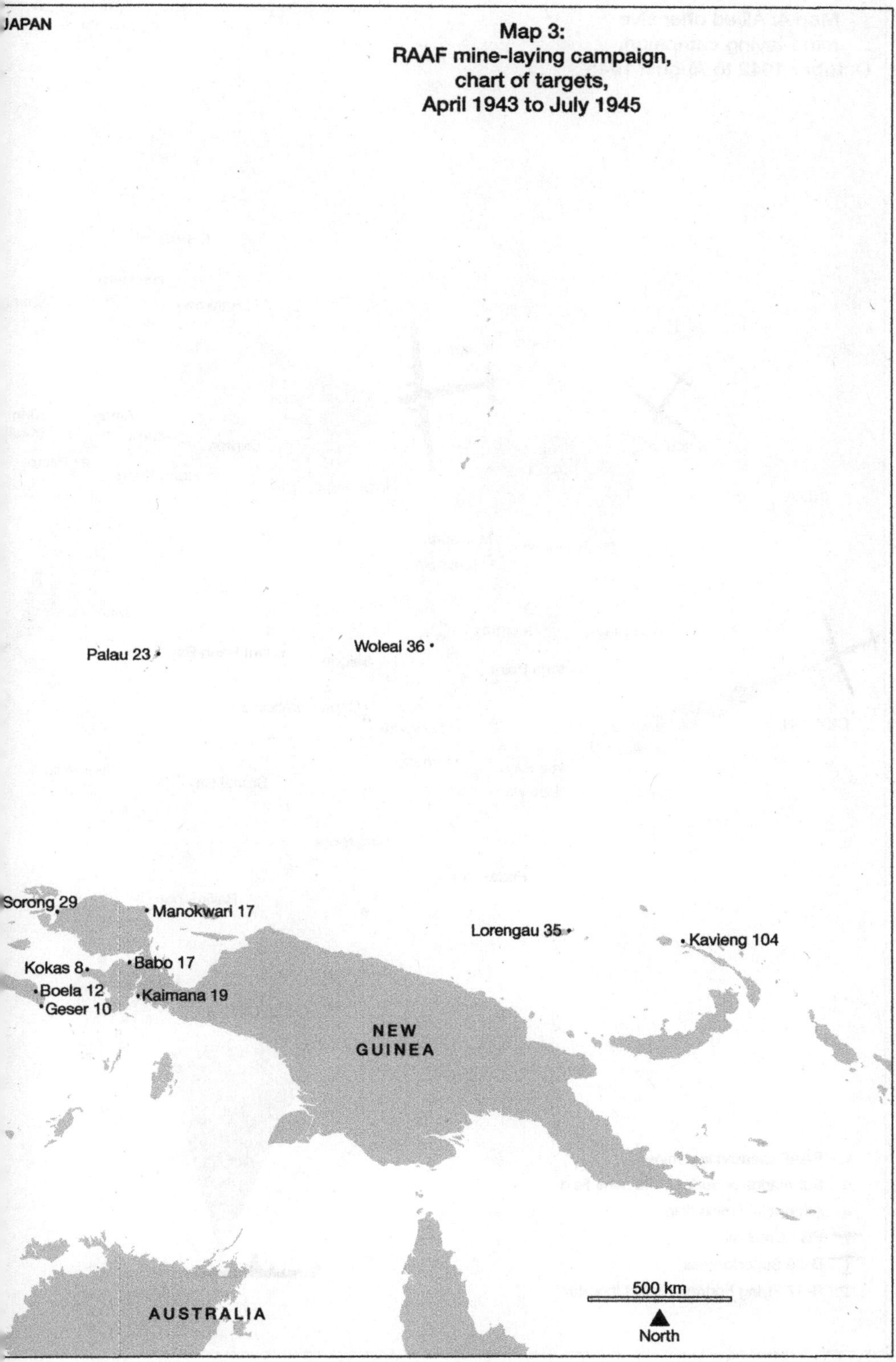
JAPAN
Map 3:
RAAF mine-laying campaign,
chart of targets,
April 1943 to July 1945
Palau 23
Woleai 36
Sorong 29
Manokwari 17
Lorengau 35
Kavieng 104
Kokas 8
Babo 17
Boela 12
Kaimana 19
Geser 10
NEW GUINEA
AUSTRALIA
500 km
North

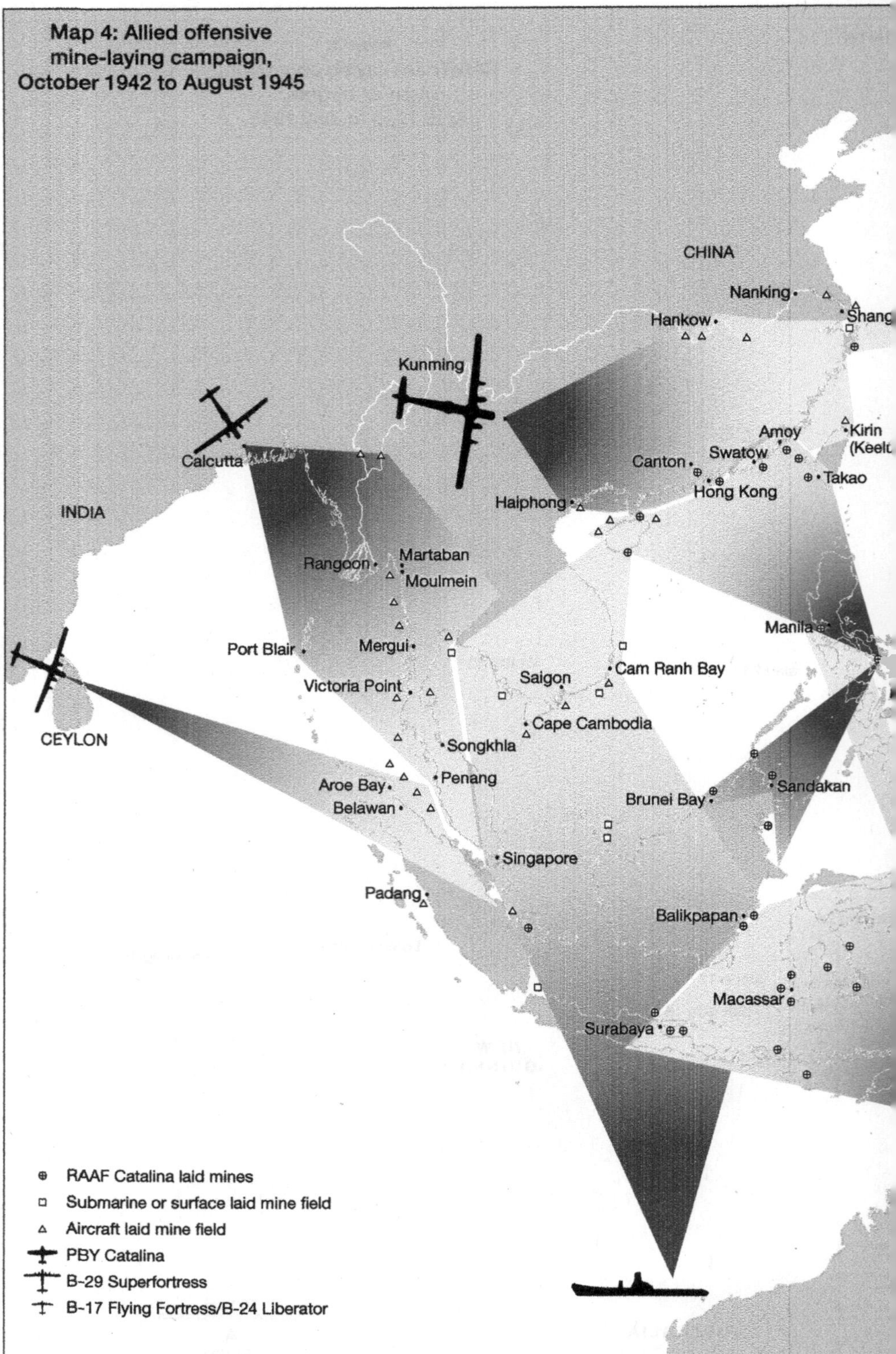
Map 4: Allied offensive mine-laying campaign, October 1942 to August 1945
CHINA
Nanking
Hankow
Shang
Kunming
Calcutta
INDIA
Amoy
Kirin
(Keelu
Swatow
Canton
Takao
Hong Kong
Haiphong
Martaban
Rangoon
Moulmein
Manila
Port Blair
Mergui
Cam Ranh Bay
Saigon
Victoria Point
Cape Cambodia
CEYLON
Songkhla
Aroe Bay
Penang
Sandakan
Brunei Bay
Belawan
Singapore
Padang
Balikpapan
Macassar
Surabaya
RAAF Catalina laid mines
Submarine or surface laid mine field
Aircraft laid mine field
PBY Catalina
B-29 Superfortress
B-17 Flying Fortress/B-24 Liberator

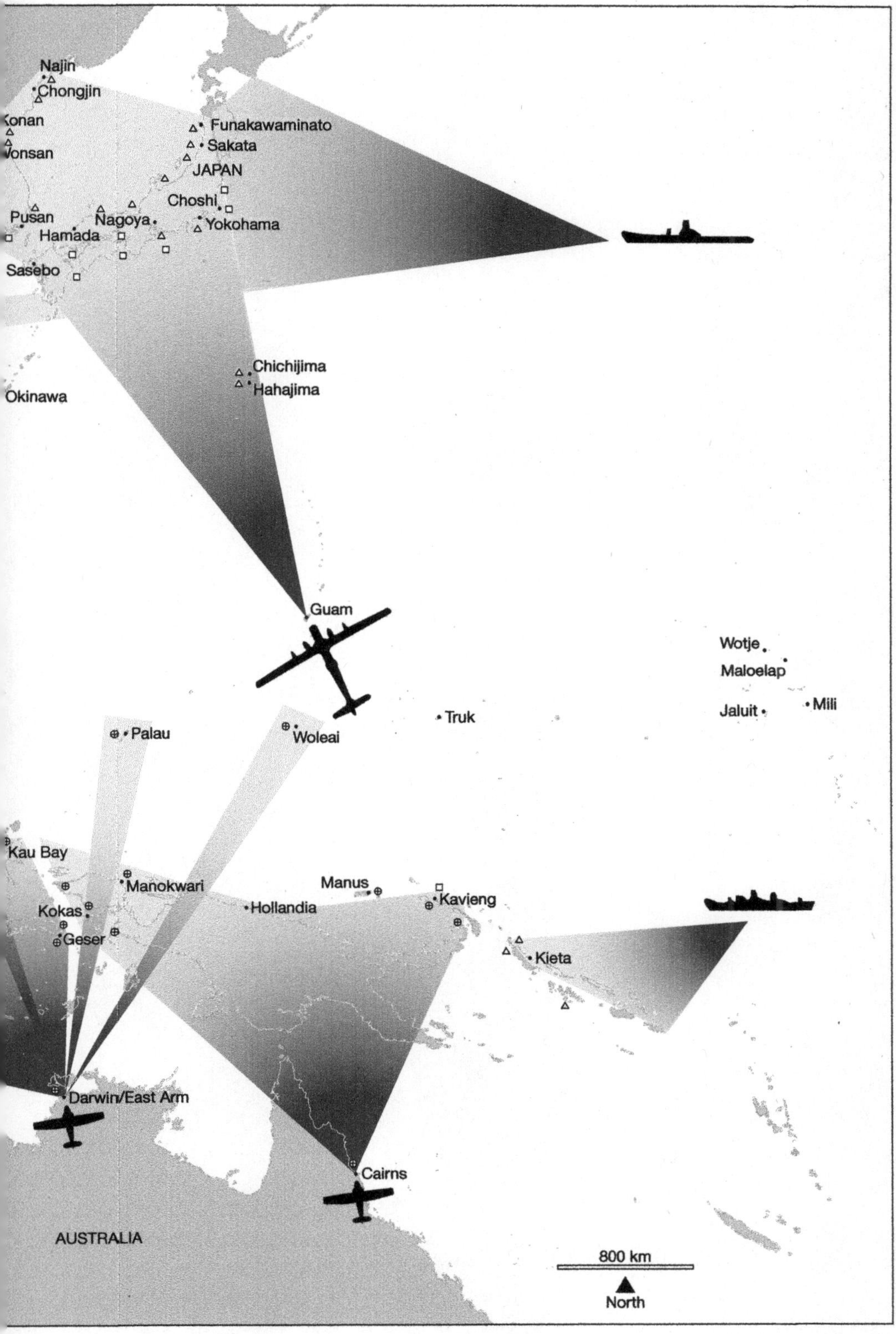

Najin
Chongjin
Konan
Wonsan
Funakawaminato
Sakata
JAPAN
Choshi
Pusan
Nagoya
Yokohama
Hamada
Sasebo
Chichijima
Hahajima
Okinawa
Guam
Wotje
Maloelap
Jaluit
Mili
Truk
Palau
Woleai
Kau Bay
Manokwari
Manus
Kavieng
Hollandia
Kokas
Geser
Kieta
Darwin/East Arm
Cairns
AUSTRALIA
800 km
North

PREFACE

On a warm day in December 1944, a young Royal Australian Air Force (RAAF) warrant officer (WOFF) named James Reginald Cleworth—known as Reg—was en route to collect a new aircraft. He happened to be enjoying some free time in Melbourne when a street photographer snapped his picture outside the General Post Office. Reg stared into the camera, giving nothing away. No smile, no frown, no hint of his thoughts, his experience, his hopes or fears. It was common for people to take photos of servicemen and women at the time to supplement their income, hoping their families would buy a copy. Reg's mother, Janet, obliged.

A navigator with 20 Squadron, flying PBYs—more commonly referred to as Catalina flying boats—Reg had been assigned to collect a new Catalina, A24-203, from the RAAF Flying Boat Repair Depot at Lake Boga, near Swan Hill, just over 300 kilometres north-west of Melbourne. The aircraft, however, was not ready, and this gave Reg some time to visit his family, who lived in Black Rock, an outer southern suburb of Melbourne. Being stationed in Darwin, almost 4000 kilometres away, it wasn't easy for Reg to get home when given leave. His stay this time would be brief, unfortunately, as he needed to journey back to base before Christmas Day.

Born in 1922, Reg was the second-eldest of four children to James Raymond and Janet Cleworth. His siblings were Dorothy (born in 1919), Nancy (1928) and younger brother Joseph Robert (1934), known as Bob to his family. As Bob remembered, 'Reg was the apple of our mum's eye . . . he could do no wrong.'

When war broke out in 1939, James knew that his son would want to join the fight. He didn't stop him, but James did warn Reg not to enlist in the army. The horrors of World War I were still fresh in James's mind, and he didn't want his son going through what he had suffered.

James had served in the 29th Australian Infantry Battalion, 5th Division, Australian Imperial Force (AIF), from 1916 to 1918, and he had vivid memories of the shock of trench warfare and gas attacks. He was seriously wounded in March 1918, near Messines Ridge, during a raid to gather intelligence on the enemy's strength. The only thing James remembered of the incident was that he 'went into Belgium and woke up in France . . . in excruciating pain'.

James screamed as he regained consciousness, and a matron stuck a piece of leather into his mouth, telling him, 'Bite down on that and stop your complaining . . . there are worse off than you.' Even so, shrapnel had lodged in his leg, creating a wound as big as a fist. Mud and debris had been forced into the wound by the shards of metal, causing an infection. The wound was irrigated, but James was still weak. The doctors thought he would die.

The AIF notified Janet, whom James had married while stationed in England in 1916, and paid for her travel expenses to be at James's side. James credited seeing his wife walk into the ward as the reason he decided that he wasn't going to die. He didn't want to leave her. He eventually recovered enough to be shipped to England, where he recuperated. That was the end of the war for James.

When Reg came of enlistment age in 1940, he decided to heed his father's advice. Initially, Reg wanted to join the Royal Australian Navy (RAN), but then chose the RAAF. He trained as an observer, passing his exams and earning a wing with an embossed 'O'. Later in the war, the RAAF redesignated 'observer' to 'navigator', changing the 'O' to an 'N'. Like many who had earned the original designation, Reg would continue wearing his 'O' wing proudly. It signified his experience in the RAAF and was, quite literally, a badge of honour.

Signing up to the RAAF proved just as dangerous as James's time in the army. Reg was sent on missions that took him far behind enemy lines. It might not have been a soggy trench, but the risk to his life was just as real. This was something that Reg kept from his family.

During training and when given his postings, Reg regularly wrote home. Nearly all the letters were addressed to his mother, but they were for the whole family to let them know he was okay. He wrote of mundane activities such as washing, darning socks, watching tropical thunderstorms and spending money on milkshakes. Movies provided the main source of entertainment. More often than not they were American, and usually came with a cartoon, which interested and amused Reg more than some of the features. With the exception of one letter he addressed to his father, Reg never wrote about his operations, close encounters with the enemy, or anything considered top secret. The closest he came to this was a reference to having 'had a long flight', and explaining that he had slept for most of the day after returning.

When Reg visited his family in December 1944, he and Bob had a quiet moment together. The curious ten-year-old asked Reg what he planned to do after the war. Bob was surprised when Reg dropped his stoic facade and said, 'I don't think I'm coming back.' There was silence as each reflected on what had been said. Bob kept Reg's confidence, never telling anyone of their short conversation, especially his mother. Reg's words, however, would remain with Bob for the rest of his life.

On 11 March 1945, an urgent telegram arrived, addressed to Mr J.R. Cleworth. It read:

> 419459 WARRANT OFFICER J R CLEWORTH MISSING STOP REGRET TO INFORM YOU THAT YOUR SON WARRANT OFFICER JAMES REGINALD CLEWORTH IS MISSING AS RESULT AIR OPERATIONS ON 7TH MARCH 1945 STOP KNOWN DETAILS ARE HE WAS MEMBER OF CREW CATALINA AIRCRAFT DETAILED FOR OPERATIONAL FLIGHT IN NORTHERN OPERATIONAL AREA WHICH FAILED TO RETURN TO BASE . . . WHEN ANY FURTHER INFORMATION IS RECEIVED IT WILL BE CONVEYED TO YOU IMMEDIATELY.

Bob, resting in his bedroom, heard his mother let out a loud cry of anguish. While the telegram didn't say that Reg had been killed, his father, knowing war all too well, quietly told Bob that he didn't think his brother would return. He also warned Bob, 'but don't tell your mother I said that'.

During this time, many families feared for the loss of their son, brother or husband, but hoped for their return. Any hope Janet had of Reg being found hiding among the forests of a tropical island or being repatriated from a prisoner-of-war (POW) camp was dashed when, in 1947, Reg was officially classified as deceased. More precisely, in a letter that arrived at the Cleworth home dated 3 April:

> MISSING PRESUMED DEAD.

Naturally, the family was devastated. Reg's mother carried her grief for the remainder of her life. His father, a superintendent at the local Methodist Sunday school, lost his faith. Bob vividly recalled his father telling him, 'I had my doubts in World War I . . . now your brother's gone, there is no God . . . it's all a lot of load of hooey [rubbish].'

The Black Rock Cricket Club, where Reg had played, named its building The J R Cleworth Pavilion in honour of Reg's popularity, contribution and sportsmanship. It remained so for some years until the grounds were taken over by a baseball club. As Bob noted, 'that's how history goes'.

No details were ever given about Reg's incident. Where and why he was flying, and the reason his aircraft went down, were not forthcoming. Bob was always curious about what his brother did during the war, though he respected his mother's grief and didn't delve too much into the subject. He was busy himself, starting his apprenticeship to become a marine engineer at the age of fourteen and, five years later, earning his qualifications and going to sea. Unbeknown to Bob at the time, he sailed around the south-west Pacific, visiting and working in the same areas in which his brother had flown operations. Bob married and shifted careers, gaining a law degree and a master's in modern history while teaching law at Macquarie University. His interest in World War I led Bob to become one of the first tour guides to take people to Gallipoli and Western Front locations in Belgium and France. He also led tours as a historian for Returned and Services League (RSL) Travel.

It wasn't until after his mother, Janet, passed away in 1986 that Bob felt he could investigate Reg's service career. In her final days, Janet had a fall and was admitted to the Royal North Shore Hospital. After her passing, Bob and his family went to collect his mother's belongings. A nurse asked Bob if he had a brother who was killed in the war. She revealed that she and other staff would hear Janet speaking with Reg, right up until her last day. Reg's death had affected Janet more deeply than anyone had realised.

Janet had kept all the letters Reg had sent, from his early training days in 1943 to his last on 28 February 1945. In that final letter, Reg wrote:

> Dear Mother,
>
> Haven't much news for you this time, but thought I'd drop you a line + let you known [sic] I was OK. Don't be surprised if you don't get any letters for a while. There will be a delay in them for a while I think.

Bob began piecing together titbits of information to uncover the truth about what his brother and other RAAF Catalina servicemen did during the war. His research led him to meet a number of veterans, pilots, crewmen and service personnel who were members of the Catalina Association. Most spoke generally of their time during the war, but a few opened up about being involved in 'secret mine-laying operations' in partnership with the US Navy—specifically the US Navy Seventh Fleet, also known as MacArthur's Navy. Bob learned that the RAAF had imposed restrictions on what the veterans could reveal about their wartime operations. Should they mention anything about the mine-laying operations, they would face legal repercussions. In 1945, the RAAF and the Australian Government decided to keep secret the development of the mines and how they were used operationally. Although the war was over, there was no knowing when or if the weapons and strategy would be needed again. Thus, all returning crews and support personnel were sworn to strict silence. More importantly, Bob discovered that Reg's 20 Squadron was one of four involved in laying mines throughout the south-west Pacific. Now he knew what his brother was doing during the war.

The more Bob met and spoke with the former Catalina crews, the better his appreciation and understanding became of the tasks and risks they undertook. He decided that he would chronicle their experiences, as much as they were willing to tell. As Bob remembered, 'interviewing Catalina veterans when they are together is a most enjoyable experience. I found it useful to have a tape recorder at the ready to catch the unexpected recollection.'

By the late 1980s, it wasn't unusual for former crew members to have written about their experiences, though most only mentioned the mine-laying operations in passing, if at all. One book, however, stood out for Bob. *The Cat Has Nine Lives* was written by former Catalina pilot Fred Robins, and featured a photo of Robins with Reg. As it happened, Reg had been Robins' navigator when they crewed a twin-engine Avro Anson, performing convoy escort in Bass Strait during 1943. The photo had been taken by the RAAF to be used for publicity purposes.

Bob was quick to make contact with Robins, who was generous in his praise for his former navigator and explained that Reg was also a good friend. They had flown together in 67 Squadron before volunteering for the Catalinas. Once they'd completed their training at Rathmines in New South Wales, Robins and Reg had been assigned to different squadrons, 43 and 20, respectively. Talking with Bob, Robins candidly admitted 'it would be a gross misstatement to say that I enjoyed mine laying, because there was always the possibility of being shot up by ships in the harbours, and flying in low at 100 or 200 feet in complete darkness was, to say the least, very dangerous'.

Bob found that there was very little in any contemporary history texts about the RAAF/US Navy mine-laying operations, let alone any reference to its success. The National Archives of Australia and relevant RAAF squadron archives also fell short on providing details and answers. Then Bob came across a 1978 book by author and historian David Vincent. *Catalina Chronicle* related anecdotes of former crew members, including some mentions of mine laying. Bob contacted Vincent and, from this meeting, Vincent introduced Bob to Ivor Collins, formerly a lieutenant in the US Navy Reserve. A mine expert who was stationed in Australia during the war, Collins worked with the RAAF for 22 months as part of the aerial mine-laying team. Vincent had, some years earlier, corresponded with Collins to record his experiences and gather information on the technical data of the mines and the work of mine officers, so he allowed Bob to view the various letters Collins had written about his time working with the RAAF.

Over time, the veterans became more relaxed with Bob and, because of Reg, accepted him as one of their own. They now began relating more details of their mine-laying experiences. Realising there was a 'huge omission' in the history books, Bob wanted to know more about the RAAF/US Navy mine-laying coalition: how it started and why, what the objectives were and how successful the strategy was. Bob soon discovered the evidence he sought was located in the National Archives and Records Administration (NARA) in Maryland, not far from Washington, DC. Between late 1945 and early 1946, all documentation about mine laying was shipped to the United States, as it was the property of the US Navy Seventh Fleet.

In February 2003, Bob took a sabbatical from Macquarie University to visit Ivor Collins at his home in North Carolina, and NARA in Maryland. Bob fondly recalled meeting Collins for the first time: 'He was an unassuming person and very proud of his association with the RAAF/US Navy mine-laying campaign. In fact, [because of] the stint he did with the RAAF, Ivor told me he didn't know if he was an Aussie or a Yank at times . . . Like many who served in World War II, he was a citizen soldier with a father who served in the Great War . . . It was a delight to know Ivor and [his wife] Shirley.'

Collins shared a lot of technical information about the program, and anecdotes from his time in Brisbane and Cairns. In later years, Bob would return to visit Collins, and Collins would visit Australia. They would take time out to travel to locations in Australia and the south-west Pacific region where the RAAF operated. Collins wanted to see and talk about how much the landscape had changed, while Bob listened and learned what it was like all those years before. They shared many conversations over the phone and via email but, as Bob remembered, 'the best exchanges were over Ivor's favourite Scotch'.

After visiting Collins in 2003, Bob set off for NARA, hoping to find flight logs and action reports giving the dates, locations and details of each mission. The staff members were helpful, but a lot of the material he requested was unavailable. He was shown some documents from the period that had been catalogued; however, they weren't what he was after.

Frustrated, Bob boarded the last bus back to his accommodation in Washington, DC, before a predicted big snow dump. With the first snowflakes falling, Bob took his seat, wondering if he would ever find what he was seeking. Just as the bus was about to set off, a man ran from the archives building and jumped on board. The slightly dishevelled man sat next to Bob, who commented, 'You just made that.' Bob's accent caught the man's ear, and they began talking. The conversation turned to Bob's reason for being at NARA. The man appreciated Bob's frustration and told him, 'Ask for me when you come back tomorrow . . . I think I can help you.'

It turned out the man was NARA's Chief Archivist, Steven Schafer. He explained that not all the archive boxes from the Seventh Fleet had been sorted. Some hadn't even been opened since their arrival in late 1945 or early 1946. Schafer was more than happy for Bob to go through them; however, there was a condition. Half-jokingly, Schafer told Bob he could do so, provided 'you catalogue the contents as you go'. It was a mammoth task.

Over two weeks, while staying with a friend of Bob's sister, Brenda Rosa, at Twinbrook, close to NARA, Bob sorted through the pile of archival boxes, going through document after document. Some of the boxes had cigarette butts, food wrappings and empty beer bottles among the 'top secret' communications. At least the sailors who packed the boxes had also decided to send their rubbish home. Bob wasn't alone in going through the material. Schafer had 'loaned' Bob a staff member to help, Barry Zerby. The two men cross-referenced the documents to match dates, information and code names to specific locations. Unfortunately, some documents were incomplete, while it appeared some were missing. Even so, the information they unearthed revealed the sacrifice and achievements of the RAAF Catalina crews, as well as the vital role they played in General Douglas MacArthur's strategic plan for the south-west Pacific campaign.

Between 22 April 1943 and 1 July 1945, the crews of the RAAF's Catalina 11, 20, 42 and 43 Squadrons conducted covert mine-laying operations in the south and south-west Pacific to disrupt Japanese naval movements, supplies and military operations, and to help block merchant vessels from delivering raw materials to Japan. Commander-in-Chief of the US Pacific Fleet Admiral Chester W. Nimitz and General Douglas MacArthur understood mine laying would be an effective strategic weapon to stop the Japanese from supplying their forces and feeding their war machine; it would, therefore, soften up the enemy for eventual US Army and Marine landings. They were proved right.

Bob also discovered that during MacArthur's campaign to regain the Philippines, he had employed the Catalina squadrons to thwart Imperial Japanese Navy attempts to supply their troops and attack the Seventh Fleet's amphibious forces. The operations were successful in protecting the Seventh Fleet at Leyte Gulf and paving the way for MacArthur to liberate the Philippine capital, Manila. Admiral Nimitz used the RAAF Catalinas to lay mines as a tactical manoeuvre, bottling up Japanese Navy and merchant ships in harbours, or preventing their access to safe waters, ensuring that the vessels were sitting ducks for Allied submarine and air attacks.

Bob would also learn neither the Australians nor the Americans led the secret operations; rather, they were a true coalition between the two countries, between the RAAF and the US Navy Seventh Fleet. Each brought its own expertise, and they worked together on strategies to hamper Japanese supply routes.

Despite the 30-year rule for the release of classified information, operations remained secret for over 60 years. In addition to former crews being restricted in what they could say—and the fact the documents were held by the US Navy—earlier historians tended to concentrate on the more spectacular RAAF contributions in Europe during World War II. Therefore, the work of the RAAF Catalinas in coalition with the US Navy became absorbed into the US records as 'Allied' actions. Similar treatment had been given to Australian, New Zealand and Canadian achievements in World War I.

There is no doubt Bob's research in 2003 revealed a little known yet crucial and courageous chapter in Australia's air-war history. And, in memory of Warrant Officer Reg Cleworth and all those who were part of the RAAF/US Navy mine-laying coalition, this story needs to be told.

1

GERMANY FIRST AND 'LIMITED OFFENSIVE' IN THE PACIFIC

1941 TO 1942

The Pacific War started when Japan attacked the US naval base at Pearl Harbor on 7 December 1941. Well before then, Japan's entry into World War II appeared inevitable. It had already signed a pact with the Axis powers, Germany and Italy, and, after invading China in 1937, it had moved against French Indochina (today's Vietnam) in 1940 to close the route by which the United States was supplying China. The United States and Britain protested, seizing Japan's assets, depriving the country of copper, iron and other essential raw materials, and laying an oil embargo upon it. Without access to oil, Japan relied on its reserves for civilian and military consumption. It was estimated these reserves would only last around two years. Japan had already planned, beyond China, to execute its Greater East Asia Co-Prosperity Sphere as part of its 'divine right' to unify Asia under Emperor Hirohito's rule. Given the situation, one of its main targets was to secure the rich oil fields in the South West Pacific Area (SWPA).

The attack on Pearl Harbor was an integral part of the Imperial Japanese Navy's (IJN) thrust into the south and south-west Pacific, and its aim was to emasculate the US Navy fleet. Japan hoped that, after the attack, the United States would spend the coming months, if not the year, rebuilding its fleet. This would then allow Japan to exploit its gains after rapidly advancing through the Malay Peninsula, Singapore, Netherlands (Dutch) East Indies (now Indonesia) and major parts of Dutch and Australian New Guinea. Japan wanted to establish and defend a strong position in areas rich in natural resources, particularly oil from the East Indies, to feed its war machine.

The surprise attack resulted in US Navy cruisers, destroyers, auxiliary vessels and eight battleships being damaged or sunk. Of the battleships, all but the USS *Arizona* would be raised. The USS *Oklahoma* was beyond repair, but the remaining six battleships would eventually be returned to service. Fortunately, none of the US aircraft carriers, including the USS *Enterprise* and USS *Lexington*, were in harbour. The Japanese launched two waves of air attacks from their six carriers, focused on the warships and airfields. A third wave had been planned, but was cancelled. Because of the improved US air defences during the second wave, the IJN didn't want to risk losing too many aircraft. The third wave would have targeted the submarine base, weapons depot, fuel storage facilities and naval yard. Had these areas of infrastructure been hit, according to Admiral Chester W. Nimitz, Commander-in-Chief of the US Pacific Fleet, 'it would have prolonged the war another two years'.

After Pearl Harbor, British prime minister Winston Churchill and US president Franklin D. Roosevelt met; they agreed to follow the Germany First strategy, which had been devised by the US Joint Chiefs of Staff (JCS) prior to December 1941, when they feared Japan would eventually enter the war and cause the United States to fight on two fronts. This strategy ensured the American war effort, men and materials, would be prioritised for Europe, and the Pacific campaign would be allocated only enough resources to keep Japan's advance at bay. It would be fought as a limited offensive campaign. The plan, recommended by Chief of Naval Operations Harold Rainsford Stark, was to wait until Germany, Italy and the other European Axis powers were defeated, and then concentrate all Allied forces on the fight against Japan.

Fleet Admiral Ernest King, the US Navy Commander-in-Chief, vehemently challenged the Germany First strategy. After all, Japan was an immediate threat, while it would be years before the Allies would be ready to launch an attack against Germany. Because of this, King held firm to an earlier view he had expressed to the JCS of the need to reinforce the bases on the Hawaiian–Australian line of communications. He said that they were essential in the preparation for an eventual American assault into the Solomon Islands, New Guinea and the Bismarck Archipelago, leading to an eventual northern push to Japan.

King also knew that not taking the fight to the Japanese would leave Australia and New Zealand vulnerable. Soon after Japan had launched its attacks, King told Roosevelt it seemed impossible to halt the Japanese thrust southwards. He argued: 'We cannot in honour let Australia and New Zealand down . . . they are our brothers, and we must not let them be overrun by Japan.' Roosevelt agreed.

King explained his strategy thus:

> [T]he best defence is offence . . . offence in those war areas where the enemy actually is, remote even though they are far from Continental US . . . it is offence which will keep the enemy engaged and occupied to such an extent that he cannot gather the means to make any serious threat to Continental US.

King hoped to keep the Japanese busy in the central and western Pacific areas—too busy to establish a solid foothold or to launch any incursions into the United States or against its Pacific allies.

In the book *Global Logistics and Strategy: 1940–1943, US Army in World War II*, authors Richard M. Leighton and Robert W. Coakley point out that, despite the Germany First policy,

> as a consequence of the immediate threat and the need to contain Japan's advance across the Pacific, American resources allocated to the defeat of Japan initially exceeded those allocated to Europe. In the first six months the US was in the war, the US Army deployed more than 300,000 soldiers overseas to the Pacific while less than 100,000 were sent to Europe.

Nine hours after Pearl Harbor, in yet another surprise attack, the IJN Air Service began a raid on the Philippines, destroying the majority of the US aircraft on the ground. Commanding the US Army Forces in the Far East was General Douglas MacArthur. By the end of December, the Japanese had taken Guam and Wake Island. One of the few places in the South Pacific where the Japanese were met with resistance was in the Philippines. In spite of efforts by the US Army, its infantry and tank corps, and Filipino militia, the Japanese landing forces advanced. President Roosevelt ordered MacArthur to evacuate. On the night of 12 March 1942, MacArthur fled Corregidor, a small island in Manila Bay, and was flown to Australia, to become Supreme Commander of the SWPA of Operations. At Terowie railway station in South Australia, on 20 March, MacArthur addressed the waiting media and proclaimed, 'I came through and I shall return.'

The Philippines held out until 6 May, when US Army Lieutenant General Jonathan Wainwright, who'd taken overall command after MacArthur's departure, officially surrendered to the Japanese. Under Japanese occupation the Filipinos would suffer greatly. Throughout the war, however, guerrilla tactics would be employed by the homeland militias to harass and prevent the Japanese from taking full control of the Philippines. Militias would also support Allied Special Forces—including Australia's Z Special Unit—that were sent in to gather intelligence and perform sabotage operations.

The British colonies of Hong Kong and Malaya, as well as the Netherlands (Dutch) East Indies, were under Japanese control by 25 December 1941, 31 January and 8 March 1942, respectively. Also, by the end of January, Rabaul on the island of New Britain had been taken, with over 1000 Australian soldiers captured. Rabaul was significant because of its proximity to the Caroline Islands, where the main IJN base had been set up on Truk Lagoon. The Japanese would use Rabaul as their headquarters, directing operations in the SWPA.

Singapore surrendered on 15 February. Winston Churchill called the Singapore defeat 'the worst disaster and largest capitulation in British history'. British losses during the fighting for Singapore were heavy, with 60,000 troops and nearly 25,000 support personnel captured. About 5000 people were killed or wounded, of which Australians made up the majority.

Five months into the Pacific War, the United States struck back in retribution for Pearl Harbor. Sixteen US Army Air Force B-25B Mitchell medium bombers were modified so they could be launched from the aircraft carrier USS *Hornet*. The Doolittle Raid, named after its lead pilot, Lieutenant Colonel James 'Jimmy' Doolittle, called for the B-25Bs to bomb military targets in Japan, and to continue westward to land in China. In the raid, around 50 Japanese military personnel and civilians were killed, and a further 400 were injured. Militarily, the bombing had little effect, but it would have psychological consequences for both the Allies and the Japanese. While the raid was a morale booster for the Americans, it only served as a propaganda tool for the Japanese. It angered the Japanese people and made them even more resolved to defeat the Americans. After the raid, the Imperial Japanese Army (IJA) swept the eastern coastal provinces of China, searching for the surviving American airmen. The IJA inflicted severe punishments on any Chinese people who were found to have aided the airmen.

By this time, Australia had been at war against the European Axis powers for over two years. The closest the war had come to Australian shores, before any Japanese threat, was when the German raider HSK *Kormoran* sank HMAS *Sydney* off the coast of Western Australia in November 1941. All crew members on the *Sydney* were lost, but the pride of the Royal Australian Navy (RAN) had inflicted severe damage on the *Kormoran*, and it was scuttled. Just over 300 German sailors were then captured and interned in a POW camp in Australia.

Meanwhile, four divisions of the AIF had been sent to North Africa, fighting with British and other Commonwealth forces against Italy and Germany. RAN vessels were sent to support Royal Navy (RN) operations in the Atlantic and Mediterranean. Australian airmen, having been trained under the Empire Air Training Scheme, were posted to England, where they served under the Royal Air Force (RAF) either in Fighter, Coastal or Bomber Commands. Likewise, some RAAF-only fighter and bomber squadrons were formed and operated in North Africa, and then went on to serve during the Allied invasion of Italy.

Like the United States, Australia had known it would only be a matter of time before Japan entered the war; Australian politicians and military officials believed that when Japan struck, it would pose an immediate threat to Australia. Therefore, in 1942, the Australian Government requested the return of the AIF. All divisions returned except for the 9th Division, which would remain in North Africa until the end of the conflict there in January 1943.

In 1940, Australia had taken delivery of 18 Consolidated PBY seaplanes—later more commonly known as Catalinas—under the US Lend Lease Agreement. Initially these planes were destined to be patrol aircraft, keeping watch over Australia's surrounding seas and oceans.

Once the Japanese thrust south began, however, the PBYs were quickly utilised as heavy bombers against enemy shipping and land-based targets.

Two Catalina squadrons, 11 and 20, were established and stationed initially in Port Moresby, New Guinea, to act as a forward-warning base. In 1941, both army and RAAF personnel were sent to man and protect the area. Keith Pinson was an airframe engineer and, later, air gunner with 20 Squadron. Stationed in Port Moresby from November 1941, he recollected, 'It was obvious that Port Moresby was Australia's most important northern base. Along the wharves and in the harbour, small and large cargo vessels of various types were gently swinging at their moorings. They seemed to move similar to horses tied to a hitching rail and presented an idyllic and peaceful scene.'

That idyllic scene would abruptly end with the Japanese advance. While New Guinea offered the Japanese some precious metals and food supplies, they mostly viewed Port Moresby as a strategic defensive location. Taking Port Moresby, and Milne Bay to its east, would mean the Japanese would have a protective barrier, should the Allies launch an offensive towards the Philippines or the East Indies. It would also, as Admiral King had feared, cut communications between Australia and Hawaii. Of course, some in Australia saw Japan's attempt to take New Guinea as a step towards an invasion of Australia. The issue of whether Japan ever seriously considered invading Australia continues to be debated.

In January 1942, Japanese aircraft began bombing Port Moresby. 'Our peaceful resting place was not for long,' Keith Pinson lamented. 'The sporadic but constant raids by silvery Japanese bombers saw to that. Their aircraft were not camouflaged as ours were, they could be seen quite clearly in perfect formation against a lovely blue sky. They realised that the weight of two or three coats of paint would make a difference to an aircraft's performance, especially on their lightly constructed Zeros.' Pinson continued:

> It was a sad day for Moresby when Jap fighters swooped around the north-eastern headland and lined up five Cats, destroying two and badly damaging a third. They were in a row at anchor on the far side of the harbour. During the raid, a fitter Armourer working on the guns of one of the Catalinas was able to fire off a few rounds but without result. Barney Ross, a Marine fitter, was lucky that a bullet hitting him lower down wasn't a little higher, and sadly, George Nancarrow, an Electrician working on another aircraft, was killed.

It wasn't only the Japanese with whom the RAAF had to contend. From the outset, in early 1942, the American airmen had a reputation for shooting first and asking questions later. There isn't a better example of this than when a pilot of a US Navy Grumman F4F Wildcat shot down a Catalina. As Flying Officer Ivan Clempson recalled, 'Our one-time Commanding Officer, Mike Seymour, was coming in to alight at a US base when an eager-beaver US pilot shot at him . . . Mike was badly injured at the time, but he did recover.'

There was a simple, somewhat excusable but near deadly reason for the friendly fire. All aircraft in service with the RAAF, prior to and at the start of the war, were marked with the British insignia, called the roundel—a red inner circle, inside a white circle, which was surrounded by an outer blue ring. In 1942, the US pilot, obviously not familiar with the British roundel, mistook the red centre for the Japanese 'sun-mark', officially known as *Nisshōki* but commonly referred to as *Hinomaru*. The Japanese used a full red circle as their insignia or roundel.

A similar incident happened in March when the first RAAF fighter unit, 75 Squadron, attempted to land their Lend Lease Curtiss P-40E Kittyhawks at Port Moresby. The Kittyhawks had been promised for so long that their arrival had become a running joke among the crews at Port Moresby, and the planes were nicknamed 'Never-hawks'. As Keith Pinson remembered:

The Kittyhawks arrived in Moresby just after lunch on 21 March 1942, four in number, the nucleus of RAAF 75 Squadron, but not to welcoming smiles. The Army gunners who were protecting the Seven Mile Strip were tired of being strafed persistently by the Japanese Zeros who harried them daily. So, when those four aircraft came in to land, the Army reception was hostile, damaging three, one beyond repair. Fortunately, no pilot was killed.

No one had ever seen a Kittyhawk before then, and the ground crews mistook the strange planes for Japanese aircraft because they had noticed the red centre of the roundel. Because of these two incidents, the RAAF quickly painted over the red centre, and the Australian roundel officially became a large white full circle within a blue ring.

The first major setback Japanese forces experienced in their move south was the Battle of the Coral Sea, 4–8 May 1942, to the east of the Great Barrier Reef, off North Queensland. Catalinas from 11 and 20 Squadron played a pivotal role in identifying the Japanese fleet as it steamed towards New Guinea. US code breakers had cracked enemy communications early in the war; intercepted communiqués confirmed the Japanese had sent a task force to take Port Moresby. Its whereabouts, however, weren't clear. RAAF Catalinas were then scrambled to search for the IJN Task Force.

The Japanese had sent a number of naval forces: one to take and hold the island of Tulagi, part of the British Solomon Islands Protectorate; the Port Moresby invasion force; and a carrier strike force to give aerial cover for the invasion. All groups set off from different locations, and the latter two planned to rendezvous off the east coast of New Guinea, then sail together to Port Moresby.

As recorded by the RAAF *Pathfinders* history magazine in 2008:

> On 4 May, Catalina A24-18, commanded by Flying Officer Allan Norman, was attacked and shot down by Japanese aircraft, probably from the light aircraft carrier *Shōhō*; Norman and his crew were taken prisoner and later executed. The search resumed on 5 May, when Flight Lieutenant Frank Chapman and his crew in Catalina A24-17 sighted the *Shōhō* and her escorts. This sighting was quickly followed by a report from Flight Lieutenant Norm Fader and the crew of A24-12 that more enemy vessels were bound for New Guinea. Next day, Squadron Leader Gough Hemsworth and his crew in A24-20 were shot down and killed after reporting the sighting of a strong enemy force heading towards the Jomard Passage [just off the easternmost tip of New Guinea].

Over the three days, the RAAF Catalinas had discovered the location both of the troopships east of New Guinea and the carriers in the Coral Sea. According to the *Pathfinders* article, this 'confirmed the immediate threat posed to Port Moresby by the Japanese . . . The Japanese plans received a further setback on 7 May when, alerted to the presence of the *Shōhō* in the Coral Sea by RAAF and other Allied reconnaissance aircraft, and Australian coastwatchers, aircraft from the USS *Lexington* and USS *Yorktown* attacked and sank the Japanese light carrier.' Now, without the air cover to support their landing at Port Moresby, the Japanese troop fleet turned back.

While the battle was considered a stalemate, the Japanese were weakened. The *Shōhō* was sunk, while another two carriers, *Shōkaku* and *Zuikaku*, were unable to be repaired in time for the Japanese planned attack against Midway (4–7 June), north-west of Hawaii. In that conflict, Japan's biggest loss was its four carriers, the *Akagi*, *Kaga*, *Sōryū* and *Hiryū*, part of the six-carrier force that had attacked Pearl Harbor. The United States lost the carrier *Yorktown* and a destroyer. The final setback came with the bloody land battle between the US Marines and the Japanese forces at Guadalcanal in the Solomon Islands, beginning on 7 August and lasting six months.

Despite these setbacks, the Japanese continued to bomb Port Moresby, revealing the vulnerability of 11 and 20 Squadron's flying boats. Keith Pinson recalled:

> On 23 April, Catalina A24-5, previously damaged on the 3 February, was destroyed by Zeros while still moored at Port Moresby. We were attacked by Japanese bombers and the Kittyhawks tangled with the escorting Zeros, coming off second best as they were unable to gain the necessary height. Our planes were no match for the Japs. The aerial combat, although not comparable with the Battle for Britain, was hectic enough for our small arena ... The sound of bombers approaching from the west, resulted in us pulling up and making a quick dive for some slit trenches dug conveniently alongside the road. Fortunately, the Jap bombs missed us ... We were just 20 feet in front of the first bomb when it hit, but safe in the trench. The second bomb landed about another 20 to 30 feet further on from our haven. Nevertheless, despite our narrow escape we were plastered with soil and rocks.
>
> The base was becoming increasingly untenable, so plans had been initiated to reposition the maintenance unit (and aircraft) to Bowen [Queensland], out of the range of the Japanese bombers ... After Bowen came Cairns [Far North Queensland] and more Squadrons being formed.

On 25 and 26 August 1942, Japanese forces attempted to take Milne Bay, on the eastern edge of New Guinea, as part of the larger plan to advance west and take Port Moresby. The Japanese landing force was stopped at Milne Bay by units from the Australian Military Force (AMF), the AIF, US engineers and RAAF ground and air forces. This was the first time the Japanese Army was decisively beaten, forcing it into a complete withdrawal. After the victory, Milne Bay became a major Allied base for the SWPA air and sea operations.

Because of the defeat at Milne Bay, the Japanese decided to go overland, from the north coast of New Guinea, following the Kokoda Track over the Owen Stanley Range. This journey through mountainous terrain proved horrendous for both Japanese and Australian AMF and AIF forces alike. The 'push' to take Port Moresby was stopped at Kokoda's Imita Ridge on 17 September 1942. The Japanese attempt ended when the Australians captured Kokoda on 2 November 1942. The Japanese were then forced, with their backs to the Bismarck Sea, to create defences on the north coast, around the villages of Buna and Gona.

The failure of the Japanese to succeed at Milne Bay and to reach Port Moresby by travelling overland—coupled with US victories at sea in the Battles of the Coral Sea and Midway, and on land at Guadalcanal—increased the importance for the Japanese to hold their bases at Guadalcanal and Rabaul. They relied greatly on the captured oil and raw materials, the retention of which became critical for their prosecution of the war. From that point on, the Japanese were on the back foot.

After the Japanese had taken the island of Tulagi, part of the British Solomon Islands Protectorate, they then advanced on Guadalcanal in early July. Once there, they began constructing a large airfield at Lunga Point to protect their major base at Rabaul and to support further planned expansions into the SWPA, principally against Fiji, New Caledonia and Samoa. The Allies quickly realised that Japanese long-range bombers would also threaten the sea lines of communication between the west coast of the United States and the east coast of Australia. They particularly identified Guadalcanal's importance as a permanent, and unsinkable, 'aircraft carrier' for the Japanese.

Following decoded intercepts and the confirmed sighting of the under-construction airfield by US Navy surveillance aircraft, the Americans decided to go on the offensive. On 7 August, in what would be the first Allied amphibious landing of the Pacific War, the 1st Marine Division, US Marine Corps, arrived on the beaches of Guadalcanal. There was little, if any, opposition, as the island was lightly defended; an IJN construction unit quickly withdrew under the pre-landing naval bombardment. Japan had not expected the United States to undertake offensive land action so early in the war, as it was only nine months since Pearl Harbor. Almost immediately, with the help of captured equipment, the US Navy Seabees, the construction unit, began finishing the airfield. It was named Henderson Field after Marine pilot Major Lofton Henderson, who lost his life leading a dive-bombing raid at the Battle of Midway.

Reacting swiftly, the Japanese counterattacked by sending in ships and troop transports, supported by land-based aircraft from Rabaul. So many ships from both sides were sunk in the many engagements in and around the Solomon Islands chain that the nearby waters to the north-west were referred to as Iron Bottom Sound. After a bitter struggle, the United States secured Guadalcanal on 15 November, though fighting would continue for another three months.

The Japanese counterattacks against Guadalcanal taxed US Navy defence mechanisms, and the Marines struggled to hold ground against an enemy desperate to recapture the vital airfield. Initially, the IJN suffered heavy losses when approaching Guadalcanal during daylight, so they switched their attacks to night, using faster vessels, cruisers and destroyers to shell the airfield and disembark troops, then retreating to safer waters by daybreak. American maritime historian Samuel Eliot Morison wrote that

> a curious tactical situation had developed that virtually saw an exchange of sea mastery every twelve hours. During daylight hours

the US Navy were dominant and after dusk the Japanese took over to discharge soldiers or freight and tossing a few shells in the Marines' direction.

To support their forces, the Japanese used 'The Slot' and Iron Bottom Sound as transport routes between Bougainville Island and Guadalcanal in the Solomons. The Slot, or New Georgia Sound, is the passage running between Santa Isabel Island and New Georgia Island. It leads to Iron Bottom Sound, the stretch of water between Guadalcanal and Savo and Florida islands. The Americans referred to this route as the 'Tokyo Express'; the Japanese called it the 'Rat Transport'. To further avoid submarine attacks, moored mines and aircraft strikes, the IJN used barges and submersible transports to navigate the shallow channels and shoals, known as the 'back streets', to deliver troops and keep them supplied, thereby thwarting the efforts of conventional naval vessels.

During the battle, US surface vessels and submarines were hard-pressed. To combat the enemy, they had at their disposal the barely adequate converted World War I destroyers USS *Tracy*, USS *Montgomery* and USS *Preble* as mine-layers, along with limited operational aircraft. Despite an underlying reluctance by a majority of the US commanders to use mines as an offensive measure, something had to be done quickly to stop the Japanese from supplying and supporting their troops.

Up to this point, Japan and the Allies in the Pacific had only ever used mines as a defensive tactic. In the European theatre, however, the Luftwaffe, the Royal Air Force and the Royal Navy's Fleet Air Arm had employed mines successfully as an offensive mode of warfare. Few Pacific commanders, of whom Admiral Chester W. Nimitz was one, advocated mines for offensive purposes, largely because mining was regarded as 'dirty' work. Mines did not discriminate between friend and foe, and extensive clearance work had to be carried out before waterborne invasions, unless sterilisers were used (sterilisers rendered mines non-explosive after a period of time). Disgorging mines without sterilisers was hazardous.

Captain Ross P. Whitemarsh, the Mine Officer on the Operations Staff of Admiral Nimitz, visited Guadalcanal when Japanese cruisers and destroyers were paying nightly visits to shell the US land forces. He suggested that mines could be laid along the path of these vessels, and heavy enemy casualties could result. He also stated that climatic conditions on Guadalcanal were unsuitable for the storage of mines. This assessment would lead to the construction of mine assembly and storage facilities in Australia, principally in Brisbane and then Cairns.

In November 1942, Lieutenant (junior grade) Ivor Collins, US Navy Reserve, assisted in the establishment of the mine assembly depots and details in Brisbane. They were initially sited at the suburb of Newmarket, before being relocated to Mount Coot-tha, and were set up to prepare mines for use by suitable American aircraft in offensive aerial mining in the Solomons.

Initially, American mines were shipped to Australia and unloaded at New Farm, Brisbane, then transported to the Newmarket depot for assembly before transfer by rail to Cairns in Far North Queensland. The transfer would be accompanied by a mine officer and an enlisted man. Their Commanding Officer (CO), Lieutenant 'Mike' Moldafsky, US Navy, travelled on the first two monthly trips to supervise operations, then Collins took over these trips in June 1943. Lieutenant Commander (LTCDR) Martin Xavier Smith, US Navy, assumed command when the depot relocated to Mount Coot-tha. In August 1943, Collins was promoted to Officer in Charge (OIC) to set up a new depot in Cairns.

Interestingly, Collins knew that his work with the US Navy would involve the aerial laying of mines as early as September 1942. The US Navy established its Mine Warfare Operations Research Group (MWORG) on 24 June that year, but it had existed earlier, albeit informally. MWORG was a home for scientists, physicists and mathematicians, both US Navy and civilian contractors. It grew from America's pre-Pacific War contact with Britain, assisting RAF Coastal Command and the Admiralty, working on problems of naval mining, anti-submarine warfare and convoy organisation. As it happened, the tactics being employed by the British, particularly aerial mining, would have even greater relevance to the US Navy in the SWPA.

Before any aerial mining was done, the job of laying mines in enemy waters initially fell to US Navy submarines. Some historians believe that this was because there were no torpedoes available at the time. This is not entirely true. The situation arose because the US Navy was having problems with a new type of torpedo. The conventional air-operated turbine-driven torpedoes had been replaced by electrically operated torpedoes, which left no tell-tale trail. The supply of these weapons, however, had dwindled due to defective depth control and exploder mechanisms. The US submariners were, therefore, ordered to resort to mine laying while the defects in these new torpedoes were corrected. The mine-laying missions in enemy waters were unpopular with the submarine crews, because they involved going into shoal waters where a submarine would be almost helpless if sighted and attacked. An alternative was needed.

A secret mailgram, written on 3 October 1942 by Vice Admiral Aubrey Fitch, Commander of the South Pacific Air Force, reveals that offensive mining using aircraft was being considered as early as September, if not earlier. In the mailgram, Admiral Fitch goes into great detail on the proposal, possible targets and the type of weapons to be used, as well as what aircraft were available and their suitability. The Catalina and the Boeing B-17 Flying Fortress are mentioned. Fitch then questions the economics of the operation, the shortage of aircraft and whether such an operation, particularly at night, would be feasible. He finishes by recommending 'against such operations until and unless the situation worsens to the extent that this "offensive" type of defensive operation appears necessary'.

As it happened, the situation on Guadalcanal did worsen. Even with knowledge of the Japanese codes, US Intelligence failed to interpret the real meaning of a rescript issued by Emperor Hirohito. In his book *Combined Fleet Decoded*, John Prados reveals that, during a liaison conference on New Year's Eve 1942, the decision was made by the Japanese to withdraw from Guadalcanal. The decision prompted the Emperor to issue this carefully worded rescript:

> The Emperor is troubled by the great difficulties of the present war situation. The darkness is very deep, but the dawn is about to break in the eastern sky. Today the finest of the Japanese Empire's army, navy, and air units are gathering. Sooner or later they will head toward the Solomon Islands where a decisive battle is being fought.

The rescript had an air of aggression and, had this been understood, further attacks by the Japanese forces would have been expected. Imperial Japanese Headquarters sped up preparations for another offensive, but its real intent was to pave the way for a rapid withdrawal from Guadalcanal and to facilitate the concealment of their master plan—holding MacArthur's forces in New Guinea so the Japanese could stabilise their fronts in the Solomons with the aim of striking back with irresistible force.

Many of the islands the Japanese tried to secure—including the Gilbert, Ellice, Marshall and Caroline Island chains and the Marianas—were not much more than coral atolls or lumps of volcanic mud covered in lush vegetation. They had a strategic value, as they straddled the major sea routes between the United States and the SWPA, but their phosphate and coconuts were of little significant value to the world economy. American maritime historian Samuel Eliot Morison wrote that Guadalcanal 'offered no natural resources but mud, coconuts and malarial mosquitoes'. However, he noted that Japan's expanse across these atolls resembled 'the webs of a giant tropical spider . . . each the centre of a defensive system supported and supplied by Japan'.

Like Guadalcanal, all of these islands served as unsinkable permanent 'aircraft carriers'. Australian historian Lionel Wigmore described the Japanese advance as leapfrogging the islands, and 'the length of each stride forward was about the range of their land-based aircraft. Thus aircraft from one captured base would support the attack on the next—if no such base was available, carrier-borne aircraft were employed.'

The Germany First policy of Churchill and Roosevelt only allowed for limited offensive actions in the Pacific, in order to focus resources on defeating Germany and Italy. By the end of 1942, however, Allied victories in the Pacific had convinced President Roosevelt the Pacific Theatre could be pursued offensively as well. Admiral King had tested and proved his theory that 'the best defense is offense'.

While it seemed the 'gloves were off', the priority would still be Germany First. Roosevelt rejected requests by the US Army Chief of Staff, General George Marshall, to scrap the Germany First plan, as he feared that the Soviet Union—which was pushing for the Allies to launch an invasion of northern Europe as early as 1943—would react badly to any abandonment of the plan. Despite the status quo being maintained, the terms 'holding action' and 'limited offensive' in the Pacific were now subject to the individual interpretations of US senior military commanders. This allowed the leaders some freedom of action to go after the Japanese, though the continued competition for resources would intensify as operations in both theatres of war were scaled up.

2

'BEWARE—THIS HARBOR IS MINED!'

EARLY TO MID-1943

Despite their losses and constant harassment by Allied aircraft, the Japanese continued to operate the Tokyo Express down The Slot to Iron Bottom Sound in support of their evacuation plan for Guadalcanal. In early February 1943, twenty Japanese destroyers departed from Bougainville Island's Tonolei Harbour, escorted by thirty Mitsubishi 'Zeke' fighter aircraft, more commonly known as the Japanese Zero. They were sighted heading with obvious intention to support the Japanese force on Guadalcanal. US fighter aircraft intercepted the destroyers, sinking the *Makinami* but losing four US Navy aircraft during the engagement. The remaining destroyers escaped further attack and headed towards Guadalcanal. To counter the move, the three US Navy mine-layers—USS *Tracy*, USS *Montgomery* and USS *Preble*—swung into action, quickly laying 300 mines to create an offensive minefield. The first casualty was the Japanese destroyer *Makigumo*, which suffered severe damage and was subsequently scuttled. This incident spurred Admiral Chester W.

Nimitz to use mining as an offensive weapon. He wanted to mine behind enemy lines, to keep the enemy boxed in.

Realising he couldn't use his mine-layers for this purpose, Nimitz quickly obtained 43 US Navy Grumman TBF Avenger torpedo bombers from General MacArthur to 'mine-in' units of the IJN in Tonolei Harbour. On 20 March 1943, the Avengers took off from Henderson Field and successfully laid their mines at the southern tip of Bougainville in the Buin–Tonolei–Kahili area of the Solomons—effectively preventing the enemy vessels from leaving the harbour. It was the first time this tactic had been employed in the Pacific War. The TBF Avenger, with little modification, could carry the 2000-pound (900-kilogram) Mk 12 magnetic mine that had been used previously by US Navy submarines.

After this successful operation, Nimitz requested an extension of the use of the Avengers so he could thwart Japanese supplies to Guadalcanal and stop them recapturing the vital airstrip. MacArthur refused, as he needed the aircraft for his Rabaul offensive. He planned to push the Japanese Army from the Huon Peninsula in New Guinea, and support Fleet Admiral William Halsey's offensive at Munda, New Georgia.

The plan to attack Rabaul, then the main Japanese naval base, was scheduled for May 1943 but delayed until June. MacArthur's US Fifth Air Force, commanded by Lieutenant General George Kenney, was to bomb Japanese airfields at Buka, Kahili, Ballale and Vila. The US Navy Third Fleet then planned to bombard the airfield at Munda on New Georgia Island at the southern end of the Gizo Strait. MacArthur was aware that the Japanese, after losing at Midway, were concentrating their efforts on building up air and port facilities in the Bismarck Archipelago, north-east of New Guinea. Japanese success in these projects would enable them to maintain pressure on the Allies and strengthen their continued thrust towards Port Moresby, allowing them to control the shipping channels between Australia and the United States. Frustrated at the lack of equipment available in the Pacific, MacArthur asked President Roosevelt to devote 'America's "entire resources" . . . to the southern Pacific', warning: 'If we are defeated in the Solomons . . . the entire Southwest Pacific will be in gravest danger.'

American maritime historian Samuel Eliot Morison believed that the aerial mining by the TBF Avengers did not pay dividends. The facts, however, show otherwise. The Avengers achieved their objective—mining-in the enemy's harboured ships—but the method was problematic. The aircraft dropped 82 mines from a height of 1500 feet (450 metres) to blockade the enemy vessels, and the mines landed in waters of varying depths. Mines that landed in deep water were ineffective, as the water pressure cushioned the explosion. Later, similar raids would see mines land on terra firma, an even worse situation. This was not precision mining. In addition, the mines were not self-sterilising. This meant they were a threat to any US submarine activity around the harbour, and would need to be swept if an Allied invasion was contemplated. Given the speed of the TBFs and the altitude of the drop, there was no way to accurately record and map the coordinates of each mine—information that would have been useful to US submarines as well as to any Allied forces involved in sweeping operations.

Former RAAF Flight Lieutenant and Catalina pilot Norman Robertson served at Port Moresby in 1941 and later with 43 Squadron, before becoming an assistant to the Air Officer Commanding (AOC) Number 76 Wing RAAF to coordinate mining in the SWPA until the end of hostilities. On the subject of the Buin–Tonolei–Kahili US aerial mining experiments with the Avengers, Robertson noted that 'these were stopped by MacArthur . . . My best recollection is that they were trialled near Bougainville in the Solomons by a mass dropping of mines . . . the method posed all sorts of hazards for subsequent minesweeping operations and was abandoned.'

However, if the aerial mining at Buin–Tonolei–Kahili was a failure, why did Nimitz want to persist with it? Clearly, he favoured the strategy and continued to implement it for the rest of the war. Nimitz 'doubted that the risk of valuable ships and lives, and the expenditure of nearly 10,000 rounds of ammunition, were commensurate with the results obtained'.

Nimitz pushed hard for aerial mining of Japanese ports and harbours, including the Shimonoseki Straits between Japan's Honshu and Kyushu islands. The straits would eventually be mined by General Curtis E. LeMay's US Army Air Force B-29 Superfortresses in March 1945. In early March 1943, however, the straits were well out of reach of any Allied bomber, and the top priority was to neutralise the enemy's resources at Rabaul to stop their desire to take Port Moresby.

It would be wrong to assume that, given his recalling of the Avengers from Nimitz, MacArthur did not appreciate the effective threat of mining. In 1904, while MacArthur was taking an oral quiz at his examinations for the rank of First Lieutenant, a colonel posed the hypothetical question to him of how he would defend a harbour with a limited number of troops. After MacArthur answered, the colonel changed the question to, 'What would you do if all the troops were withdrawn?'

MacArthur ardently replied, 'First, I'd round up all the sign painters in the community and put them to work making signs reading, *BEWARE—THIS HARBOR IS MINED*. These signs I'd float out in the mouth of the harbor. After that I'd get down on my knees and pray. Then I'd go out and fight like hell.' His answer obviously impressed, as MacArthur was awarded his silver bars.

Back in 1942, during the Guadalcanal campaign, a young Royal Australian Navy (RAN) officer named Lieutenant Commander (LTCDR) Palgrave 'Pally' E. Carr was seconded to the RAAF. He was an acknowledged torpedo expert, with flying experience in the Netherlands East Indies. The bulk of Carr's experience, which included aerial mine laying, was gained when he was attached to the Fleet Air Arm in UK, European, Mediterranean and Indian Ocean waters.

Even before Nimitz's use of and success with the TBF Avengers in aerial mining, Carr had long thought that the RAAF Catalinas would be a suitable aircraft to do the job. Vice Admiral Aubrey Fitch and Captain Ross P. Whitemarsh had both suggested using Catalinas to Nimitz, but the US Navy Catalinas were unavailable as they were already heavily involved in other operations.

With his aircraft knowledge, Carr understood the Catalina's potential and, later, he was able to exploit the aircraft's long-range capability and load capacity. The Catalina was, in fact, Australia's first modern, long-range heavy bomber since World War I. It was capable of carrying a payload equivalent to that of a B-17E Flying Fortress. Although the B-17 was being used in the Pacific, it gained greater glory during its service as a daylight bomber in raids over Germany.

Carr passed on his thoughts to RAAF Group Captain William Norman 'Hoot' Gibson, who was Senior Staff Officer to RAAF Air Vice-Marshal William Bostock—and Bostock relayed the idea to MacArthur's office. In late February and early March 1943, the RAAF—in cooperation with US Mine Warfare Officers from MacArthur's staff—commenced mining experiments using Catalinas at Moreton Bay, off Brisbane, Queensland. It would have been quite a sight for the Brisbane locals, seeing wave after wave of Catalinas flying along Moreton Bay at low altitudes—between 100 and 200 feet (30 and 60 metres)—then dropping dummy mines and sharply peeling away.

These manoeuvres were conducted under the watchful eyes of US Navy mining experts LTCDR Shirley L. Quimby US Navy Reserve, physicist and member of the US Mine Warfare Office in Brisbane; LTCDR Ellis Johnson US Navy Reserve, an underwater ordinance expert with degrees in Science and Engineering from Massachusetts Institute of Technology (MIT); and Lieutenant Ivor Collins US Navy Reserve, also a graduate from MIT and from the US Navy Mine Warfare course at Yorktown, Illinois. Collins would accompany RAAF Catalina crews on trial flights to determine their maximum altitude while carrying four Mk 13 mines under the wings. He recalled the limit was between 11,000 and 12,000 feet (3300 and 3600 metres).

The success of these and other tests paved the way for Bostock to volunteer RAAF Catalinas for aerial mining. He passed on the suggestion to MacArthur through Lieutenant General George Kenney on 29 March 1943. MacArthur accepted the offer, opening the way for Carr to implement his skills.

The coalition of RAAF and US Navy mining experts was then assembled, including Carr and Bostock on the Australian side, and Quimby, Johnson, Collins and Lieutenant Kenneth L. Veth, US Navy, on the American. It was a mixture of skill and talent. All members of the team had knowledge or experience of the aerial mining in Europe, except Collins, who was specifically a mine ordinance expert with a deep knowledge of the weapons at his disposal.

The brief for the operation was simple: to implement a strategy of blockading enemy ports and channels. The sinking of ships was not important, but it would be a pleasing by-product if it occurred. In any case, having ships bottled up in harbours with no access to safe cover would make them easy pickings for US Navy and Army bombers, submarines and surface vessels. Either way, the mines would directly or indirectly result in the sinking of enemy shipping. More importantly, the mines would limit or prevent Japan's access to and shipment of raw materials to feed its war machine, hampering its ability to exploit its gains. Also, the mines would put a stranglehold on Japan's supply chain, limiting or preventing it from delivering troops and supplies to reinforce its strongholds.

US Navy Intelligence would identify the targets, but Carr was left to deal with them. Quimby, with all his experience, was happy to allow Carr a free hand to implement the mine-laying strategy. The RAAF/US Navy mine-laying operation was a true coalition between the two Allies, with neither claiming nor exercising command over the other.

In March 1943, the RAAF had approximately thirty serviceable Catalinas, and all were flying boats. The amphibious version, which could be used on sea or land, did not arrive until December. Being a flying boat, the Catalina wasn't reliant on land-based airstrips. It had a long range and was more than capable of deploying the aerial mine as an offensive weapon.

Sir Richard 'Dick' Kingsland, former commander of 11 Squadron, believed that the Catalina was chosen because it was the only long-range heavy bomber available. The American-built Consolidated B-24 Liberator also had the capacity and range, but was not available to the RAAF until 1944. In any case, the Catalina had the advantage of being able to alight and refuel on the ocean using submarines or surface tankers as advanced operational bases (AOBs), thereby increasing its range. A Liberator was restricted in how far it could fly before needing to return to its base to refuel. Kingsland felt the Catalinas' performance 'was undoubtedly [due to] the calibre of the crews who flew and maintained them', adding that 'the Catalina was the only suitable aircraft available in 1943 in the Pacific for mine laying'.

Kingsland was a daredevil of a pilot and certainly took the Catalina to its extremes. His official obituary, written for the Australian National University archives, details his exploits with a Catalina while commanding 11 Squadron. 'RAAF veterans still recall the day he used one of these lumbering aircraft as a dive-bomber to destroy Rabaul wharf, despite a heavy barrage from Japanese guns.'

The Catalina was designed and built by Consolidated Aircraft Corporation in San Diego, California, to meet US Navy requirements in 1933. The design of the aircraft was, quite literally, a flying boat. The fuselage or 'hull' was boat-shaped, and the aircraft was fitted with floats that lowered and retracted at the wingtips. As the type continued to be developed in the pre-war years, two large 'blisters', between the wing and the tail, were added. The blisters were made from clear perspex, offering all-round vision during search and rescues, and where the self-defence machine guns were positioned. Its original designation when used by the US Navy was PBY (PB for Patrol Bomber, while Y was the designation given to the manufacturer). When the RAF took delivery of the aircraft, they renamed it Catalina after the small island off San Diego, in respect of its heritage. The RAF had, at that time, a tradition of naming its bombers after places, such as Lancaster, Stirling, Blenheim and Hampden. The RAAF followed suit, as did the United States before war's end, and the name Catalina is now synonymous with the flying boat. The aircraft is also known affectionately as the Cat.

To confuse matters, the Royal Canadian Air Force (RCAF) followed the RAF naming methodology, but did not exactly follow the RAF nomenclature. They named their PBYs Canso, after the Strait of Canso between Cape Breton Island and the mainland of Nova Scotia, Canada. The name originally chosen by the RCAF was Convoy, but this was discarded in favour of Canso because the former was easily confused with ship convoys.

Another added notation was the Catalina type or version, marked by a numeral placed after PBY. There were six versions, including the PBY-5—the fifth version of the aircraft—which was the type used by the RAAF. To indicate the aircraft was amphibious, an 'A' was placed after the numeral (as in PBY-5A of the US Navy version). The RAAF would eventually make modifications to some of its Cats for mining operations, which would have its own designation, PBY-5A(M), and be recognised by the US Navy as a wholly Australian variant.

Apart from the RAAF Catalina's bombing and mining capabilities, it was used in search and rescues, to escort convoys, transport VIPs, deliver Australian Z Special Unit operatives behind enemy lines, and distribute much-needed supplies to coastwatchers. Coastwatchers were a mix of civilian and military personnel keeping watch and communicating enemy movements behind the lines. Between 1943 and 1944, there were 75 coastwatch outposts in New Guinea and surrounding islands in the SWPA.

Catalinas also performed long-range reconnaissance to keep the enemy on their toes, a point not missed by MacArthur. In a communiqué to Australian prime minister John Curtin in 1942, MacArthur noted: 'Catalina squadrons are rendering magnificent service in long-range reconnaissance and in long-range bombing missions.'

So that the Catalina could perform its task as a mine-layer with minimal risk of losses, it was decided the aerial mining operation would be conducted at night. Vice Admiral Aubrey Fitch had doubts about this strategy. In his mailgram of October 1942, he stated that 'the accuracy of positioning mines from aircraft at night is debatable'. In a further step, to conceal the aircraft from enemy observers and anti-aircraft batteries, as well as enemy aircraft, it was decided to coat the Catalina in all-black matt paint. Thus, they became known as the Black Cats.

The first mine-laying operation was planned for Wewak, on the northern coast of New Guinea. Intelligence reports identified an airfield being built by the Japanese at the location; this threatened Allied operations on the island and in the broader SWPA. However, as much as those in MacArthur's General Headquarters wanted to see the approaches to Wewak mined, in reality the Catalinas couldn't do the job. The tests performed in Moreton Bay had proved that a Catalina with a full mine load was incapable of attaining the desired altitude to safely cross

New Guinea's Owen Stanley Range. Consequently, Bostock recommended the abortion of the plan to mine at Wewak and suggested that the approaches to Kavieng, on New Ireland, should be mined instead.

The Japanese were developing Kavieng as an intermediate anchorage between Truk Lagoon and Rabaul. Enemy shipping was prevalent, making the approaches to Kavieng an ideal target. Admiral Nimitz would have been absolutely delighted with this plan. At the time when MacArthur refused his request for an extension of the use of the Avengers, Nimitz had intended to use them to mine the anchorages at Kavieng to frustrate Japanese attempts to support its Guadalcanal operations. Now the Catalinas would be fulfilling Nimitz's plan.

Bostock and Carr decided to lay two minefields at Kavieng: one in Silver Sound, and another in Ysabel Passage. On 22 April 1943, eight RAAF Black Cats, each carrying two mines, took off from Cairns for Silver Sound; because of the distance from Cairns to Kavieng, aircraft refuelled at Port Moresby or Milne Bay. Unlike most other bombers of the period, the Catalina didn't have an internal bomb bay. Bombs, torpedoes and mines were all attached under the flying boat's massive wing, which spanned 104 feet (31.7 metres). In most cases, the crew had to carry an equal number of mines on either side of the wing to keep the aircraft balanced. If no torpedo rack was available, mines were attached to the under-wing bomb rack using metal cable slings.

The mines—each weighing upwards of 1060 pounds (480 kilograms)—were loaded on a flat-hulled vessel called a scow and manoeuvred out to the moored Cat. Once the scow reached the Cat, it was held in position by being moored to the wing struts of the aircraft. As the mines were transferred from the scow to the aircraft, the Cat would sink a bit, and the scow would rise. This, coupled with the bobbing movement of the water, meant that the handlers had to be very flexible at the knees and to be careful with their heads, not to mention the heavy weapon. Hand-operated winches were then attached to the upper side of the mainplane, through which steel cables were passed. These cables were looped around the mine, and the mine was winched into position by the loading detail.

The mission to Silver Sound was wholly successful, despite accurate light to medium anti-aircraft fire from the enemy. The second minefield in Ysabel Passage was laid a few nights later, and follow-up mine laying of these targets would continue up to 30 June. On 15 July 1943, the Japanese light cruiser *Nagara* fell victim to the mines that had been laid at Kavieng and was forced to proceed to Truk Lagoon for repairs. It was put out of action for a considerable period.

Sergeant Douglas 'Doug' Sykes, 20 Squadron, was a member of Pilot Officer (PO) Tom Blackley's crew, one of the eight aircraft flying that first mission to Kavieng. Sykes recalled:

> As it turned out we were the first aircraft to arrive at the target area. The Japs were night flying, with flare path down. They signalled us to land, we signalled back, flew along the flare path and then laid our mines ... the first two in the Southwest Pacific Area as I understand ... very accurately, and then stood off and watched. About three more of our aircraft did the job before the Japs woke up that something was going on. Then the rest copped a bit of rubbish ... The next day 'Tokyo Rose' reported that Catalina Flying Boats had raided Kavieng and their bombs fell harmlessly into the sea.

Tokyo Rose, whose real name was Iva Toguri, was an American-born Japanese woman who hosted a Japanese propaganda radio program, *Zero Hour*, aimed at the Pacific Allies. Although she called herself Ann or orphan Ann, the American soldiers nicknamed her Tokyo Rose, and it stuck.

The Japanese reaction to Tom Blackley's arrival was not surprising. During the early Catalina sorties, the Japanese mistook the low-flying aircraft for their seaplanes and, therefore, lit up the harbour for them to land. This helped the Catalina crews to sight their target better. In time, however, the Japanese learned about the Catalinas laying mines, and they became a lot less welcoming.

Incidentally, there is no reference to Sykes' account in the Unit History of 20 Squadron or 11 Squadron, other than an entry from the time that recorded: 'All aircraft completed POPSY No.1 successfully. Accurate opposition from ships and shore. Full details by safe hand to AOC RAAF Command and AOC NEA.' POPSY was the code name given to the target area (the approaches to Kavieng). Confirmation of Sykes' observations was recorded in the RAAF's *Report on Mine-laying Operations—Kavieng—April and May 1943*. It reads:

> PO Blackley was the first to reach the area. He made one run and dropped both mines successfully at 1313Z from 300 feet. After leaving his datum and before dropping the mines, he touched the water with no ill effects. He encountered no opposition but a ship signalled him with a green Aldis type lamp.
>
> WGCDR Green dropped his mines two minutes later from 900 feet. Medium A/A [anti-aircraft gunfire] burst closely behind him during his run.
>
> SQNLDR Vernon made his run at 1330Z in the same area as PO Blackley. Both mines released simultaneously on the position of the first drop. He continued his run inadvertently over the ship that signalled Blackley fifteen minutes earlier. This ship opened fire with medium and light A/A. SQNLDR Vernon sustained five shrapnel holes in his port float, one hole in the hull and four large holes in his port wing caused by explosive bullets. He turned west on being fired upon and encountered more A/A fire from another ship. He returned to Cairns direct.

The remainder of the report confirms that all other aircraft, with the exception of that of Squadron Leaders Stilling and Stokes, and Flight Lieutenant Clarke, encountered accurate anti-aircraft fire:

> FLTLT White came in last, by which time the defences had a very good idea of height and speed of our aircraft. He encountered very accurate medium A/A and was forced to turn to port to avoid it. He dropped his mines on this run from 1000 feet at 1418Z about 1000yds north of the planned position but in good water.

The times in the report are given in coordinated universal time (UTC), abbreviated as 'Z'. It is the international equivalent of Greenwich Mean Time (GMT). The UTC system allows all aircraft throughout the world to use the same 24-hour clock and in the same time frame. To establish local time on a meridian, hours are added or subtracted as necessary. For example, 13.13Z at Kavieng would have been 03.13 local time at Kavieng.

The round trip to Silver Sound of around 3600 miles (5800 kilometres) took approximately nineteen hours. Future sorties sometimes lasted over 24 hours. In Europe, an average round-trip bombing sortie from England to Berlinwas around seven to eight hours.

Apart from topping up fuel at Port Moresby or Milne Bay, all flights from Cairns to Kavieng were nonstop. The navigators did not have the benefit of today's satellite-assisted global-positioning systems (GPS). All they possessed was a chart, the stars and a sextant to help them navigate in the hours of darkness. As former skipper Tom Broughton, 42 Squadron, remembered:

> The distances involved, and absolute dependence on pinpoint accuracy for success, placed extreme demands on the physical endurance and skills of the crews, particularly the navigator. The flights were low, long and deeply fatiguing ... navigation relied on very little more

than a compass, a map, pencil and an advanced ability to count. At the back of all crews' minds also was the fact there was no fail-safe rescue machinery if things went wrong. If you managed to get down there was the sea to contend with . . . if you reached shore, there was the jungle. If you beat both, yet were captured, you could expect to be executed, mostly by beheading.

3

NOTHING LEFT TO CHANCE

APRIL 1943 TO JULY 1945

Royal Australian Naval Lieutenant Commander Pally Carr meticulously planned every detail of the RAAF/US Navy coalition mine-laying operations. He obtained charts of the areas, but occasionally they were inaccurate—and some hadn't been updated since the mid to late nineteenth century. It was necessary to call upon the knowledge possessed by Burns Philp Master Mariners, and former harbour pilots, who had guided ships through the islands in that part of the Pacific. Wing Commander Brett Hilder, 20 Squadron—a former Master Mariner with Burns Philp—became a valuable asset during the planning stages.

As well as the charts, Carr would also check water depths, currents, weather reports, surveillance photos and land features. From the latter, he would select a datum, a fixed point to mark the start of the run to the target area. This was mostly a land feature, such as a headland, river mouth, small atoll or shallow reef, which was easily seen and wouldn't move or disappear. From the datum, he would measure the distance to the target—the most effective place to lay the mines, depending on the water depth—and then use the speed of the Catalina to calculate how long in seconds it would take the aircraft to fly from the datum to the target. During the approach, the pilot would confirm his speed as they flew over the datum; the navigator would start the stopwatch and count the number of seconds to the target. This allowed the Catalina crews to accurately plot every mine they laid, assisting with any future sweeping of the area prior to Allied landings. It also helped to facilitate the clearance of ports and shipping channels when hostilities ceased.

There was little room for error when laying the mines, even when under anti-aircraft fire. As former skipper Tom Broughton recalled:

> Once the run had been commenced, absolutely nothing must be varied by the tiniest margin, direction, height or speed of the aircraft until the run was complete. Otherwise, the arithmetic failed and the mines missed the channels . . . the aircraft must run dead straight and level until all mines had been cleared.

Should a sortie be aborted, the mines were often unable to be carried back because this would consume too much fuel. Carr plotted dumping areas for such an eventuality. These locations were specifically chosen to be well away from shipping lanes, so the mines did not become a hazard to Allied shipping. This strategy was acknowledged and applauded by the US Navy Commander-in-Chief, Fleet Admiral Ernest King.

All operations were also planned in close cooperation with US submarine commanders, who were comfortable in the knowledge RAAF Catalinas would be performing the bulk of the mining within harbour approaches and the narrow channels between the islands. The submariners were made aware of mining operations so they could plot a course around the mined area, or just stay away. This also gave them the opportunity to go hunting for any enemy ships that were outside the harbours and channels, waiting for the mined area to be swept.

Carr left nothing to chance. All targets were mined at night from low altitudes, to achieve surprise and accuracy. In most cases, the mines were released from below 200 feet (60 metres). So that pilots could fly confidently at these levels in almost complete darkness, they used radio altimeters. Initially installed for torpedo work, the altimeters proved invaluable for mine laying, as Rees Hughes of 43 Squadron explained:

> It only had a little aerial and was a small box with three lights on the control panel, orange, green and red. It was extremely accurate and ideal for the mine-laying missions. It could be set to any altitude and was much more accurate than the aneroid type altimeter that depended on atmospheric pressure and had to be set from time to time. The radio altimeter emitted radio waves that bounced back from the surface of the sea. It was a beautiful piece of equipment ... we could not do without them. It was so accurate that, because of the slow speed of the Catalina, the needle would fluctuate with the wave height.

The first operation at Kavieng was performed in moonlight. As in Europe, it was decided that moonlight—known as the bomber's moon—would allow for easier recognition of the datum points, so the mines could be accurately laid on target. Only part of the second operation was carried out in moonlight, but it was still successful. This proved that moonlight was not necessary; in fact, a moonless night was a safer option for the crews. Wing Commander Athol 'Attie' Wearne, who would become 20 Squadron Commanding Officer (CO) in 1944, acknowledged this change in tactics:

> It was obvious too on the first two operations the Japs could see better in the light of the moon and their reception committees [were]

more active. So, from these operations our first tactical principle was evolved and accepted, namely, heavily defended targets were mined in the dark of the moon. Although this principle was adhered to when possible throughout the campaign, there always had to be a couple of bunnies to test a new target or datum point to determine the defences.

Flying in darkness over large stretches of water without visual aids, RAAF navigators used a mix of navigational tools. When the sky was clear, they utilised celestial navigation (astronavigation). This involved using the stars to guide the aircraft to and from a target over many kilometres of ocean, just as early seafarers had done to find their way to harbour.

Former squadron leader David Vernon DSO, of 11 Squadron, recalled a time when this type of navigation helped him and his crew return safely. They had been on a night-time bombing mission, attacking a Japanese airbase at Babo, near the western tip of New Guinea, when

> a shell entered the aircraft near the Second Pilot's feet, went past my head, then came in contact with the main electrical circuit, cutting off all lights, also severing the power source for the automatic pilot. A shell fragment cut the Engineer's cheek, but not badly.
>
> For a while, I thought I might have been wounded, as there was warm fluid running down my neck and back. But being so busy flying the Cat at low altitude on a dark night . . . unable to see the instruments to help me, and still under AA fire . . . there was no time to investigate. I struggled to keep the aircraft on course and climbing out of the danger zone. Later we discovered that the warm fluid was hydraulic oil from the ruptured autopilot system. A check revealed no other damage or injury, however, here we were some 1500 kilometres from our refuelling stop at Horn Island [next to Thursday Island], with no illumination for the essential flight instruments or anywhere

> else in the aircraft. Luckily, the Navigator had a torch to provide some help with his now most essential task of guiding us over this great expanse of water, the Timor Sea.
>
> Fortunately, we were flying towards the East, so we could observe the stars as they rose, and the Navigator was able to determine from his Astro Nautical tables which star would appear above the horizon in the direction we needed to go. So, off into the blackness we went with the Navigator pointing out which star I was to follow. This required frequent changes to keep us on our proper course, as the earth's rotation caused the selected star to move off the required track. Because of the density of stars in the tropical sky, it was only with extreme concentration that one could continue steering by the selected star. As dawn broke we were relieved to find ourselves right on track as we came in sight of the islands near Cape York. I set the aircraft down off Horn Island, taxied to a mooring, and was pleased to see that the hull patch over the shell hole was keeping the water out.

During overcast nights, the technique of dead reckoning was employed. This is the process of plotting the current position by using a predetermined landmark or point. By calculating the elapsed time from this point, the airspeed of the Cat and its course, navigators were able to determine their current location. This called for a high degree of skill, and would be repeated at regular intervals throughout the flight to track the aircraft's progress. Very few RAAF aircraft were lost due to poor navigation techniques. Sadly, as confirmed by Lieutenant Ivor Collins, US Navy Reserve, this was not the case with US Army Air Force and US Navy aircraft flying in the SWPA and over the Australian continent; on too many occasions, aircraft were lost.

Keith Hamilton, who was a flight engineer with 11 Squadron, believed that the loss of American planes might have been due to the tendency for US navigators and pilots to rely too much on their Bendix radio compasses. This was a radio-position-locating device that, although excellent as an adjunct to navigation skills, also required knowledge of the location of radio transmitters, both civilian and military. It obviously worked for them over the North American continent, but not in the SWPA or over outback Australia.

The Bendix Corporation had designed the RA-10 receiver early in 1939, and it became standard equipment on US Army Air Force and US Navy aircraft built by Martin, Vought-Sikorsky, Douglas and Consolidated Vultee. It was also used on many RAF, Soviet Air Force and South African Air Force aircraft. Using the Bendix, a navigator or pilot could—by taking the bearings of two or more broadcast stations—plot the intersecting bearings and locate the relative position of the aircraft. This, however, required some knowledge of the local terrain. In the United States, where their training was carried out, a lost navigator could tune in to the Bendix and pick up a few stations that could be readily identified. In most cases these were commercial radio stations. After a few cross fixes had been plotted, the navigator would know where he was.

This was not always the case in northern Australia or the SWPA during the 1940s, when few radio stations existed in this largely undeveloped area. Even if a call sign or the name of a town was picked up, it was likely that the US aviator had little idea of its location. By using the Bendix in an unfamiliar region, the navigator could become hopelessly lost if he failed to apply the basic checks on his navigation. It is known that a number of US airmen lost their lives by flying too far inland or out to sea until they ran out of fuel. Later, the improved automatic radio compass was developed and used on most commercial airlines and a majority of Allied bombers.

To further protect the operations—should the Japanese intercept any communications—secret codes were used based on the mining codes adopted by the RAF. The British chose to refer to mining as 'GARDENING' and mines as 'VEGETABLES'. The minefields were coded after plants, such as ARTICHOKES, ONIONS and DEODARS. A similar methodology was adopted by the RAAF to confuse Japanese Intelligence. The RAAF referred to mining as COURTING, DINING, SERENADING or DANCING (chosen at random for each mission), and each minefield as FILLY, HARLOT, POPSY, GIRLIE and so on. As new targets were added, minefields were codenamed after loose women to enhance security.

According to RAAF Group Captain Norman P. Engel, former operations armament officer and member of the first mine-laying planning team, the codes were devised over a beer in the Naval and Military Club in Brisbane. They were informally adopted in April 1943 and first used for mining in the Kavieng area. On 5 June, Air Vice-Marshal William Bostock began referring to mines as FILLIES.

In the Squadron Unit Histories, some of the record entries do not include a code or location for the target in their reports. Former Wing Commander Athol 'Attie' Wearne said that this was probably because some airmen who wrote up the reports were more meticulous than others, and 'most were glad to get back from a long mission and only made a cryptic notation, such as "Mission successful" . . . after all, there was a war on!' Unfortunately, such entries have made it virtually impossible to match some codes with their mine targets.

The secret coding system for identifying targets was officially adopted in July 1943. An extract from an instruction issued by Wing Commander Reginald Bruce Burrage, 11 Squadron CO and later CO of Number 76 Wing Headquarters, emphasised that the codes were only to be used for mining operations. Any geographical names and references to mines or mine laying were not to appear in the same signal as any of the code words. In addition, the bearings and distances of each mine laid or not laid were to be coded.

In this extract from an original message discovered in the Australian archives, the adoption of the code and recording system is explained:

> A code system has been adopted for use in the formulation of despatches concerned with aircraft minelaying operations. Except in regard to terminology, this system is identical with that used in Great Britain ... Minelaying is referred to as 'COURTING', or 'SERENADING', etc. Areas in which mines are laid are designated by such terms as 'POPSY', 'FILLY', 'FAIRY', 'BLONDIE' etc. A set of area charts upon which area 'pin points' or 'Datum Points' are inscribed has been prepared . . . Thus a typical minelaying operational despatch reads as follows:
>
> COURTING OPERATION IS TO TAKE PLACE NIGHT OF 17TH OR 18TH MAY AS FOLLOWS X FOUR SMALL POPSYS ON TRACK 205 DEGREES SIX HUNDRED YARDS FROM CIRCLE 7 SPACED FOUR HUNDRED YARDS X THREE HUNDRED YARDS X THREE HUNDRED YARDS.

Written in December 1943, a secret letter to the AOC (Air Officer Commanding) of the North Eastern Area (NEA) in Darwin uses an example of the code. A copy of the letter was forwarded to Lieutenant Commander Shirley Quimby, US Navy Reserve, US Mine Warfare Officer, in Brisbane:

> COURTING OPERATIONS DECEMBER/JANUARY
>
> 1. The following operations are to be carried out by aircraft of 11 SQN and 20 SQN, commencing December 19th:—18 large American and 18 small British DARLINGS
> 2. The North Eastern Area is to initiate each operation in the above programme by the normal form green to the Units concerned and to the AORC

3. The following schedule for the above programme is suggested: -
   a. 18 December—8 aircraft carry 18 small British and 7 large American females to DARWIN, each of 7 aircraft carrying 2 British and 1 American and the remaining aircraft carrying 4 British.
   b. 19 December—6 aircraft serenade DARLING, returning to DARWIN
   c. 21 December—6 aircraft serenade DARLING, returning to DARWIN
   d. 23 December—6 aircraft serenade DARLING, returning to DARWIN
4. In the event that 8 aircraft are not available for dispatch to DARWIN on 18 December, a minimum of 6 may be so assigned. It is desired, however, that a reserve of 1 or 2 aircraft be made available at DARWIN if possible.
5. Details of the mine-laying plans will be communicated to the North Eastern Area and to the SQNs concerned by hand of Lieutenant Commander QUIMBY from the Allied Naval Command.

Signed Group Captain for Air Vice-Marshal,
AIR OFFICER COMMANDING, RAAF COMMAND, AAF.

In keeping with the coding system, the codename Shecat was given to Yampi Sound, off the north coast of Western Australia, one of many advanced operational bases (AOBs) used by Catalina crews during raids. AOBs weren't just land bases, but were also US Navy Seaplane Tenders or submarines with which the Black Cats would rendezvous at sea. Catalina crews would use the latter AOBs more frequently as the war progressed and the distance to their targets increased.

After the Kavieng missions, the RAAF continued to mine almost every strategic target within the range of their Catalinas. It was soon decided that modifications to the original design of the aircraft were needed to improve the Cat's maximum performance levels, extending its range or increasing its bomb load. Ultimately, these changes enabled results far beyond what the original designers, Consolidated, had contemplated.

In May and June 1943, a report for the mine-laying operations at Manus Island and Kavieng revealed that by

> taking off the following items: internal heating unit, oxygen bottles and equipment, de-icer boots, tunnel and pilots armour plating, smoke screen gear, self sealing cells and the NORDEN bomb-sight . . . the dry, unbombed, no ammunition Tare weight was reduced to 18,000 lbs [8000 kg]—with a crew of nine, . . . full tanks, . . . oil, full ammunition & 2 x Mk XII mines of 1600 lbs each [total 1500 kg] the all up weight was 35,600 lbs [16,100 kg].

The removal of most of these items compromised the Catalina's defences. Given the low altitudes at which the Cat was flown, losing the armour plating and self-sealing cells from the fuel tanks would make it vulnerable even to rifle fire by Japanese troops. To their credit and courage, the crews accepted these changes as necessary for undertaking their task efficiently. After the changes were made, the Catalina's only defence was its few guns, all-black camouflage and, ironically, its low speed. As former Wing Commander Brett Hilder observed, the Catalina 'flew so slow you could park it in the clouds and wait for the enemy fighters to disappear'.

Former airframe engineer and air gunner Cyril Payne noted that, as far as an increased risk was concerned, 'we flew at about 50 feet [15 metres], not much could get under you at that height and, if you did get hit by anti-aircraft or jumped by a Jap fighter, that stuff wouldn't have made much difference. It would have been [the] end of section for you.'

The modifications were completed at two Flying Boat Repair Depots (FBRD) established during the war. Number 1 FBRD was at Lake Boga, near Swan Hill in Victoria. After the shock bombing of Darwin on 19 February 1942, and the raid on 3 March that destroyed flying boats and the maintenance facilities at Roebuck Bay near Broome, Western Australia, Lake Boga was chosen as a safer proposition for service and repair as it was outside the known range of Japanese carrier-based aircraft. The Lake Boga depot was designed to look like part of the township from the air. Pretend houses with fake fences were constructed, and the sergeants' mess resembled a town hall. Today, part of the site is a popular Catalina museum. The other depot, 2 FBRD, was at Rathmines, on the Central Coast of New South Wales, around 140 kilometres north of Sydney.

Despite requests by the RAAF for Consolidated to deliver PBYs without the armour and other additions, Consolidated wouldn't comply. They were making the PBYs to US Navy requirements, so all PBYs—regardless of their destination—were fully fitted out. The RAAF made their own modifications, removing the armour, self-sealing cells and, on the PBY-5A, the landing gear. All these changes resulted in a reduction of the aircraft's overall weight, allowing the aircraft's range to be extended; it could also carry a heavier mine load over shorter distances. With these modifications, plus the use of seaplane tenders or submarines as AOBs, the mining of distant targets, hitherto impossible, was now achievable. Catalinas could top up fuel at the AOBs; in some cases, the seaplane tenders also provided accommodation and rest stops for the crews.

Only PBY-5s were modified at Rathmines. The amphibious PBY-5As and some PB2B-1s and 2s—more recent models built under licence by Boeing in Canada—were sent to Lake Boga. Forty-six PBY-5As were converted to PBY-5A(M)s.

After removal of the landing gear and hydraulic equipment from the PBY-5As, the wheel bays were faired over with metal sheeting. The port wheel bay was converted to house the Auxiliary Power Unit (APU), and the starboard wheel bay became a food locker. In effect, the modified amphibians had been returned to a standard PBY-5 flying boat. By removing the self-sealing cells from the mainplane's integral fuel tanks, the fuel capacity was increased by 936 litres, restoring it to its original fuel capacity of 6600 litres.

Former sergeant and airframe engineer Bert Jones, who had worked in maintenance and flew missions with 20 Squadron, was in charge of the modifications at Rathmines. He handpicked his crews and, when the pressure was on, worked around the clock to convert two aircraft every three weeks. Jones noted that the weight of the armour plate protecting the navigator was so great, 'each piece took one man all his effort to lift it'.

Jones and his team strengthened the Cat's body by riveting a heavy-gauge duralumin strip along the fuselage. This modification was also done at Lake Boga. Suggesting a good-humoured rivalry between the two FBRDs, Jones said his crew was better than 'Scotty' Allan's, an earlier commander at Rathmines FBRD. Allan had left Rathmines to take charge at Lake Boga.

George Urquhart Allan—or 'Scotty', as he was affectionately known—was an experienced aviator. Born in 1899 at Forgandenny, Scotland, he trained as a pilot in World War I and flew Sopwith Camels against the enemy—that is, until he was found to be underage. After the war, he re-enlisted with the RAF, learning to fly heavy bombers and specialising in night flying. Scotty joined the RAAF in 1940. When asked how many flying hours he had under his belt, his response was 'ten thousand'.

Scotty was part of the crew that flew the first RAAF Catalina to Australia and, in February 1941, he was posted to Rathmines to set up a Catalina Training Establishment. Scotty's pupils, of all ranks, learned how to fly the Catalina, how to anchor it and how to handle armaments, as well as anything else necessary to keep the Cat safe both in the air and on the water. In the early months of 1942, experienced RAAF Catalina pilots flew with leaders of the US Army Air Force bomber formations to aid and advise on tactics. The US Army and Navy air arms held the RAAF Catalina pilots in high esteem, thanks to Scotty's thorough training. He was later awarded the Air Force Cross (AFC) for his excellent training record—during his whole tenure, he had no fatalities. Scotty reached the rank of Wing Commander before being honourably discharged in December 1944 and going on to work as a pilot for Qantas, and later as a consultant.

As for Bert Jones, he would serve the remainder of the war at Rathmines, being discharged in October 1945. He remembered his time in maintenance fondly: 'The Catalina men, particularly the Operational Squadron crews, made many lifetime friendships, which seem to grow stronger as we become older.'

The US Navy, of course, had their own Catalinas, and even their own Black Cat Squadrons. US Black Cats attacked IJN night convoys using torpedoes and bombs, and blasted the decks of ships with their .30-calibre and .50-calibre machine guns. It has been said that US Navy Catalinas were not employed for mine laying because US Navy crews were not happy about removing protective armour from their aircraft. RAAF Flight Lieutenant Norman Robertson, the person most familiar with the strategies employed, noted that '[it] was a distinct possibility that this was the case . . . but again, it would be doubtful if there was anything in writing about anything like that. However, the possibility should not be discounted.'

There is no written record in either Australian or American archives to say why US Catalinas weren't chosen for mine-laying missions. Any reticence US Navy crews had about removing the weighty defensive gear probably should not be interpreted as a refusal to undertake the missions, but rather as a desire to obey an order from Admiral King, Commander-in-Chief of the US Navy. On 15 February 1942, King demanded that 'US Navy aircraft be equipped with self-sealing tanks and fitted with armor for the pilots and observers'. As such, US Navy crews were just exercising their right as imposed from above.

Former RAAF airman John Gibson, of 43 Squadron, said, 'In effect, we had the same privilege. We did not have to volunteer, and the RAAF airmen were asked or given the opportunity to volunteer for the Catalina mine laying. Not much different really.'

Another reason the US Navy didn't conduct the night raids is believed to be the problems they faced navigating because the Bendix system was unsuitable for the conditions in the SWPA. Ray Byfield, also with 43 Squadron, remembered a potentially awkward moment when chatting with some US Navy personnel over a beer one night. The Australians questioned the young US Navy sailors about life in the United States and about Hollywood movie stars. Then the Australians answered the sailors' questions about the different services, in particular the AIF, and the conversation turned to why Australian Catalinas were being employed as mine-layers. Byfield explained:

> The Americans were intrigued by the AIF and aware of their good reputation ... then came the inevitable question when one said to us, 'Why are you here? We have our own Catalinas, crews and mines, why are you here?' There was silence. We had to think of an acceptable answer, as we could not criticise their navigators. We replied, 'Our navigators are specially trained for this type of mine laying ... that's all.' The answer was accepted ... 19-year-old Australians to 19-year-old Americans.

4

MINING OPERATION SUFFERS A SEVERE BLOW

MID TO LATE 1943

Almost as soon as the RAAF and US Navy began their mine-laying operations, new and improved weapons became available. In August 1943, new mines arrived that had delayed arming mechanisms (DAMs), consisting of colour-coded washers made from a soluble salt material; each colour represented a different length of time before the washer would dissolve when immersed in the sea. The DAMs were an anti-sweeping device designed to frustrate the enemy's mine-clearance operations, as they could be set for a variety of time periods.

Then there was the introduction of the period delay mechanism (PDM). This enhancement allowed a certain number of ships to pass over the mine—up to eight, as confirmed by Ivor Collins—before it exploded. Together, DAMs and PDMs allowed for greater control over the activation of mines. For example, the DAM could be set to arm six days after planting, with the PDM triggering the mine when the fourth ship passed over it after it had been activated.

To further complicate sweeping operations for the enemy, magnetic mines—which relied on vessels being metal for them to activate—were joined in the Allied arsenal by acoustic mines, which were activated by the noise generated by the ship's engines and propellers. A mixture of mine types could be planted. Later, a mine was developed that combined both magnetic and acoustic capabilities. It was almost impossible to sweep it. The fitting of sterilisers became a necessity so the mines would be rendered inactive after a predetermined period. Mines planted early in the campaign were not fitted with sterilisers.

Former armourer Ray Byfield graphically explained the logistics of laying mines:

> [A] shallow water mine is a 2000 lb [900 kg] cylindrical object [similar to a torpedo] . . . it's not a big ball with spikes . . . it is something that lies on the bottom of the sea in harbours or a waterway. When released from the aircraft a drogue [a sort of parachute] opens out. This makes the mine fall straight and at the right entry angle when it hits the water. Some plates are held together by a soft shear pin that shears on impact and releases a ring that has vanes attached. The water strikes the vanes and rips away the cotton drogue to prevent tides shifting the mine and giving away its position. The mine then lies on the bottom of the sea, under the water. Nothing happens except water dissolves a salt washer that is seven centimetres diameter by three centimetres that holds the arming pin.
>
> When . . . the washer [dissolves], a spring-loaded arming pin descends and arms the mine . . . the more compressed the salt, the longer it takes for the mine to be armed.
>
> Salt compression is identified by the various colours, depending on the delay required. Sometimes a mine can lie there for weeks and not be armed . . . This delayed activation causes the enemy a lot of

headaches in clearance operations, because, until all the mines are located and rendered neutral, the harbour is useless to ships.

The most difficult type of mine to sweep is the combined magnetic and acoustic. To activate the mine and set it off there has to be the sound of the ship accompanied by its magnetic field. Being magnetic doesn't mean the mine will pop up and hit the ship. The magnetic operation is simple . . . take a look at the needle on a compass, then pass any piece of steel past the compass, the needle will turn. In a mine the needle is a 'switch', so that when the needle reaches a pre-set point it makes an electrical contact and if the acoustics are right—BANG!

The travel of the compass needle is a way to pick up the size of the ship to be blown up . . . the length of the time for the needle to travel 180-degrees is an indication of the size of the ship.

Of course there are tricks. For example, what if the enemy convoy is protecting a big important ship? The mines, or a mine, can be set so that it will not be activated until maybe six, or any number of ships, go over . . . then the big one comes over—GOTCHA!

The mind boggles at the sneaky things that can be done. The triggering of the mine needs a combination of acoustics and magnetics to work and makes it harder for the enemy to find and neutralise it.

Great secrecy surrounded the mines. The technological advancements of the weapons—the DAM and PDM mechanisms, the sterilisers and the incorporation of both magnetic and acoustic sensors—and the speed with which these technologies were adopted are a credit to the people involved and an amazing achievement for the time. Because of this, all crews were ordered never to drop a mine in shallow water or on land. If they couldn't get to their target, they would either have to return with the mines or 'dump' them at the predetermined location along their track. The mines could never fall into enemy hands. It was feared that if the Japanese found an intact mine, they could develop countermeasures that would render the mines useless. This happened early in the European Theatre when, in 1939, the British collected a discarded magnetic mine that had been jettisoned by the Germans in, of all places, the River Thames. This allowed the British to develop countermeasures and ensure safer travel for their convoys.

To outwit the mine-laying operations, the IJN would send a ship ahead of its convoy to act as bait. This would be a vessel with a skeleton crew that they were willing to sacrifice for the defence of other ships carrying important cargo. They hoped the ship would explode the mine or mines, making it safe for the convoy to proceed. However, the Allied strategy of applying the DAM and PDM, as well as using a mix of magnetic and acoustic mines, thwarted the Japanese; the IJN had no real solutions for this problem. They started using wooden-hulled vessels to transport troops and supplies in the back-street channels to avoid the magnetic mines, but this was no defence against acoustic mines.

Despite all the careful planning by Pally Carr, and the advanced technologies being used in mines, there appeared to be a problem in October. An urgent message was sent:

> To: North Eastern Area RAAF Command
> From: 11 SQN, 13 October. For Senior Air Staff Officer
> Use of British B200 females, to date three, repeat three British Mines have exploded on hitting the water. One on the night of first of October, one on the night of the fifth of October. All dropped from 400 feet. Consider there is grave danger of an explosion on the surface of the water which would almost certainly result in the destruction of the dropping aircraft. Recommend that use of these mines be stopped and investigation made as to the reason for the exploding. Alternatively that they be modified to carry parachutes. Understand these females have received very little maintenance since arrival from overseas.

The British Mark IV Assembly B200 mines were filled with one of two explosives, either amatol (weighing 680.388 kilograms) or minol (691.728 kilograms). The first mine mentioned in the report was dropped at Pomalaa, Sulawesi, Netherlands East Indies, and observed to explode prematurely after it had entered the water. The second was in Manokwari Harbour on the Vogelkop Peninsula, Irian Jaya. The third mine was dropped at Waingapu, Sumba, Netherlands East Indies. The Mine Warfare Officer's report to Washington, DC, noted that a total of four out of sixteen Mark IV Assembly B200 mines dropped up to 20 October had exhibited this fault. Tests were carried out using drogues, and this was thought to resolve the problem. Further investigations were made when another premature explosion occurred after a mine entered the water at Kaimana, south-east of Manokwari.

Given how low the Catalinas flew, an exploding mine was a huge problem for the crews. Former RAAF skipper Bryan Monkton gave an account of what it was like to be blown up by your own mine for *Blackwood's Magazine*, a quarterly periodical in the United Kingdom that ceased publication in 1980. Having released his first mine successfully, Monkton made his second run and released his last mine. This time, the drogue didn't deploy. Monkton wrote:

> Damn and blast, I curse to myself. What a bloody waste of time and effort, dragging that hulking mass nearly a 1000 miles only to have it lie on the sea bottom, impotent and useless. Then . . . the clouds above are lit by a great, blinding flash and the next instant the 'Cat-boat' bucks as though kicked by a giant boot from below. At the same time, the tail of the aircraft is thrown up, the nose goes down into a steep dive and the control yoke slams back into my stomach.
>
> The remote chance has happened, and two thousand pounds of high explosive have erupted right under our feet!

> [A]s we plunged headlong at the sea, I had no time to dwell on the possible cause while the effect was putting us in such peril. I snap out the autopilot and heave hard on the control yoke. To my surprise it comes back without much effort, but the movement seems to have no immediate effect on our nose-down attitude. We are going to hit the water in a matter of seconds unless I can get the nose up quickly. My horrified stare takes in the radio altimeter, which indicates we are now less than a 100 feet from the surface.
>
> 'Power!' I yell. 'Quick! Full power!'
>
> Abbot [Monkton's copilot, also known as Second Pilot], never the fastest to react as a rule, on this occasion moves with the speed of light. In one swift action he slams the propeller controls and throttles forward and there is instantly a surge of power from the two engines. All this has taken less than 20 seconds and during this time my eyes have remained fixed on the instruments that foretell so clearly our impending fate. The radio altimeter now reads less than 50 feet while the vertical speed indicator still shows we are going down. I brace myself mentally and physically for the shock of crashing into the sea. In those few critical seconds I am almost in a trance, still with the control yoke pulled hard back. The needle of the radio altimeter now begins to kick erratically between zero and 50 feet, a sure sign we are almost on the surface. But then the needle steadies momentarily on 30 feet and, as I watch unbelievingly, reads 50, 60, 70, a 100 feet! We have miraculously missed the sea—but by how much one can only guess.

The crew is shaken, but there are no serious injuries—just a few cuts and bruises. The Cat, however, is in worse shape. Holes dot the fuselage, and fuel begins leaking from the tanks. The engineer regulates the amount of fuel being used, attempting to conserve what they have. Consulting with the navigator, Monkton realises that they don't have enough fuel to get them home. He breaks radio silence and sends a 'mayday', in preparation for ditching the Cat in the ocean. As they are still in enemy territory, Monkton hopes a rescue party will reach them before the Japanese do. Monkton says to his crew, 'There is nothing more we can do now but pray.'

Suddenly, the engineer yells to Monkton that the left engine's fuel gauge is reading empty, and the right is low. Yet, both engines are running. Monkton now has a choice. He can ditch the Cat while over water, and hope for a rescue. Or, if he continues on his course, he will soon be over land—'and once we start to cross it, we shall be committed to the possibility of a forced landing in hilly bush country, which would mean almost certain disaster'.

The left engine begins to fail. Monkton orders the engineer to feed the left with fuel from the right. Both engines now purr again. Monkton commits to crossing the island in order to reach the AOB: 'Slowly, painfully, the ground creeps beneath us, and each minute seems like an hour. Abbott and I scan the terrain constantly, searching in vain for any flat area where we might get down.'

Despite both fuel gauges now reading empty, the engines continue to run and Monkton prays. The crew are bracing themselves for a crash-landing, when 'slowly but surely we pass over the ground until, hardly daring to believe our luck, we approach the shoreline and [are] within reach of safety'.

Ignoring identification protocols, Monkton quickly sets the Cat down and is met by US Navy personnel in their work boat ready to drag the Catalina onto the beach. Monkton continues:

> The hard-boiled crew chief, his US Navy cap on the back of his head and a stubby cigar clenched between his teeth, pokes his head through the open hatch. 'Whatsa matter wit' you Aussie guys?' he growls. 'Why all the panic to beach th' ol' bucket?'

'You'll find out soon enough, Chiefy, if you don't hurry,' the engineer tells him happily as he watches the water rapidly swirling in over the floorboards.

There was never any 'fix' to stop mines exploding if they hit the water hard without the drogue deploying. This would just be another occupational hazard the crews would have to live with while doing their job. Thankfully, this occurrence was rare.

As if laying mines wasn't complicated and hazardous enough on its own, someone decided to make it even more so. During the early mine-laying days, the 'higher-ups' resolved that the RAAF Black Cats should also carry torpedoes on their mine-laying runs so they could have 'a crack' at any enemy ships floating about. After laying the mines—which was the primary mission—the Cats should then torpedo any ships in harbour.

Former flight engineer Keith Hamilton, of 11 Squadron, vividly remembered taking on this precarious order:

> The torpedo operation and run was different, it involved a low level run to line up on the target . . . Our skipper proceeded to the target after laying his mines, but the exercise proved less than effective. The aircraft encountered heavy fire from the moored ship as well as from gun positions in the vicinity. We were forced to take violent evasive action with a heavy torpedo under one wing . . . a second run was attempted with the same results as the first. The skipper did his best to line up the ship and release the torpedo and then to break away.

On his return to base, Hamilton's skipper filled in the report sheet, writing that the mine laying was successful. As for the torpedo attack, he noted that the torpedo had narrowly missed the vessel, headed for the beach and 'probably sunk a truck nearby'.

Whoever decided on this operation persisted with it until 30 September 1943. That night, while attempting a torpedo run, a Catalina was lost. Just one person survived the flight.

It was commonplace for Mining Operations planners to join sorties as observers, to see for themselves what the crews experienced in case there was anything they needed to change to make the operation smoother. On 30 September, Pally Carr—the brains behind the mine-laying strategy—joined the crew of 20 Squadron's Catalina A24-67. While other Cats on the mission were just laying mines, A24-67 also acted as an observation craft and was tasked with torpedoing any vessel in the harbour. After the other Cats had laid their mines, Flying Officer Douglas McDiarmed brought A24-67 around to launch a torpedo at an anchored ship. Heavy anti-aircraft fire caught the Catalina, and it came down near Pomalaa, south-east Sulawesi. McDiarmed and Carr were the only survivors, with McDiarmed badly injured. The Japanese captured them in the early hours of 1 October and began their interrogation. McDiarmed, sadly, died the next day after being brutally handled by his captors.

Carr, on the other hand, was dressed in his commander's RAN uniform and taken to Surabaya. He kept to the story that he was on board the Catalina as a naval observer for the torpedo attack and for ship-recognition purposes. The Japanese interrogators failed to discover his role as director of the mine-laying operations, and they remained unaware of the prize they had in their possession. Had they known, it is almost certain that he would have been executed by beheading, the 'dishonourable death' reserved for Catalina aircrew.

At the start of the RAAF/US Navy mine-laying operations, the IJN thought that Allied submarines were invading the channels and harbours undetected and laying the mines. The Japanese never considered that Catalinas were doing the job, because they believed their harbours and ports to be beyond the range of the aircraft. Eventually, the Japanese discovered the mining was the work of modified RAAF Black Cats.

They saw the mine-laying operations as a serious threat and an act of 'terrorism' outside the normal conventions of war. They would behead any captured RAAF Black Cat pilots or navigators, identifying these crewmen as being responsible for the terrorist act. That said, it didn't stop other crew members receiving the same treatment from their captors.

Carr was held in captivity until the end of the war. His contribution was acknowledged in the US Seventh Fleet Mining Report to Fleet Admiral Ernest King. Paragraph 15 of the report dated 20 October 1943 states:

> LTCDR P. E. Carr, Royal Australian Navy (RAN), OiC of Section Ops 3 (T) of the RAAF Command, Brisbane . . . in close cooperation with the 7th Fleet staff, has guided the aircraft minelaying campaign in the Netherlands East Indies since its inception, and it will be extremely difficult to replace him with an officer of equal knowledge, acumen and energy.

Military historian George Odgers recorded Carr's capture as a severe blow to the Seventh Fleet mining campaign. Odgers noted that Carr had worked hard and enthusiastically to plan its inception, acknowledging his expertise, wide knowledge of the Netherlands East Indies and awareness of the financial benefits of aerial mining.

To Carr's credit, his successors—LTCDR Denis W. George OBE, RAN Reserve, and LTCDR Shirley Quimby US Navy Reserve—did not alter the principles of his planning. Before his capture, Carr had written a paper on aircraft mine-laying procedure. Visiting the RAAF Command Headquarters in Melbourne in 1945, Carr learned his paper had been included in the RAAF Air Publication. He was pleased and commented 'that there had been no changes and that the procedures and methods worked out for our early efforts had proved successful enough to become standard up to the end of the War'.

Torpedoes weren't the only additional weaponry carried by the crews on mine-laying missions. Incendiary bombs also formed part of the arsenal during the early months. Incendiaries were, in the words of Ray Byfield, 'fiendish weapons' that consisted of a cylindrical body with a welded tail plate to control trajectory. The steel hemispherical nose welded to the body held a non-delay percussion fuse plus 680 grams of white phosphorus in a bakelite (hard plastic) container. On contact with the target, the percussion fuse activated and caused the bakelite container to break. This resulted in the phosphorus mixing with rubber benzoyl in the incendiary, generating an enormous pressure that would blast the welded tail plate off the end of the cylinder, causing the body to spin like a Catherine wheel and spray the ignited mixture over everything. The mixture could eat through steel roofs; the rubber stuck to whatever it touched, while the phosphorus burned any combustible material.

The British used incendiaries against the Germans from early in the war. So severe was the damage caused by the weapons, the Germans complained to the Geneva Convention, calling the weapons 'inhumane'. Ray Byfield worked with these volatile bombs and was told by his superiors, 'if the phosphorus gets on a finger . . . "cut" that finger off or the phosphorus would keep eating up your arm'.

Incendiaries were used as additional weapons, particularly by those Cats involved in bombing raids. Once they had hit their primary target, they would have a secondary target to 'light up', usually an airfield or ammunitions storage building. The area around the second target would be lit with flares, and then the incendiaries were dropped out of the blister by hand to cause as much damage as possible. When the mine-laying sorties began, some crews continued carrying incendiaries so they could menace the enemy. Mine-laying crews were never given secondary targets—it was purely an opportunistic situation, where crews would attack any enemy sighted on their way back to home base.

RAAF Command became concerned that this practice exposed the crews to unnecessary risk, as it revealed their position to the enemy and made them vulnerable to attack—not to mention that mishandling the bomb in flight would be fatal to all on board the Cat. A directive was soon issued to cease such bravado:

> Enthusiastic Catalina Captains have, in the past, made a practice of strafing likely targets encountered en route home from mining missions. Some have carried bundles of incendiaries to enhance the fun . . . [leading to] their exposure to needless and usually profitless jeopardy. [Crews are not] to carry bombs of any description when engaged in minelaying operations, [or] to carry out any strafing of ground installations or shipping unless this is directly required to discourage opposition during its mining run.

Not wanting to have their 'fun' totally taken away, the crews came up with an ingenious substitute 'bomb'. An unknown aviator discovered that if they placed a razor blade in the neck of a beer bottle and then dropped the bottle at altitude, it made a whistling noise very much like a real bomb. Crews would carry these homemade 'bottle bombs' to confuse the enemy. Because they didn't explode and didn't need to be accurate, the bottle bombs never exposed the crews to any danger. The Japanese could hear a bomb falling, but they didn't know where it was coming from or where it was going to land—and they had no idea if or when it would explode. This would have had the enemy diving for cover—mission accomplished. Though some crews may have been tempted to drop a flare to watch the enemy's reaction, thankfully they were happy to imagine the scene rather than take that risk.

5

EVERYONE HAD THEIR JOBS TO DO

Membership of a mine-laying Catalina crew was voluntary. Each volunteer, despite having already earned their wing or wings, would undergo further training and testing before being accepted. Taking off and alighting a Cat on the sea were vastly different to doing so in an aircraft on land. In bad weather, land-based aircraft would be grounded. For a Catalina, alighting on choppy or rough seas was necessary during rescues or if the weather turned as the crew returned from an operation.

These rough-water alightings were perilous, as former flying officer Richard 'Dick' Udy, wireless air gunner (WAG) of 43 Squadron, remembered:

> It was taken for granted that we were always on hand for emergency rescues in the open sea if any of our planes crashed. To prepare for such eventualities, at the end of our operational training programme, we would go to do rough water alightings in Broken Bay [Central Coast, New South Wales]. This was a tricky business because, instead of flying onto the water with a great skid, peacefully, as we usually did,

> to alight in rough water we had to gradually lose flying speed as close to the water as possible and then, when the plane stalled, fall with a crash on top of the swell. The strain on the thin metal skin of the plane and the battering we all had on impact meant that we would only do this in really desperate situations in the open sea . . . nowhere else.

Even before attempting a rough-water alighting, Udy and his crew quickly learned how dangerous this procedure was. When they arrived at Rathmines for training, their 'first duty was to act as pallbearers to a crew who had died doing this very thing at Port Stephens', about 90 kilometres north of Rathmines FBRD.

Pilots, navigators, engineers, wireless operators, armourers and gunners were all highly skilled and rigorously trained. Not all graduated—but those who did were specialists in their area. In addition to being skilled airmen, all volunteers had to be able to swim. Given that the Cats operated from water and, if the aircraft was forced to 'ditch', it would most likely alight on water, the RAAF required all crew members to be competent swimmers. They didn't want to lose any servicemen to drowning. This, however, didn't stop some non-swimmers from wanting to join the ranks, such as George Findlay, a former navigator with 20 Squadron. Findlay was stationed at East Arm, Darwin, with Reg Cleworth:

> Reg and I were brother navigators, he was on Ross Schulz's crew and I was on Lance Stedman's crew . . . I remember Reg very well, as an intelligent, earnest, capable and likeable guy. I also remember with great affection the two flight engineers, whose names I have forgotten but whose faces are still clear in my memory. I believe that I owe my life to a couple of members of Schulz's crew and Reg, and either or both of the engineers could have been the fellows involved . . . I cannot remember.

Findlay had been helping Reg set the compasses on his Cat on a stinking hot day. After they had finished, Reg suggested that they all go for a swim. Findlay noted that 'they were not to know that I had dodged every one of the weekly swim exercises'. However, the coolness of the sea was too inviting, and Findlay jumped in with everyone else and

> commenced to practice my aquatic art, that of floating on my back. After 30 seconds in accordance with my usual practice, I pushed down my feet to touch the bottom. I touched bottom alright, but with my head underwater. Drifting out to sea and making desperate but only partially successful attempts to keep my head above the water and to avoid swallowing same. I kept trying to catch the attention of the others who were jumping off each other's shoulders and making a lot of noise near the slip. At last I heard someone say, 'he's fair dinkum'. Out swam at least two and, with a lot of difficulty, hauled me in from some 50–60 yards out to sea. I was a fool. There is a 28-foot rise and fall of the tide at Darwin and at that time, it was going out, with me with it. I have remained ever grateful to them.

Findlay's crew was originally scheduled for a mine-laying mission in the China Sea, but replacement orders were given for them to collect a new Catalina from the United States. This meant that Ross Schulz's crew, taking A24-203, flew the mission. Findlay remembered his reaction to hearing that Schulz's plane 'went in', a colloquial phrase used when an aircraft was lost in action:

> We were in Cairns waiting transport to the US when news reached us that the Schulz crew had not returned. I am sure for a considerable time I was very close to becoming severely psychotic. All aircrew were close knit. After the swimming incident, Reg and the two engineers were special people. They were unselfish men. I was almost

certain that they had lost their lives and quite illogically blamed myself and, in fact, the whole crew. It was as though, like cowards, we had pulled out and Reg and his crew, my friends, had taken our place. Of course, the decision was made quite outside the knowledge of our crew, but at the time my mind would not accept that. It was our fault, my fault.

Servicemen and women share a bond forged by the defence arm to which they belong, be it army, navy or air force. The bond becomes stronger as they share experiences and suffer losses. Both air and ground crews, regardless of the squadron to which they belonged, were bonded in training and during operations by the aircraft they flew and serviced. Therefore, whenever a crewman or an entire crew was lost, those remaining experienced survivor guilt. Tom Broughton, former skipper with 42 Squadron, explained: 'It was a feeling, especially if you knew the crew as I did Ross Schulz, why these chaps? They didn't deserve to go. Why not us?' Years later, when talking with veterans, their foremost recollections and thoughts still focus on those they had known and lost.

There were nine crew members on a Catalina. The pilot, also known as the skipper, a second pilot known as second dicky, a navigator who was also the bomb aimer, first engineer, second engineer, first wireless operator and gunner (WAG), second WAG, an armourer who was also a gunner, and a rigger who was yet another gunner. As an armourer, Ray Byfield remembered that 'all aircrew were trained to operate, strip and reassemble the machine guns and clear a jammed weapon, a task that could be all too frequent'.

On 26 June 1944, Reg Cleworth wrote home while in training:

Had a dose of training today, 3½ mile cross country in heavy boots, then bayonet drill + lecture on foot hygiene. Spent the afternoon at the rifle range using rifle + Tommy gun, so apparently we are to be infantry

> as well as aircrew when we leave. If we get too much I'll transfer to the A.I.F. We only need an artillery course + we could fill any job it offers.
>
> Well, love to all from Reg.

After graduating, all crew—apart from pilots—were awarded the single wing badge worn as part of their uniform. The badge displayed AG for air gunner, or WAG if they were a wireless operator. Armourers and fitters all had AG on their wings. Fitters were ex-ground staff volunteers who looked after the engine mechanics, airframe and controls of the aircraft, and had trained and qualified as air gunners. They were carried as specialist staff to conduct daily inspections away from base, no matter how remote. When attached to an aircrew, fitters were promoted to acting sergeant. If they were no longer needed as crew members, they could revert to ground staff and their former rank as corporal or leading aircraftman. Once they had been awarded their AG wing, however, nobody could take it away. As Ray Byfield recalled, 'It remained with them forever, so there!'

As far as rank was concerned, once the aircraft was in the air, seniority was put aside as everyone had their jobs to do and was treated equally. This was because the skipper may be a Flight Sergeant, yet the wireless operator could hold the rank of Flight Lieutenant. On land, the WAG outranked the skipper, but not so in the air. When on an operation, the entire crew relied on each other; instructions were sought from whoever had the better experience, dependent upon the situation. In fact, some crews refused to wear their rank insignias on ops to show they were part of a team.

Keith Hamilton, former flight engineer with 11 Squadron, gave further insights into how the crews operated:

> A navigator was responsible for all navigational functions and to act as a bomb aimer who guided the aircraft on the mine-laying runs.

> Only one navigator was carried which meant he would, at times, be required to work long hours with minimum relief, and to snatch a rest and relief whenever he could. During mine-laying operations he called off the time in seconds to the target from the datum point and would be assisted in that task by the second pilot.
>
> The WAGS were trained to cope with any electrical problems that may arise during a mission and . . . assisted other crew members with the aircraft's mooring and slipping operations. When at action stations, one manned the bow machine gun, the other the wireless equipment.

Two engineers were jointly responsible for the operation of the aircraft's engines and auxiliary equipment. As Hamilton explained from firsthand experience:

> The First Engineer, or Flight Engineer, monitored the fuel flow meters and operated the fuel transfer pump switches, engine mixture and controlled all fuel operations. During flight he would record all instrument readings on the control panel at 20 minute intervals. The entries in the aircraft's logbook were later analysed to assist in the maintenance of the aircraft. His main station was at the control station in the superstructure supporting the mainplane, located in the wing, above the pilot. The Flight Engineer also supervised engine start-ups and the retraction and lowering of the floats . . . the Flight Engineer's decision could strongly influence a Skipper deciding if any action was to be taken should a mechanical problem arise that may require a mission to be aborted.

The second engineer operated the auxiliary power unit (APU) used for generating power for engine starts. A 28-volt petrol-driven generator, it supplemented the aircraft's storage batteries at start-up. His action station was to man the downward-firing tunnel machine gun in the rear of the aircraft. This, according to Hamilton, was not a simple procedure, as it required the operator to be suspended by a harness from the roof (deck head) of the tunnel compartment. In this position, he could swing over the top of the gun, which had a hinged mounting so that it could be swung out of its storage position, and slot through a large hatch that opened in the floor of the rear compartment. Hamilton only operated this gun during training, never on operational sorties.

Former fitter Cyril Payne remembered that some skippers, in order to save weight, did not carry the tunnel machine gun on mining operations because 'we often flew below 10 metres to avoid enemy radar contact . . . any self-respecting enemy pilot would not fly that low'.

Those who carried the tunnel machine gun were able to use it to strafe the Japanese navy and army personnel who were taking pot shots at the low-flying Cat with their rifles. The aim was to keep the enemy's heads down to stop them doing any serious damage to the Cat or its crew. As all of the armour plating and self-sealing fuel cells had been removed from the Cats, the Japanese Arisaka rifles—the Type 38 used by the army and, particularly, the more powerful Type 99 used by the Imperial Japanese Army Air Service (IJAAS)—could easily penetrate the aircraft. It may have needed a lucky shot to bring a Cat down, but given the plane's slow speed and the zeal of many angry soldiers all shooting at once, the odds were in the enemy's favour.

The armourer stored and maintained all the weapons on board—the machine guns, ammunition and the crew's ground weapons—and collected any spent cartridges for recycling. During action stations, he manned one of the two .50-calibre machine guns. In the event a Cat was shot down and the crew survived, they had at their disposal some very basic weapons: two .303 rifles, each with two five-round magazines, and one American Thompson submachine gun with two twenty-round magazines. Each crewman also had his own .38 Smith & Wesson revolver with twelve rounds of ammunition. With this arsenal, as Ray Byfield commented, 'they expected us to fend off a marauding Japanese Army . . . good luck!'

An armourer's main duty was to check the correct mines were loaded onto the release hooks under the wing and, of course, to be sure the release hooks worked, particularly where parachutes were fitted to the mines. He also assisted the navigator with launching flame floats or sea markers to help in plotting the course to the target. Byfield recalled that 'the Navigator never got any rest, so it was a pleasure to be able to assist a little'.

As its two engines were close together, the Catalina was more difficult to manoeuvre than other flying boats. Consequently, armourers helped with mooring the Cat and applying the drogues as required when taxiing. The armourer also assisted in preparing the meals and keeping the aircraft clean and tidy.

Catering on long flights was shared among the crew members. Although a RAAF ration of consumables was issued to each aircraft, it was not unusual to have these supplies supplemented by a crew member who had cultivated a rewarding friendship with one of the mess supply staff. Often the cardboard scrounge box would contain steak and eggs, vegetables, bread and butter, tins of canned fruit, condensed milk, fresh fruit and other 'goodies' for the crew's meals on a flight. In addition, the crew would chip in and buy packets of biscuits or the occasional cake.

After departure, the engineer closest to the galley would switch on a hotplate ready for the preparation of the evening meal by another crew member. He would also heat a container of water ready for tea- and coffee-making.

The Catalina's galley was equipped with a set of pressure cookers. These new devices were unknown to many Australians during World War II, but were helpful aboard the Cat. In addition to the special lids preventing spillages in rough weather, the pressure cookers made it easy to get a meal together for the entire crew in a reasonable time. After a meal, or a round of coffee and tea, the dishes were washed and stowed neatly away. It was a matter of great pride to have a clean aircraft. It didn't go down well to come on board a Cat and find a dirty galley left by a previous crew. Sometimes, however, terrible flying conditions and near-disastrous operations were encountered, and these were valid excuses for an untidy galley.

The cooking smells would eventually drift up to where the flight engineer sat. He would open the sliding window and, by cupping his hands and holding them out through the window, he was able to direct fresh air into the Cat; this also served to cool the aircraft. Other crewmen would perform a similar operation by taking turns to hold their arm out of the blister compartments, directing cool air into the fuselage. There was no air-conditioning, so this was the only way to get some relief from the almost year-round tropical heat and humidity.

Because of the sweltering conditions and the natural heat emanating from the nine crew members all crammed in together, the environment within the aircraft was extreme. Shirts were considered optional for most crew members. Flying caps, shorts, socks and regulation flying boots were all that most men wore. Even then, it didn't stop them from sweating profusely.

Lieutenant Ivor Collins, US Navy Reserve, preparing to join his first mine-laying sortie as an observer, decided to take his flying jacket, which had a thick leather outer and a plush woollen lining. As he waited at the jetty with the crew for the small launch to take him to the Cat, the skipper, Flight Sergeant Bob Honan, queried the jacket. 'What's that for?'

Collins answered, 'I believe it gets cold up there?'

Giving a typically laconic response, Honan told Collins, 'Leave it behind . . . we don't fly that high.'

In the early morning hours, with enemy territory far behind, the skipper and most of the crew would head for the bunks or some convenient 'padded' corner and quickly fall asleep. The navigator, having calculated the course home and given the headings to the pilot, would probably doze off with his head cushioned on a life preserver placed on the plot table. One WAG would be 'listening out' on the appropriate frequency in case there was a 'mayday' call or an incoming coded message. The two crew members in the port and starboard gun stations—the 'blister' compartments—would almost certainly be dozing in their seats, although technically they were meant to be on watch. The engines would be throttled back to an easy cruising speed, and the aircraft—having dropped its load and used half its fuel—would, with its large wing area, be little more than a powered glider. The noise levels would now be considerably lower throughout the hull. Catalinas were notorious for being one of the loudest aircraft.

Evidence of the effects of the noise was revealed by Michael Nugent, a former fitter and engineer with 113 Air Sea Rescue, who served on Catalinas after the war. Many years after retiring from the RAAF, Nugent's wife complained that he was losing his hearing. He reluctantly saw a hearing specialist in Sydney, Dr Baker. When Dr Baker examined Nugent's history and discovered he had flown in Catalinas, the doctor's immediate response was: 'No need to test you, you're deaf.' Baker had examined many former Cat crew members, and found they all had hearing problems. It was an occupational hazard.

While on an operation, crew members would not sleep for twelve hours or more. As the adrenaline from the mission waned, it was easy for them to doze off. The duty pilot would tend the autopilot and keep a watch on the course. The other pilot's seat could be occupied by anyone tasked with making conversation and keeping the duty pilot awake. At his station, the engineer would also be constantly battling to stay awake, with nothing but a wall of hypnotic green dials in front of him. He would be continually watching the clock to ensure all engine readings were entered in the logbook. It was at these times that the engineer would attempt to chat to the duty pilot on the intercom. Sometimes the duty pilot would realise there was no response from the engineer. The first recourse was for the duty pilot to flip all the signal lights on at once, flashing them until the engineer responded. This system was used during operations and proved foolproof in comparison to using the intercom. Conversation via the intercom was difficult to understand with the engines at full throttle. Even without the guns firing, speech could be hopelessly garbled. Also, most microphones and earphones had deteriorated in the humid conditions. If the duty pilot received no response to the blinking lights, he would awaken his companion to take control, and go back to the engineer's compartment to give his leg a good shake. If the engineer received no response from the cockpit, he would drop down from his perch and give the duty pilot's arm a nudge.

Many times, a Cat sailed on quietly in the early morning hours under the sole command of the autopilot, which was quite reliable if set up properly. Generally, though, the pilot, engineer and one of the WAGs would be sharing these quiet hours. Someone might get the Bendix working and check on a few navigational fixes or even find some good music to while away the hours.

Of course, not all operations offered crews the luxury of rest periods. On 22 August 1944, Reg Cleworth wrote to his father to tell him of his first 'close encounter', which gave his crew a sleepless night.

Dear Dad,

Just a few lines to let you know, I had my baptism of fire two nights ago. Operating from this spot, we went about 700 miles to do a job. Went through the islands just about dark, and didn't get jumped.

Had a good night right up to the target, then things went a bit haywire. Pinpointed ourselves just South—then flew out to sea, and somehow went past, and it was nearly an hour before we finally were right for our job.

Flew right over one of their ships on the way. Made our run, had to turn nearly vertically to avoid a mountain and, while levelling out, a ship let us have it. I saw the tracers going past, but didn't even feel scared—must have been so satisfied at finding and completing the job. About an hour later petrol leaked into the bunk and engineer's compartment, and the boys couldn't smoke till we got back again.

Came back over Timor and saw hundreds of lights all over the island. First-light showed up just then and a pretty good watch was kept till we got well clear. Got back about nine-thirty a.m. after 17 hours straight.

Went up to the mainplane and found out how lucky we were. An explosive bullet went through the engine nacelle and penetrated the tank—hence the petrol leak. It just missed the oil tank as well, so we were pretty lucky. Also got another harmless one through the wing. Quite an exciting time for the first trip.

The C.O. was very tickled when we got back, as we were the only ones to find our target, and that was a smack in the face to the old-hands, of course.

Well cheers to you.

From your son, Reg.

P.S. Didn't even mess my underpants.

Alan Lancaster was an engineer on board Catalina A24-63, flown by Flight Lieutenant Eddie Ham, on a mine-laying op in the Woleai Atoll area:

> We had on board the Squadron Intelligence Officer [Flying Officer Paul Lachal] to observe the progress of a Japanese fighter strip under construction at Woleai Atoll. We had successfully laid our mines and were stooging around over Woleai at about 1500 feet [450 metres]. There was plenty of cloud above us. We dropped a flare over the target

> area so that the Intelligence Officer could get a better view. The flare ignited prematurely just below the aircraft, throwing our shadow onto the cloud ceiling not far above us. The Jap searchlights picked us up and their Bofors started throwing rocks at us. Fifteen hundred feet is about point blank range for a point-five inch machine gun and about the same for a Bofors. I was manning the tunnel gun and had it popped out. I could hear the Bofors and they got on to us and, to the best of my recollection, we were hit twice or a second one must have been mighty close. It was quite dramatic to say the least.

A24-63 was hit, resulting in the perspex dome being blown out of the blister turret, and a jagged hole—5–7 inches (13–18 centimetres) in diameter—being created in the hull, threatening to sink the Cat on alighting. Lancaster continued his recollection:

> There was wind rushing in everywhere and it was dark. The Skipper [Eddie Ham] came down to take stock of things and the Armourer, Sergeant Ron Ely, who copped most of the shrapnel on the blister gun, died in the Skipper's arms . . . Sergeant Norm Phillips was also killed. The Squadron Intelligence Officer was hopping around with a severe wound to his foot which later had to be amputated. He was traumatised and in shock.

Lancaster had to attend to the wounded Intelligence Officer and attempt to seal the hole in the hull. As he noted, 'I quickly arrested the bleeding, put a temporary dressing on him, and the Skipper, I think, put him on one of the bunks. I was covered in blood, there was quite a bit of it floating around. I then went to fix the hole.'

All Catalinas were supplied with leak-stoppers for such eventualities. A leak-stopper was shaped like a truncated pyramid, with a toggle bolt and batten attached. It would be manipulated through the hole, and then the batten would be put in place and twisted to tighten up the toggle bolt. Once tight, a piece of sponge rubber would then seal the hole. After that, plasticine supplied with the kits would be put over the repair to seal any irregularities. Lancaster grabbed his leak-stopper:

> I had to modify the stopper, and I can't remember to this day how I did it. I had to manipulate the T-piece into the hole because it was not as big as the hole, there were frames in the way. I probably filed a piece off, but anyway, I managed to get it in place and tightened it up on the sponge rubber and slapped the plasticine over it. I had to get the APU ready so that the bilge pump would be able to be started in the event the seal wasn't perfect and there was a leak . . . but when we landed at the Admiralty Islands the repair worked perfectly.

After patching up FO Paul Lachal, then repairing the hole, Lancaster remained in the hull of the aircraft for the remainder of its journey, caring for the wounded officer and cleaning up as best he could:

> What annoyed me the most . . . and it's funny how little things dominate . . . the other Engineer decided to leave me down below to fix the leak, nurse the wounded and clean up. Not a pleasant task. He decided to look after things up in the engineer's compartment in comparative comfort and did not even come down to relieve me during the flight back.

Given the condition of the aircraft, it was to the crew's credit that A24-63 was able to make it to its AOB, the USS *Tangier*. Lancaster continued the story:

> When we arrived back at the base, the Cat was hoisted aboard the *Tangier*. It was a big ship with a flat after-deck, capable of having

> three Cats carefully stacked on it. The crane that lifted the aircraft on board was capable of lifting a Catalina on board with all of us in it. The ship not only looked after Catalinas and Mariners [an American patrol-bomber flying boat] but also was home to the US Submarines that were operating in the area. We didn't stay on board but were flown back in one of our other Catalinas to Cairns. Our two comrades were buried on the nearest Island, which was Los Negros.

Lancaster recalled that on another occasion, when returning from a bombing raid, the Catalina began running low on fuel. For the Cat to reach home, the skipper ordered the crew to ditch anything weighty and superfluous to their immediate needs. Lancaster and the others threw out whatever they found not bolted down, 'including the ammunition'. Then they had a brainwave:

> Because we hadn't fired the guns for a while, we thought it would be a good idea to fire the ammo rather than dump it. This we did. It was rather stupid really. We didn't stop to think that we were only jettisoning the bullets, and all the cartridge cases would drop back into the aircraft, only to have to be picked out of the bottom of the aircraft. A time-consuming process. Also, it was quite uncomfortable when the odd hot cartridge case dropped down the top of your flying boot . . . which made you hop about a bit. The Armourers were not all that happy about having extra cleaning on the guns either. You live and learn.

Whenever the nine crewmen of a Catalina took to the air, their lives were literally in the hands of those who maintained the aircraft. The pilots, navigators, wireless operators, engineers and gunners all relied on the skill and dedication of the ground crews to keep the Cats floating on water and flying in the air—otherwise they would not be able to complete their tasks and get home safely.

Tom Broughton, skipper with 42 Squadron, acknowledged that

> much has been written of the exploits of aircrews but their lot in the main, by comparison, was not unpleasant. They enjoyed rhythms of life that were denied to ground crews.
>
> The practice was for Catalinas from Karumba and Melville Bay to fly to Darwin for a programme of missions, return to their base after a week or so, rest for a few days then repeat. This provided breaks in routine which were not sufficiently appreciated at the time. On the other hand, ground crews were locked at an isolated location without much other than their work to occupy their minds and energies. There was the arrival and departure of their aircraft every so often to break up the pattern but little else. It is not hard to imagine that for many a young man each day could assume a maddening sameness that cruelly tested their stoicism and mental endurance.
>
> That they continued to do their work with exactitude and dedication under difficulties imposed by tropical conditions is deserving of equal recognition, and even perhaps higher praise, than the aircrews whose life had variety. This has been seldom given except by the aircrews themselves whose lives depended upon the skills of the ground crews.

Keith Pinson, fitter and air gunner with 20 Squadron, added:

> The 'Black Cats' and the Airmen, both aircrew and the ground staff who kept them flying, must never be forgotten. It was through their efforts that the RAAF Catalinas gained quite a place in the history of the war. It has been said that of all the aircraft that operated in

> the Southwest Pacific, the Cats were constantly employed on operational missions, dropping torpedoes, bombing, laying mines off the coast of China, and in the shipping lanes and harbours elsewhere in the theatre, to well and truly earn their motto, 'The First and Furthest'.

The Flying Boat Repair Depots at Lake Boga, near Swan Hill in Victoria, and at Rathmines, on the Central Coast of New South Wales, were kept busy converting the Cats for mine-laying operations and also performing major repairs. Sergeant Bert Jones was posted at Rathmines and served for a time with 20 Squadron. He admits that

> very little has been written about the aircraft maintenance personnel and their service during World War Two, particularly the Catalina men. Their work became specialised, and they were seldom posted to other squadrons. Being well trained and totally committed to their work, they were also aware that the safety of the aircrews depended on them.

Early in 1942, Jones was put in charge of the major-repair section at Rathmines FBRD, where they were tasked with repairing Catalina A24-10, which had returned from an operation with a broken back:

> We had to rebuild the bunk section behind the step [the rear of the aircraft where the fuselage angles up to the tail section] and, as we could not get spare parts, had to make them as needed. It took 10 of us, 12 weeks to complete the work on A24-10 . . . I'm pleased to say that it flew throughout the war, and was later sold.

Another aircraft with a broken back was flown down from the islands. The crew had performed a makeshift repair, keeping the plane together with a braced length of timber over 10 metres long in the centre of the hull. According to Jones, his team worked '12-hour shifts . . . to complete the work in six weeks'.

In July 1942, all the men from the major-repair section were posted to Port Moresby to assist with the maintenance of operational Cats. Jones was given orders to go to 9 Squadron, stationed at Bowen in Far North Queensland:

> I was due to leave on the Saturday morning, but on the Friday afternoon, the [Commanding] Officer told me that I was to remain at Rathmines, and Corporal Fred Rivers was going in my place. When he arrived at 9 Squadron he was attached to HMAS *Canberra*, but sadly, a few weeks later, the ship was sunk during the Battle of Savo Island in the Solomon Islands, with heavy casualties . . . I remained at Rathmines until August 1943, when posted to 20 Squadron, Cairns [Far North Queensland].

Jones acknowledged that work on an operational squadron was more relaxed than 'the pressure-cooker atmosphere' of the repair depot at Rathmines. There was also a special camaraderie that developed between all personnel working with squadrons, and

> we became part of a close-knit and very dedicated team. When the Catalinas came in for repair, we sometimes worked till midnight, to have them serviceable for the next day. Our serviceability record was highly regarded. The Squadrons were very active, mining harbours and shipping lanes over the whole of the Southwest Pacific . . . carrying out bombing raids on Japanese wharf and airbase installations . . . flying in, bringing out, and supplying Coast Watchers. Also on shipping convoy work and air-sea rescue. The aircraft and crews were often in the air for up to 22 hours, sometimes longer.

In September 1944, 20 Squadron was relocated to East Arm, Darwin, in the Northern Territory. Jones noted that

> at times, some of the maintenance fitters and Radar technicians were called upon to fly as temporary crew members, at an extra two shillings [20 cents] a day. I did about 90 hours in the air, and some others did much more than that. On two occasions we were away for three weeks, and another time we were at Shecat for 10 days on mine-laying work. After 16 months with 20 Squadron, I returned to Rathmines and was in charge of the General Section.

Sir Richard Kingsland epitomised Catalina crews and the men who serviced the operational squadrons by saying of them, 'they didn't see themselves as heroes or anything special . . . but, special . . . very special they were'.

6

KEEPING UP THE PRESSURE

EARLY TO MID 1944

By the beginning of 1944, the RAAF/US Navy mine-laying operations were proving to be a real headache for the Japanese. So much so, just hearing the drone of a Catalina's twin Pratt & Whitney engines in the dark of night was enough for the Japanese Navy to cease ship movements and begin sweeping harbours and channels for suspected mines. This is verified by the *Report on Mine-laying Operations by the RAAF between 22 April 1943 and 31 July 1945*, which was written by RAAF Command in September 1945. On page 17, the report states:

> It was found that on many occasions the enemy expected that mines had been laid by the aeroplanes carrying out these duties and [as] a result 'decoy' tactics were instituted. These decoy tactics were carried out at all important targets and consisted of providing a proportion of the mine-laying aeroplanes [to make] a 'dummy' run to be carried out in a remote area from the actual minefield on completion

> of their mine drop. These dummy mine-laying runs were combined with reconnaissance duties wherever possible. In addition, when a secondary mine-laying target was located en route to or from the primary target, one or more aeroplanes were often ordered to fly at a low altitude over this secondary target in order to provide the enemy with the impression that mines had been laid. The sighting of enemy minesweepers operating these dummy areas on subsequent nights has proved that these tactics were often successful.

In the first year of the mine-laying campaign—April 1943 to March 1944—the RAAF Catalinas were very successful and had a serious impact on the Japanese war economy. Enemy ships were lost, including three at Kavieng. By far the greatest result was the dislocation of enemy shipping, causing a delay in oil shipments. The Japanese were forced to expend a considerable amount of energy in minesweeping. They employed 30 ships and 1500 men in the Netherlands East Indies alone, and were forced to increase their defences. This was not a bad outcome for the part-time activity of two, then later four, squadrons of what some referred to as 'slow and obsolete' Catalinas.

By 1944, the European Theatre had changed dramatically from the previous year. The Germans and Italians had been defeated in East and North Africa by British, Commonwealth, South African, French, Polish, Czechoslovakian and American forces. The Allies had landed in Italy. Benito Mussolini was sacked as the country's prime minister and exiled by Italy's King Victor Emmanuel III. Italy then surrendered in September 1943 and, a month later, did an about-face and declared war on Germany. The Germans, however, continued the resistance in Italy and stopped the Allied advance at what was known as the Gustav Line, which ran through the town of Monte Cassino. Since the victory at Stalingrad in early 1943, the Russians had had the Germans on the defensive, pushing them back to their border with Poland. All that remained was an offensive to open a western front in Europe. This offensive, codenamed Operation Overlord, had been secretly planned for months leading into 1944 by Britain and the United States. It was scheduled for June, though the actual date would depend on the weather.

Buoyed by the actions in Europe and the successes in the Pacific, President Roosevelt allowed his JCS to press on with their offensive plans to secure the Solomons, New Guinea and New Britain, with the ultimate goal of pushing the enemy back and taking the war to the islands of Japan. After Admiral Chester W. Nimitz had achieved his goals in the central Pacific region with the Gilbert and Marshall Islands campaign between November 1943 and February 1944, the Americans began a series of softening-up missions aimed at weakening Japanese land-based air power. They wanted to limit Japan's ability to counter future Allied amphibious landings. General Douglas MacArthur and his newly formed Seventh Fleet, along with amphibious commander Admiral Daniel E. Barbey, were beginning amphibious landings along northern New Guinea and the surrounding islands. MacArthur's doctrine was 'hit 'em where they ain't', meaning that he chose locations where the Japanese defence was minimal, avoiding strongly held areas. His strategy succeeded.

The Japanese had lost most of their main aircraft carriers, but during 1943 they were rebuilding their carrier strength and hoping to face off against the US Navy and retake control of the Pacific. However, throughout that year, most of their experienced carrier-based fighter and bomber pilots were killed or injured. Unlike the Americans, the Japanese failed to value their battle-hardened pilots, to rotate their duties and use them to train new recruits. Soon, the usually stringent selection process to become a pilot in either the Japanese Navy or Army Air Force was dropped, and replacements were being rushed through their training and put into action. This only resulted in greater losses of aircraft and men. Despite this, the Japanese land forces doggedly defended their territories because the Japanese High Command did not want to lose access to the much-needed oil on Borneo and in the Netherlands East Indies. It also held the belief that Japan could still defeat the Allies.

Two ports supplied the majority of the Japanese oil needs. Balikpapan, on the island of Borneo, was a major port and the site of a large aviation fuel refinery producing and shipping some two million barrels of bunker fuel and aviation spirit monthly. The other was Tarakan, north of Balikpapan, which had a storage capacity of over seven million barrels. It produced a high-grade bunker fuel that required little or no refining, so it could be used straight out of the wells.

In 1944, the war was moving too quickly for submarines or slower surface craft to mine some strategic targets. To reach areas deep behind enemy lines, such as Balikpapan, Surabaya and Halmahera, AOBs were established. It was not practical for these bases to be on land, as there was no time to wait for acquired ground bases to be made secure. Instead, US Navy Seaplane Tenders were used in this role. While some were purpose-built for the task, others were converted minesweepers and destroyers.

The US Navy Seaplane Tenders used by the RAAF during the mine-laying operations were the USS *William B. Preston,* located mainly at Cygnet Bay and then Heron Haven in Western Australia; the USS *Childs,* at Yampi Sound, north of Broome; the USS *Tangier,* at Morotai Island in the Halmahera group of eastern Netherlands East Indies' Maluku Islands; the USS *San Pablo,* at Lombrun Bay in the Admiralty Group; the USS *Heron,* at Jinamoc in the Philippines and at Lombrun Bay in the Admiralty Group; the USS *Currituck,* at Jinamoc; the USS *Wright,* at Woendi Island, which was an atoll south-east of Biak and part of the Netherlands East Indies, and the USS *Orca,* at Lingayen Gulf in the Philippines.

The RAN had its own purpose-built Seaplane Tender, HMAS *Albatross*, but it had been sent to Britain in 1938 and put into service with the RN as payment for HMAS *Hobart*, formerly HMS *Apollo*. HMAS *Albatross* would be used as a landing-craft repair ship on 7 June 1944, as part of the flotilla supporting the continued invasion of Normandy, Operation Overlord, which had begun the day before.

The RAAF Catalinas' regular involvement with the US Navy Seaplane Tenders began in February 1944. The Tenders, which also serviced US Navy PBYs, provided the Cats with fuel stops, repairs and running maintenance close to the target areas; they carried spares and were fitted with well-equipped workshops. Weary Catalina crews appreciated the mess facilities, which were far superior to those of the RAAF. The Tenders also had the additional advantage of flexibility, as they could move to virtually any location along a route if necessary. This was ideal for mining operations. In some cases, US Navy submarines were substituted as AOBs.

In February, both 11 and 20 Squadrons staged through the USS *William B. Preston*, a converted destroyer nicknamed the *Willie B.* At first the ship was anchored at Yampi Sound, codenamed Shecat, and used to mine Balikpapan on 22 and 24 February. The AOB was moved to Cygnet Bay, and operations against Balikpapan continued on 20 and 24 April. The USS *Childs*, a World War I vessel, took over the role of AOB at Yampi Sound.

A RAAF Beaufighter squadron from Derby covered the *Willie B*'s location at Cygnet Bay during daylight hours, with Boomerang fighters on call if needed. Staging from Cygnet Bay to Balikpapan was a long haul of 945 nautical miles (1750 kilometres), which forced the Cats to fly through enemy territory in daylight hours. To avoid radar detection, the Catalinas flew as low as 10 feet (3 metres). During the first operation against Balikpapan, little opposition was encountered; on subsequent trips, the anti-aircraft fire became heavy and deadly. One Catalina was shot down over the harbour, and others were badly holed. By mid-1944, Cygnet Bay had been abandoned in favour of Shecat, which would be used continuously as an AOB until the end of the war.

As MacArthur planned his amphibious landings at Hollandia, western New Guinea, the RAAF/US Navy coalition mined Woleai Atoll in the Caroline Islands. The target was reached via a US base on Manus Island.

As additional support for the operations at Hollandia and Aitape, the Catalinas mined Balikpapan, Manokwari, Kaimana and Sorong in an attempt to close the harbours. According to *The Report on Mine-laying Operations by the RAAF between 22 April 1943 and 31 July 1945*, these operations in April closed the Balikpapan Harbour for nine days and resulted in the sinking of one destroyer.

Former flight engineer Earle Evans of 20 Squadron recalled that the

> early use of US Navy Seaplane Tenders was the mining of Surabaya, the important Japanese troop transfer port on the northern coast of Java. Our Catalinas, before moving to Darwin, flew from Cairns across country to Darwin. Then, after loading mines, departed in the early afternoon to reach enemy territory after dark. We would arrive at the target area after midnight. After laying mines we withdrew to the south, flying across Java to alight at about 0730 at Heron Haven in the Dampier Archipelago on the north-west coast of Australia to refuel from the US Seaplane Tender USS *William B. Preston* ... a 24-hour rest period would be taken before flying to Cairns. From there the Catalinas returned directly to Cairns, sometimes tracking directly to Cairns and sometimes via Darwin. The unbroken flying time of this sortie was of the order of 20 hours.

Evans recalled a less auspicious time when his Cat needed emergency repairs and the crew called in at an AOB. The Cat's fuel tank had been ruptured by enemy fire during a mine-laying mission. The mines were delivered successfully, but the loss of fuel meant that the aircraft's range was limited and it couldn't reach its home base of East Arm at Darwin. A decision was made to return via the USS *Tangier* at Morotai, make running repairs, take on fuel and then continue to Darwin. This necessitated breaking radio silence to alert the USS *Tangier* and to obtain permission to refuel. The captain of the *Tangier* granted the clearance and issued instructions for the aircraft to ignore the security radar approach, which was a predetermined zigzag course to physically identify any approaching aircraft as friendly. In normal circumstances, this zigzagging was done to avoid breaking radio silence. As the Catalina approached the *Tangier* in a straight line, however, every other ship anchored around Morotai Island started to fire at it. The captain had obviously failed to pass on vital information to his fellow seamen.

As Earle Evans explained,

> rather than risk it, our Skipper alighted on the water a fair distance away. The *Tangier* then sent a boat to pick the crew up and towed the flying boat to the Seaplane Tender. On arrival, the Catalina's crew, led by their Skipper, stormed up the accommodation ladder. The Yeoman on the quarter deck stopped us and insisted on 'piping' us aboard . . . this was a US Navy and RN tradition extended to visiting officers. For some strange reason it was still being observed by the *Tangier*, even though they were in a war zone.

Evans said his skipper, 'still fuming after the unfriendly welcome that had nearly blown us out of the sky, told the Yeoman "to stick your bosun's pipe up your arse and take me to your bloody skipper!" The Yeoman's jaw dropped, perhaps in shock, and [he] obliged by taking him to the tender's Captain.'

One of the 'back streets' used by the Japanese transports to avoid contact with US submarines was Laut Strait, on the south-eastern tip of Borneo. Running between Laut Island and Kalimantan, it was a corridor used by the enemy en route to Balikpapan. Blocking this strait forced ships into deep water, where US Navy submarines were waiting with torpedoes.

Ray Byfield remembered laying mines in this area during 1944. On one occasion during the Cat's first mine-laying run, only one mine dropped—the other failed to release. The skipper, Flying Officer Jeff Bergman, was forced to make a second run at the exact height of 150 feet (46 metres), on the same course and speed. During the second run, Bergman's attempt to release the mine with the jettison toggle was unsuccessful. As Byfield explained,

> we gained height for the third run, put the Cat into a dive, then released the jettison mechanisms, making them active at the point of pull out and managed to release the mine . . . by this time, I think every Jap was out of their dormitories, which were visible in the moonlight, and shooting at us with every weapon they had. A problem for us was that so much fuel had been used in the three attempts to release the mines, and that if the mine, weighing 2000 pounds [900 kilograms], did not drop, we may not have had enough fuel to carry the thing back to Darwin. As it was on that operation, en route to Laut out from Darwin, we had to top up at the AOB at West Bay in Western Australia.

Despite meticulous planning to 'surprise' the enemy and avoid casualties, there were always those inevitable 'close encounters'. Keith Hamilton, flight engineer with 11 Squadron, described an incident when his crew met heavy ground fire, and several hits were felt that were thought to be insignificant. They had a rude awakening some hours later when water started flooding into the hull on alighting:

> The Skipper immediately put on the power and became airborne. It was discovered our large five-man dinghy had been perforated with two large holes about a metre apart. The enemy heavy bullets or cannon shells had pierced the hull under where the dinghy was stowed beneath the Navigator's table. The aircraft's tool kit provided the leak-stoppers to plug the holes sufficient to allow the aircraft to alight again. The five-man dinghy was not so lucky. Heavy calibre bullets had ploughed through several thicknesses of rubberised fabric

> before coming to a stop. The Navigator was considered very lucky because, at the time of the hits, he was working at the table on the homeward plot. Had the dinghy not been under the plotting table, he would have certainly collected one of them. We were lucky that bullets did not enter the fuel tanks in the wing to produce disastrous results. The self-sealing had been removed and it is possible the aircraft would have become another statistic. A later inspection at our base revealed the aircraft had been holed in three other places.

On 19 April, during another op, Hamilton's Catalina was over the target when there was a rapid bump-bump felt throughout the aircraft. Hamilton noted that 'the Skipper felt the control column shake and checked out the crew on the intercom. In seconds, except for the Second Engineer at the tunnel gun position, all crew reported "Okay"'.

Hamilton remembered that Roy 'Curley' Richards, an air gunner, came over the intercom and, referring to the second engineer, said, 'He must be okay, his gun is still firing.' Curley then quickly added, in typical gallows humour, 'Unless he's gone with his finger wrapped around the trigger!'

At that moment, the gun stopped firing. As Hamilton observed, 'The Second Engineer burst out of the rear compartment clutching his leg, yelling, "I've been hit!"'. Hamilton continued:

> We removed his flying boot quickly and discovered a piece of aluminium extrusion in his bloodied calf from one of the hull stringers. It had passed through the leather upper of his boot into his leg. Luckily the injury was little more than a scratch, but the shell only missed his leg by a millimetre! It was the result of a large anti-aircraft shell piercing the fuselage, disintegrating a stringer, to continue out through the top of the hull parting the rear control cables on the way through. That was the 'bump-bump' the crew felt. Fortunately, the shell did not explode . . . either it was a 'dud', or it had been set to explode at a

> higher altitude [than] the aircraft had been flying. It was a close call . . . If it had exploded, it would have killed the three gunners within the fuselage and the stern of the aircraft. But we were lucky! As we learnt later, another Catalina was hit in the same place that night, resulting in the immediate death of two crewmen, Sergeant Ron Ely and Sergeant Norm Phillips, and the 20 Squadron Intelligence Officer lost his lower leg in the explosion. Miraculously, that aircraft made it back to base!

Jim 'Blue' Henwood, a corporal who was part of the ground maintenance personnel with 11 Squadron, offered a different perspective of mining operations in 1944. He gave an account of the interaction between American and Australian servicemen, and what life was like on an AOB:

> Although I was not a crew member of any Catalina, I was associated with Cats in 11 Squadron most of my five and a half years' service with the RAAF. The reason being that every time I flew, I was dreadfully airsick and unless the flying was perfect, most of my time was spent trying to fill the slush can . . . for want of a better word.
>
> On 8 April 1944, 11 and 20 Squadrons, operating together, were given the task . . . at the request of Admiral Nimitz . . . of laying 1000-pound [450-kilogram] mines in the Woleai Atoll area in the Caroline Islands. Eight of our aircraft took off from Cairns . . . you can imagine these 'kites' loaded with four big mines, plus crew and maintenance 'bods', racing at full throttle to get off the 'drink'. It was a bit hair-raising to say the least, but all made it okay.

Despite his chronic airsickness, Henwood flew with 11 Squadron that day. The first stop was Milne Bay. After being collected by the Marine Section and ferried to shore, the crew all heard 'a few loud thumps. Apparently, they had dropped a couple of hand grenades in the water, sped off, and then collected a nice array of fish . . . so we had fresh fish for tea.'

Henwood wasn't only on a mission for the RAAF—he had also been sent on a mission by a higher authority:

> As we were boarding at Cairns, our base Padre gave me a bottle of Corio Whisky, shocking stuff, to trade with the Yanks for American cigarettes. That night, the drill was, the Yanks would walk through the camp offering 10 cartons for a bottle of Scotch. No takers . . . but one bloke's cry got to me: 'Come on Aussies, I have a Jeep and a WRAAC [Australian female Army soldier] and I need some Scotch.' So, I settled for 14 cartons [a carton being 200 cigarettes].

When Henwood arrived in the Admiralty Islands, he found his task of procuring cigarettes a whole lot easier, as 'we were allocated to two American Tenders [and] ours was the USS *Tangier*, also the USS *San Pablo*, and while on board we could buy as many "cigs" as we wanted for 33 cents a carton, so out came my spare kit bag, filled up and locked!'

Even though there were cigarettes aplenty, you could not light up wherever you pleased on the USS *Tangier*. In the front hold there was diesel fuel; the rear had 100-octane aero fuel. There were smoking lamps positioned throughout the vessel. As Henwood pointed out, 'If the smoking lamp was out, strict observance took place, or a quick trip to Eternity was possible.'

During Henwood's stay on the *Tangier*, a battered US submarine berthed alongside and, one by one, the crew appeared dressed in whites. He was taken aback when the captain of the submarine came up and

> was grabbed and tossed into the water. Then, one by one, the crew were dunked . . . hilarious to watch, but apparently the whole crew had been promoted while at sea, and this was the accepted ritual for such occasions. Then they all went below, changed, and came up to pay their respects to the [*Tangier*'s] Captain.

The food onboard the AOBs was far better than the offerings at RAAF messes back home. Henwood explained that

> for lunch, we would start off with a large self-service tray with small compartments, pass along a line of cooks to receive portions of beautiful food, topped by a huge T-bone steak and freshly baked bread. Sitting opposite a Yank, I noticed he was looking at me intensely and inquired why . . . 'Waal,' he drawled, 'I know you Aussies have some funny eating habits, but you're the first guy I've seen putting jam on his meat.' And so I was . . . I thought it was chutney!

Henwood was on the *Tangier* on 19 April, the day Alan Lancaster's Catalina A24-63 came in after a mine-laying mission in the Woleai Atoll area. The Cat had been hit by either a 20- or 25-millimetre anti-aircraft shell, which exploded in the blister compartment, killing Sergeants Phillips and Ely, and severely wounding Flying Officer Paul Lachal, the Intelligence Officer. Henwood remembered:

> Emergency repairs enabled the flying boat to be flown back to set down alongside our base ships, where it was hoisted onto the aft deck of the USS *Tangier*. There was much to be done, and substantial repairs made for A24-63 to be airworthy. It was a rule at that time, 'if you fixed it, you flew in it', so the Skipper [Flight Lieutenant Eddie Ham] said to me, 'OK Blue, strip it down and fly with me.' So we removed anything that wasn't absolutely necessary and flew all the way to Cairns in one hop.

On Henwood's return to home base,

> the Padre was overjoyed when I handed him 14 cartons for his bottle of Scotch. And my 'locked-bag' lot, which mostly belonged to friends,

> were soon dispersed. It was always good for bargaining when I came home on leave, to have on hand, a packet or two of smokes . . . it was marvellous how they [the Americans] could procure unobtainable items from under the counter.
>
> But war is a silly business at any time, and you think you will forget, but you never do.

By the end of the first half of 1944, the Allies had captured the Solomon, Gilbert and Marshall islands, and the Papuan peninsula of New Guinea that included three airfields at Biak considered important by General MacArthur. These airfields put the islands of the Philippines within range of American bombers. The Japanese still held the Philippines, as well as the Caroline, Palau and Mariana islands. Admiral Chester W. Nimitz's plan was to bypass the Philippines, as well as the Palau and Caroline islands, and seize the Mariana Islands and Taiwan, which would cut communications between the Japanese mainland and its forces in the south and south-west. Taking the Marianas also meant that Japan would be within range of the new Boeing B-29 Superfortress long-range bomber, with its operational radius of 1500 miles (2400 kilometres).

Meanwhile, MacArthur had advanced through New Guinea and secured most of the northern area. He did so expecting to eventually launch an attack, via Morotai, on the Philippines to liberate the islands, thus fulfilling his promise of 'I shall return'. In preparation, MacArthur had built up large forces in the SWPA. The Japanese, expecting an attack somewhere on their perimeter, thought that it would most likely be on the Caroline Islands, north of New Guinea and west of the Philippines. Given this, they decided to go on the offensive. They rallied their forces for a major attack on the US Navy aircraft carriers, hoping that a decisive win would give them air control of the Pacific once again. The Commander-in-Chief of the IJN Combined Fleet, Admiral Soemu

Toyoda, prepared to enact the plan—codenamed Operation A-Go—in June 1944.

The US Navy's bombardment of Saipan in the Marianas—and the eventual landings of the Second and Fourth Marine Divisions, and the US Army's 27th Infantry Division—took the Japanese by surprise. The IJN First Mobile Fleet, commanded by Vice Admiral Jisaburō Ozawa, steamed north from the Caroline Islands to expedite their offensive against the US Navy Fifth Fleet, commanded by Admiral Raymond A. Spruance, a veteran from the Battle of Midway. The encounter, known as the Battle of the Philippine Sea, would be the largest and last carrier-vs-carrier battle of the Pacific conflict. It would also expose the inexperience of the Japanese army and navy pilots.

On the first day of battle, 19 June, the IJN launched 373 carrier aircraft against the US Navy, of which only 130 returned to the carriers. Subsequently, many of these aircraft were lost when US Navy submarines sank two of the largest IJN fleet carriers, *Taihō* and *Shōkaku*. After the second day of the battle, a light carrier, *Hiyō*, was bombed, torpedoed and sunk by US Navy and Marine aircraft. In addition, more than 433 carrier aircraft and around 200 land-based aircraft were destroyed. Operation A-Go was also supposed to involve land-based aircraft support from Japan's airfield in Guam, but most of these were destroyed by the Americans well before Ozawa's First Mobile Fleet was even in position.

The Japanese pilots were outnumbered and outclassed. One US Navy pilot from the USS *Lexington* commented during the debriefing on the first day, 'Why, hell, it was just like an old-time turkey shoot down home!' The engagement then became known, historically, as 'The Great Marianas Turkey Shoot'.

The Americans lost only 23 aircraft on the first day. The second day's airstrike against the IJN First Mobile Fleet resulted in greater losses, due to the time of the raid and the aircraft having to exceed their flying limits. For this late-afternoon strike, 226 aircraft were launched but only

115 made it back intact. Reaching the IJN fleet at dusk, twenty were lost to enemy action, while the remainder ran out of fuel returning to their carriers, or crashed when attempting to land at night. The pilots and crews were rescued by supporting ships throughout the night and into the next day.

During the Battle of the Philippine Sea, 109 Americans lost their lives. It is estimated that as many as 2987 Japanese died. Most of the Japanese casualties were crews who went down with the three fleet carriers and eight other surface vessels that were sunk.

If the IJN had any hope of regaining control of the Pacific, it was now completely dashed. Operation A-Go was, quite literally, Japan's last-ditch attempt to turn the war in its favour. The Japanese had gambled and lost. Their remaining carriers and carrier-based aircraft were too few to defend the existing fleet without land-based support, and could never be used offensively. Instead, the Japanese would use the carriers as decoys to try to lure the US Navy away from protecting its amphibious landings, leaving the Japanese battleships to pound the Allied land forces and the supporting Allied naval vessels. The Japanese carriers would become sacrificial lambs.

Admiral Chester W. Nimitz had begun his plan to bypass heavily defended islands to get as near to Japan as possible, providing him with the opportunity to bomb the mainland in preparation for a subsequent landing. General Douglas MacArthur, however, wanted to first liberate his beloved Philippines before pushing north. The decision was, ultimately, in the hands of President Roosevelt. Both Nimitz and MacArthur believed strongly in their own strategy, and would now compete for the president's favour.

7

THE MANILA RAID

MID TO LATE 1944

When General Douglas MacArthur first faced the media after arriving in Australia from the Philippines in 1942, he said, 'I shall return.' The US War Information Office had asked MacArthur to change the 'I' to a 'we', but he had refused. To MacArthur, the war was personal. His reputation was at stake. The American public saw MacArthur as 'America's First Soldier'. After all, it appeared that MacArthur was the only 'soldier' who had tried to fight back against the Japanese during their initial attack.

After MacArthur made his personal pledge to the Philippines, Filipino president Carlos Romulo told a local journal, 'America has let us down and won't be trusted . . . but the people still have confidence in MacArthur. If he says he is coming back, then he will be believed.' Interestingly, MacArthur asked the Filipinos to use his words to stay strong and take the fight to the enemy. MacArthur's words did become a slogan for the partisans, and the Filipinos used guerrilla tactics throughout the occupation, denying Japan full control of the islands.

Admiral Chester W. Nimitz, of course, wanted to bypass the Philippines—or, at least, use some of its islands as stepping stones to reach

Formosa, now Taiwan, just off the east coast of China. He didn't want to waste resources against what was believed to be a heavily defended region, when he could go straight to areas within bombing distance of mainland Japan. As well as cutting supplies to and from Japan—thus starving the homeland and its outer territories—his plan would allow the Allies to bomb Japan in preparation for a land invasion that would, hopefully, see Japan surrender. Once Japan was defeated, all other occupied areas would be handed over without a shot being fired.

At a meeting with President Franklin D. Roosevelt in Hawaii on 27 July 1944, Nimitz outlined his purely military plan. MacArthur, however, countered Nimitz's plan. From a military point of view, MacArthur believed that Formosa should not be taken until they had secured the northern Philippines. Without the most northern island of Luzon under their control, an invasion of Formosa would suffer from an over-stretched supply chain, as it was far from the nearest available Allied base. MacArthur didn't disagree with Nimitz's plan, but he felt that holding the Philippines would better serve Nimitz's objective of taking the war to Japan—their shared objective.

With an emotional and politically motivated argument, MacArthur told President Roosevelt the United States had a 'moral obligation' to liberate the Philippines. He reminded the president of the thousands of Allied POWs, let alone civilians, who were suffering under the occupation. He also warned: 'Filipinos could forgive us for failing to protect them from the Japanese in the first place, they would even forgive our failing in an attempt to rescue them, but what they would not forgive was our not even trying to free them.' MacArthur got his way.

President Roosevelt decided the Philippines would be liberated, and that Nimitz would also continue his 'island hopping' towards Japan. MacArthur planned to invade Mindanao, one of the southern Philippine islands, as an initial stage of his Philippines assault. To get there, he would first conduct an amphibious landing on the island of Morotai, halfway between New Guinea and Mindanao, in September.

During July 1944, the RAAF continued mining Surabaya in the Netherlands East Indies, and two more targets were added: Bima Bay, on the island of Sumbawa, and Buton Strait. These were all staged through Yampi Sound after Cygnet Bay had been decommissioned.

An incident occurred during an operation to Surabaya that shocked everybody concerned. Four aircraft had taken off in the afternoon for the sortie, and about two hours later one of the Catalinas made a faint mayday call. The first message said, 'About to alight.' A little later, a second message said, 'Down in sea under attack.' Because of the security precautions at Shecat, all messages to aircraft had to be routed by short-range radio to the RAAF Beaufighter base at Derby, in Western Australia, and then on to Darwin. Catalina Headquarters at Darwin immediately recalled the remaining three aircraft, instructing them to return direct to Darwin. An Air Sea Rescue (ASR) unit was placed on stand-by for the next morning, and a US submarine operating in the area was also alerted.

Pandemonium reigned that night, as no aircraft returned to Darwin. The next morning, Shecat had an air-raid warning alert. Then, about an hour after dawn, the Catalina that had sent the mayday arrived at the AOB. The three other Catalinas alighted at various locations on the north-west coast. None of the aircraft flew to Darwin. Due to the strict observance of radio silence, the Cats had not received the recall message until after they had dropped their mines. As it turned out, to the relief and frustration of all concerned, the wireless operator of the 'shot down' Catalina had only been practising his radio calls. He hadn't realised he had inadvertently broadcast his tests.

During 1944, it became clear to the mine-laying planners that the campaign was highly successful—by December, only six aircraft had been lost, of which two crews had been saved. One aircraft lost for every 95 sorties was a good result, considering the risks involved. Because of the continuing success, three squadrons were assigned to full-time mining in September and directed by Number 76 Wing in Darwin, where two of the squadrons, 43 and 20, were based. The other, 42 Squadron, was stationed at Melville Bay, on the north-eastern tip of the Northern Territory.

Late in September, Admiral William 'Bull' Halsey's Third Fleet launched aerial raids against the Philippines as part of a series of attacks in preparation for the invasion of the Palau Islands, 885 kilometres east of Mindanao. During the raids, fast carriers launched their aircraft against enemy airfields and naval facilities in the central Philippines and all the way south to Mindanao. Pilots reported they destroyed 478 aircraft and sunk 59 ships.

Halsey's 'probing' of the enemy's defences showed them to be weak. He immediately contacted Nimitz and MacArthur, and suggested the invasion of Mindanao be cancelled in favour of an invasion of Leyte Island, in the central Philippines. This would cut months off MacArthur's timetable. MacArthur agreed, and so began plans for the Battle of Leyte.

Nimitz transferred significant naval forces from the central Pacific to the Seventh Fleet, known as MacArthur's Navy, in preparation for the attack. An amphibious force supported by US and RAN surface vessels, the Seventh Fleet was under the operational control of Admiral Thomas C. Kinkaid. MacArthur had been requesting naval support against land targets from Nimitz the entire war, but had been refused because Nimitz believed his naval forces were better employed in the central and southern Pacific. Nimitz didn't want to be caught short against the Japanese Navy. Now MacArthur was given additional battleships, cruisers, destroyers and some light carriers that were originally designed for anti-submarine warfare. Halsey's Third Fleet was also permitted to take part; however, Halsey kept command of his fleet and carriers, and reported directly to Nimitz, who was determined not to let MacArthur have everything.

After a four-hour naval bombardment, the US Sixth Army began their landings on Leyte Island on 20 October. Japanese defensive action varied along the many beachheads. Within an hour of landing, most were established and had received heavy equipment and supplies, while the landing at Red Beach, near the city of Tacloban, took around four hours to secure. It was at this beach that MacArthur was filmed walking through the surf and proclaiming, 'People of the Philippines, I have returned. By the grace of Almighty God, our forces stand again on Philippine soil.' MacArthur had successfully landed over 60,000 personnel and 100,000 tons (90,700 tonnes) of supplies.

The Japanese countered the Allied invasion with three naval forces: Northern, Centre and Southern. The Northern Force consisted of what was left of the IJN carriers, while the other two had heavy battleships and supporting vessels. The Japanese plan relied on the Northern Force being spotted first and drawing away the US fleets, so the Centre and Southern Forces could then attack the landings. Ironically, the Northern Force would be the last of the IJN's fleets to be sighted by the US Navy.

On 24 October, the US Third Fleet made contact with the IJN Centre Force and beat off its offensive, sinking the Yamato-class battleship *Musashi* and crippling the cruiser *Myōkō*. Centre Force then retreated. The Southern Force had also been located and was attacked by US Navy bombers but sustained only minor damage. At this time, Halsey was notified of the Northern Force carriers. Unaware it was a decoy, Halsey advanced away from Leyte to combat what he saw as the main threat. He also believed he had crushed the Japanese Centre and Southern Forces, and that they were limping home. Halsey was wrong.

Admiral Halsey's decision to engage the Northern Force—which is still a matter of contention—left the northern flank of Leyte undefended. Kinkaid's Seventh Fleet was the only protection available for MacArthur's ground forces. As the Third Fleet steamed away, the Japanese Centre Force turned around and returned to Leyte.

The subsequent naval battles—the Battle of the Sibuyan Sea, the Battle of Surigao Strait, the Battle of Cape Engaño and the Battle off Samar—would become known collectively as the Battle of Leyte Gulf. It was the largest naval battle in history, and was the very last ship-to-ship engagement. In addition, it was the first battle in which Japanese aircraft carried out organised kamikaze attacks. A kamikaze, which translates to 'divine wind', was a Special Attack Unit that undertook a suicide mission against the Allied navies. Japanese pilots would use aircraft filled with explosives to make their attacks. Small boats and manned torpedoes were also used. It was seen as a means to stop the Allies from reaching Japan, as the war had turned against Imperial forces.

On 21 October, HMAS *Australia* is believed to have become the first official casualty of the kamikaze strategy when a Japanese Val Aichi 99 bomber dived on the ship. American maritime historian Samuel Eliot Morison, however, believed it was not a planned suicide attack—as would happen en masse four days later—but rather it was committed on the pilot's own initiative. Similar attacks by damaged Japanese aircraft had occurred as early as 1942. This reflects the Japanese doctrine based on the samurai Bushido code: loyalty and honour until death. To surrender and be captured were seen as acts of cowardice and an insult to Emperor Hirohito, and would disgrace the family of the airman. In any case, HMAS *Australia* was badly damaged; its captain, Emile Dechaineux, was among those who survived the attack but later died of their wounds. Three officers, three sailors and four unidentified personnel died. Sixteen officers and 49 sailors were wounded.

As the IJN and Army Air Service continued their attack, the situation became desperate. It was obvious they were determined to regain Leyte at any cost. The US Seventh Fleet, under Kinkaid, was confronted by a strong offensive from the IJN, which, at the time, included the world's largest battleship, the *Yamato*, sister ship to the *Musashi*. Kinkaid was in a perilous situation that prompted him to cable Admiral Halsey for help, hoping he would send support from his Third Fleet. Halsey, who was heavily engaged against the Northern Force, received the message on 25 October: 'My situation is critical. Fast battleships and support by air strikes may be able to keep enemy from destroying CVES [escort carriers] and entering Leyte . . .'

The naval battle ended the next day when the IJN's Central and Southern Forces withdrew to Brunei Bay to replenish supplies and repair their battle-damaged fleet. Kinkaid's Seventh Fleet, however, was then relentlessly attacked by kamikaze aircraft. He was still fearful of an IJN return to Leyte Gulf through the Balabac Straits, the quickest route from the Japanese base at Brunei Bay.

On 27 October, Kinkaid cabled a dispatch to MacArthur: 'After 17 days of battle, my fast carriers are unable to provide extended support for Leyte . . . The pilots are exhausted and the carriers are low on provisions, bombs and torpedoes. When will land-based air take over at Leyte?'

Contemporary US reports confirm that this communiqué compelled MacArthur to request the RAAF mine the Balabac Straits. He feared, if the IJN fleet were allowed to return by the straits, they would be attacking a crippled US Navy Seventh Fleet. The Americans were aware the Japanese had defensively mined the straits, so they had sent US submarines through each one to locate the mine-free channels. However, there was insufficient time to use conventional mine-laying craft, making aerial mining necessary. The RAAF Catalinas were sent to plug those gaps, forcing the IJN fleet to take the longer route through San Bernardino Strait, north of Samar.

At last light on 7 November, eight Catalinas from 20 and 42 Squadrons departed Darwin for Morotai, where the USS *Tangier* was anchored. Each aircraft carried four Mk V 1000-pound (450-kilogram) British mines on the 1700-kilometre flight. At the briefing on 9 November, a 25-knot (45-kilometre-per-hour) headwind was forecast for most of the operation.

On 15 November, seven RAAF Catalinas departed for the trip to Brunei Bay. The mission to 'bottle up' or 'mine-in' units of the IJN fleet that were undergoing repairs and replenishing supplies in the bay was completed successfully, and no opposition was encountered. To complete the job, on 16 November bombers of the US 13th Air Force attacked the trapped fleet, scoring direct hits on a battleship and a heavy cruiser. It was the first time in the SWPA that mines had been employed to close a harbour for the specific purpose of trapping ships for a subsequent bombing attack. In all, the RAAF Catalinas flew ten sorties, planting twenty British and American mines in the harbour.

One of the Cats from 20 Squadron was A24-87, piloted by Ross Schulz and with Reg Cleworth as the navigator. They were unable to reach the primary target due to the increased fuel consumption caused by a strong headwind. Loaded with two Mk V British mines, A24-87 was forced to lay its mines at the alternate target of Sandakan, on the north-eastern tip of Borneo (now Sabah).

In late October, no doubt aware of the upcoming flights, Reg Cleworth wrote a letter home, knowing it would be some weeks before his family would hear from him again. He wrote:

> Dear Mother,
>
> Just a few lines to let you know that we have been fairly busy this week. Things have been going along O.K. I will be pretty short as I haven't any news apart from flying + that's not interesting.
>
> The food has been pretty good lately + that is quite a change for the better. Will be fairly busy this coming week + will write you a long letter at the end of it.
>
> Well, must close now, sorry it's so short but can't help it.
>
> Love to all,
>
> Reg

Even while the Allied land forces were still meeting resistance at Leyte, MacArthur was planning his next move—an amphibious landing on the island of Mindoro, a stepping stone to Luzon and the Philippine capital, Manila. Further mining of the Balabac Straits by RAAF Cats would become a defensive cover for the Mindoro landings. The mines had to be planted as close to the landing date as possible, to preclude any successful attempt at sweeping by the enemy. Because of the heavy and unexpected resistance during the Battle of Leyte Gulf, the Mindoro landing was delayed from early December to mid-December. The RAAF/US Navy planners had to choose whether to wait and plant the mines at the later date, or use DAMs. The first alternative was impossible, as there were not enough accommodation facilities available on the USS *Tangier* for the number of men in the RAAF Catalina crews. So the second option was adopted, and DAMs were used.

The eight Catalinas used for the operation carried a full load of mines from Darwin to Morotai. In addition, a number of B-24 Liberators ferried mines from Darwin to Morotai to be used by the Cats on subsequent ops. This was the first operation in the SWPA in which Liberator bombers were used to deliver mines. Although this delivery plan was completed, the USS *Tangier* would not be available as an AOB for as long as originally planned. This meant that eight additional Catalinas were sent to Morotai to speed up the operation.

The mining of the Balabac Straits required 22 sorties. These were completed on the nights of 28, 29 and 30 November, and sixty British and American mines were planted. After the mission, Intelligence officers were pleased to learn that no crews had been lost, as they had expected losses to be as high as 75 per cent.

The IJN withdrawal after the Battle of Leyte Gulf amazed the Americans. There is no doubt the US Navy was secretly pleased. Ray Byfield, armourer with 43 Squadron, which was involved in the Balabac Straits mining, was given a book many years after the war titled *Decisive Battles of World War II: Individual stories by 14 high-ranking officers' friend or foe*. It includes an article by General Douglas MacArthur, 'Leyte Gulf', in which he writes that 'the IJN Fleet disappeared all of a sudden during the night, secretly sailing to their naval base at Brunei Bay'.

The Allied fleet would have been caught like sitting ducks had the IJN remained. The help needed by the US Navy Seventh Fleet had not arrived due to a break in communications. Cable and radio messages were being sent frantically during the various battles, but Admiral Halsey received Kinkaid's cable late, due to a 'backlog'. Even so, one of the reasons why the IJN slipped away was the fierce defence put up by the Seventh Fleet. Japanese Vice Admiral Takeo Kurita, Centre Force, believed he was facing a task force from Halsey's Third Fleet and not an inferior fleet consisting of PT boats and outdated escort carriers, battleships and destroyers. So effective was the Seventh Fleet's coordinated surface and air defensive actions, it caused confusion among the IJN Centre and Southern Forces, leaving them disorganised. This is why Vice Admiral Kurita called for 'all ships, my course north' so they could regroup.

After the battle, it would take some time before the US Seventh Fleet could stock up and recover. MacArthur, in his article, made no mention of the fact that, while his fleet was being supplied, the RAAF Cats stepped in and possibly saved his navy and ground forces. Because of the secrecy imposed on the missions, Ray Byfield did not know the reason for the Balabac Straits operation. He noted that 'as crew members we were not told of any of this, our superiors reckoned what we didn't know we couldn't repeat . . . too true'.

In the short period from 9 November to 14 December, RAAF Catalinas flew 110 sorties and planted 250 British and American mines in enemy waters. MacArthur's requests were on a 'must-do' basis, and all pre-planned mining operations were put on hold.

During the defence of the Leyte landings, the United States lost one light carrier, two escort carriers, two destroyers and one destroyer escort.

Four other ships were damaged, including HMAS *Australia*. Over 200 aircraft were destroyed, and there were an estimated 3000 Allied casualties. The Japanese lost a total of 26 warships: one fleet carrier, three light carriers, three battleships, six heavy cruisers, four light cruisers and nine destroyers. Additional ships were sunk in Brunei Bay or as they tried to make their way to Singapore or Japan for repairs. The Japanese also lost an estimated 300 aircraft and had over 12,000 casualties. It was a decisive victory for the Allies.

While the USS *Tangier* provided a much-needed AOB for operations to Brunei Bay and the Balabac Straits, its anchorage at Morotai was still being defended by the Japanese. Effectively, the location was on the front line, as Ray Byfield soon realised:

> Before leaving Darwin we were issued with steel helmets . . . being puzzled we asked why? 'Dunno, you'll find out,' was the answer. The procedure for our seaplane tender, the USS *Tangier* at Morotai, was to up-anchor and hide among some islands. When this occurred the lowly members of the crew had to sleep on board the Catalina at its mooring. One night at Morotai, when we were not working, we were a bit concerned . . . when the Americans took Morotai from the Japanese they stood their battleships off shore and blasted away . . . not one palm tree was left standing whole . . . Sleeping on the Cats a short distance from the mangroves, that were probably in Jap hands, made us wish for a few Aussie soldiers. The Americans had joked to us saying, 'Guess where your Aussie AIF are going?' pointing to the jungle. They had admiration for the AIF [who] were not impressed when the news communiqués reported that, 'Americans have taken Morotai and the Australians are mopping up'.
>
> On the occasion we were there, as the night came, we were entertained by a Jap bomber dropping bombs on the airstrip. An oil storage tank got hit, creating a big fire. We were told later that a bay of four

> Liberators [B-24s] 'went up'. The Americans threw up tons of anti-aircraft flak at the Jap, who was caught in the beams of a searchlight, when we heard 'Pst! Pst! Pst!' . . . as one we yelled, 'shrapnel', and dived for our tin hats that, incidentally, were inadequate for protection against hot pieces of shrapnel . . . what goes up must come down! The US Army Air Force followed the Jap bomber to locate its base and fixed the problem. Later in Darwin, maintenance riggers found a piece of shrapnel in our Catalina's tail.

According to Byfield, he met a very different breed of American while on board USS *Tangier*. The sailors were older, bigger, cigar-chewing, really experienced 'Yanks'. They complained about the RAAF Catalinas being there, saying that had it not been for the mine-laying mission, they would have up-anchored and been at Biak replenishing stores and having a rest—well away from any Japanese bombing raids.

Byfield also noticed that nearly every sailor on board the vessel was adorned with self-made ornaments. They were made from silver and worn on pierced ears. Those sailors not already wearing these ornaments often had thick cotton saturated with antiseptic on their recently pierced ears in preparation for an ornament:

> They wanted our sixpenny pieces [then nearly pure silver] but not at inflated prices. Some of our boys wanted a lot more for their sixpence. No way! The US sailors had been to Australia and [were] only prepared to offer the equivalent to sixpence in exchange. They were seasoned sailors, and it seemed their ornaments became contagious, as almost all in the crew appeared to have them, but they were very well done.

Being stationed at Morotai did have its advantages for the Cat crews, especially when American Thanksgiving fell on 30 November. The Aussies were treated to a luxurious menu consisting of stuffed olives, sweet mixed pickles, cream of tomato soup, croutons, roast Tom turkey, sausage dressing, cranberry sauce, giblet gravy, baked spiced ham, creamed potatoes, candied sweet potatoes, buttered asparagus tips, French peas, cabbage and pineapple salad, finger rolls with butter, cherry pie and ice-cream, hard candy, cigars, cigarettes and coffee. Byfield said, tongue in cheek: 'What, no tea?'

Ron Black was a pilot officer on Catalina A24-81, and recalled an unexpected incident that occurred on 7 November. When the Catalinas first arrived,

> after alighting at Morotai a mooring buoy was sought. Reg [Cleworth, seconded from A24-87], who was Navigator, picked out what appeared to be just the job and they taxied in and moored. Later the buoy proved to be a reef marker. The tide dropped and the Cat was holed on the reef in the navigation compartment. This required patching and the aircraft was hoisted aboard the USS *Tangier* to effect repairs. Reg was not unpopular as this meant a breather for all and a change in diet. Whilst on the seaplane tender we managed to get an issue of a type of gym boot which was easier to move around the aircraft in than the RAAF issue.

On 20 November, Reg Cleworth wrote home:

> Dear Mother + all,
>
> Here we are again, hale + hearty, very tired though as I have been pretty busy this week. Haven't much news that I can tell you although quite a lot has happened that would be interesting to write about, but is taboo . . .

Reg continues, writing about receiving letters and a cake, and then goes on to tell everyone, 'Have been lucky enough to get a pair of

American rubber soled boots which are beautiful for running around the aircraft in.'

From Leyte, MacArthur now planned to move on to Mindoro on 15 December. The island would be used by MacArthur as an airstrip to launch fighters and bombers in support of the major landings on Luzon. To assist with the Mindoro landings, MacArthur needed the RAAF Catalinas to 'bottle up' Japanese warships in Manila Bay. This operation involved more aircraft than the usual mine-laying missions—where a maximum of six aircraft were used on any one occasion—and strict formation flying was considered necessary to minimise losses. Manila Bay was, at the time, a strongly defended harbour and posed some difficulties for a mining operation with the slow-flying Catalinas. A report was prepared by Sergeant C.E. Loetel US Navy Reserve on the perceived problems. It was transmitted from the Seventh Fleet to the US Navy Commander-in-Chief (COMINCH) in Washington, DC. The issues facing the RAAF Catalinas were:

1) Where to locate the field so as to effectively close the bay and yet keep the a/c [aircraft] away from strongly defended areas such as Corregidor, Cavite and Manila town,
2) What was the best track into and out of a bowl-shaped bay,
3) How to gain entrance to the bay with a minimum of warning to the enemy, and
4) How to get all a/c into and out of the bay in minimum time.

The calculations used for the operation were based on the width of the target, the depth of the water and the dimensions of the mines used. The result of those calculations indicated that an effective closure of the port could be obtained using 60 mines, representing 24 sorties.

Experience in the SWPA had shown that it was usually possible to mine a new target on the first night with little or no opposition. Given

Manila Bay's strong defences, it was decided all sorties would occur on the one night to minimise losses. The location in the bay most suitable for mining was an 8-mile (13-kilometre) stretch of water between Lukanin Point and San Nicolas light station. A mine laid at this point would close off the north and south channels; it was at least 5 miles (8 kilometres) from Corregidor and a safe distance from heavy anti-aircraft batteries. A second line of mines would be laid from the Timalan River mouth and from Calibuyo Point, out as far as 12 miles (19 kilometres), on a course of 360 degrees true. This second field straddled the most direct route from the entrance of Manila Bay to the Manila docks. Aerial photos of the east coast of the Bataan Peninsula and the opposite side of the bay, in the vicinity of the datum points, were requested. A bombing diversion was also requested to protect the Catalinas from night fighters—B-24 Liberators would strike at a military target to draw any enemy fighters from the vicinity of the mine drop.

To delay detection by enemy radar stations as long as possible, a track was planned for the aircraft to be flown below 100 feet (30 metres) in certain areas. This would bypass all radar stations, except those in Manila and the one on Lubang Island. The latter stations could give an advanced warning 15–30 minutes before the aircraft reached the target. To prevent this, machines emitting high radio frequencies were used to jam the radar, and strips of tinfoil called 'window' were released into the air to confuse the signal.

To perform the operation in one night, 24 Catalinas were needed. So that all aircraft spent a minimum amount of time in the target area, it was planned for them to take off separately and circle in the general area until all were airborne. When airborne, the Catalina carrying the jamming equipment would fire a Very flare and lead the aircraft, in formation, to the target at a speed of 90 knots [165 kilometres per hour]. When they reached the target, the 24 Cats would divide into two groups. Group A, consisting of fifteen aircraft, would mine from the Bataan side of the bay.

Group B, with nine aircraft, would mine from the opposite side. Each group had to fly in a non-intersecting course across the bay and out the other side.

Each aircraft was to make its mining run as soon as the target area was reached and to execute the run smartly, without manoeuvring around to find datums. If datums were missed, skippers were instructed to get an accurate fix on the point from which the mining run began and go round again. Each group was to fly at different heights, but each aircraft within the group was to fly at the same altitude.

Only eighteen serviceable Catalinas were available at 76 Wing at Darwin, so six Catalinas from 11 Squadron were called in for the operation from Rathmines. Because of this starting point, the 11 Squadron aircraft made a flight totalling 9000 miles (14,500 kilometres). For a single sortie, it probably set an all-time record for a Catalina operation in World War II.

The AOB for the mining of Manila Bay was supposed to be ACORN 30, the codename for a land-based AOB on Jinamoc Island at the head of Leyte Gulf. When it was discovered that the base facilities at ACORN 30 could only provide for twelve Catalinas, it was decided that twelve Cats would fly directly to Leyte, and the remaining twelve would go to Woendi Island and, on the morning of the operation, proceed to Leyte to refuel. It was also determined that the B-24 Liberators normally used for ferrying the mines could not be accommodated at the airstrip at Tacloban, the main city on Leyte. All mines for the op, therefore, had to be transported by the Catalinas. This involved changing the operation schedule, and resulted in sending the first group of aircraft one day earlier from Darwin, allowing for an overnight stay at Woendi.

The six 11 Squadron Catalinas from Rathmines departed for Darwin on 9 December. One landed at Brisbane to pick up the US Navy Mine Warfare Operations Officer. On 10 December, the six aircraft arrived in Darwin. The next day, twelve loaded Cats from 11 and 43 Squadron took off for Woendi in daylight, flying directly past the Tanimbar Islands and between Aroe and Kai Islands, then over New Guinea to Woendi. After refuelling and an overnight stay, they departed for Leyte, arriving late on 12 December. Accommodation was provided ashore on Jinamoc Island, and the Seaplane Tender USS *Heron* was available to service the aircraft.

Aboard the USS *Currituck*, a second Seaplane Tender at Jinamoc, on 13 December, arrangements were made for weather and general intelligence briefing for the crews at 1300 the next day. Whether it was mentioned to the crews or not is unknown, but intelligence reports predicted a 60 per cent loss of aircraft. Despite the careful planning, it would be difficult to avoid the strong anti-aircraft batteries around Manila Bay.

At Tacloban, two radar-jamming machines—one for 150 megacycles and the other for 200 megacycles—were obtained, as well as 720 units of 'window' and 'rope'. While window consisted of bundles of thin strips of tinfoil, which when dropped from a plane obscured the aircraft by producing myriad echoes on the enemy's radar screen, rope consisted of much longer aluminium strips, which looked like a large bomber aircraft on radar screens. A US Navy Ferret Catalina carried the two jamming machines and 120 units of window and rope, while a spare RAAF Catalina from 43 Squadron was used to drop 600 units of window and rope. At Far East Air Force Headquarters, flak intelligence for the Manila area was procured. Unfortunately, no aerial photos or information regarding anti-aircraft and searchlight positions around the datum points were available. Not knowing the full extent of the defences at Manila Bay made the use of window and rope essential for the operation.

The second group of thirteen Catalinas, which included the spare, departed Darwin on 12 December and arrived at Woendi Island late the same day. At Woendi, crews were briefed on mining runs and on the general plan of the operation; the Cats were refuelled and crews departed for Leyte on the evening of 13 December. Arriving early on 14 December, they received last-minute details about the track to the target, flak intelligence and weather.

That same morning, aboard USS *Currituck*, individual briefings for the first group took place. Commanders of 43 and 11 Squadrons were briefed on the track to the target, while the Intelligence Officer of 43 Squadron was briefed on escape points, radar locations, flak intelligence and other essential business. The US Navy Mine Warfare Operations Officer was briefed on run-out times, altitude, evasive tactics during the mining run, releasing sequence for dropping mines, and mine characteristics and jettison procedure. No alternate target was assigned for this mission, because the primary target was a must.

Among the skippers were four very experienced pilots, who were also the commanding officers of each of the squadrons: Wing Commanders Keith Bolitho of 11 Squadron, Athol 'Attie' Wearne of 20 Squadron, 'Bluey' Costello of 42 Squadron and John McMahon of 43 Squadron.

All mining Catalinas were loaded with either two Mark 25 or four Mark 26 Mod.1 mines and 1000 gallons (3800 litres) of fuel. This large fuel load was necessary to allow for the sustained flight, from sunset on 14 December until first light on 15 December.

Take-off for the target commenced at 1630. One aircraft failed to depart because of unserviceable radar equipment. Still, as planned, the others circled in the vicinity of Leyte until all were airborne. The Very signal was given, and the Catalinas then flew in formation to their target.

As the RAAF Catalinas arrived over Manila Bay, it was observed that all ground lights in the vicinity were turned on. The element of surprise had been achieved. The crew of 11 Squadron reported inaccurate small-arms fire from the vicinity of Lake Taal and Naic, while 43 Squadron reported inaccurate machine-gun and rifle fire from the east coast of Bataan Peninsula and its opposite shore. Aircraft from 20 and 42 Squadrons reported that no ack-ack (anti-aircraft fire) or searchlights were encountered. However, heavy anti-aircraft fire was seen coming from both the small island of Corregidor and Manila, where two B-24 Liberators were bombing an airfield as the diversion.

The US Navy Ferret Catalina that accompanied the mining aircraft managed to jam all seventeen of the enemy's radar stations en route, and the stations ceased transmitting as the mine aircraft approached. The spare RAAF Cat from 43 Squadron dropped liberal amounts of window and rope, which was no doubt responsible for the absence of formidable opposition during the mining operations. This was possibly the first occasion that rope had been used in the Pacific Theatre.

All aircraft that found the target made their runs with only minor difficulties. Two had problems caused by the electric mine release failing to operate. Because of this, they each laid four mines in pairs instead of singularly.

The only casualty was A24-64, 'The Dabster' (meaning the best) of 43 Squadron, skippered by Flight Lieutenant (FLTLT) Herb Roberts, who hailed from Perth in Western Australia and was affectionately known as 'Black Robbie' by fellow crew members. The official records from *Casualty Branch of US Army Forces Western Pacific* reads simply that the aircraft 'failed to return' (FTR). No distress signal was received and the reason for its loss is unknown.

Ray Byfield was nearly part of that crew. After A24-64 had returned to Darwin from the Balabac Straits op, two of FLTLT Roberts' regular crew—the armourer and one of the engineers—had gone to Cairns. They had not returned by the time the Manila Bay raid was being planned. Roberts informed Sergeant Jim Robinson, an engineer, and Byfield that they would be replacing his two crew members. Just before A24-64 was due to depart, the regular armourer and engineer arrived—so Robinson and Byfield were not required. Then suddenly, Roberts' other engineer took ill, and Robinson was, again, seconded.

A24-64's flight was to a datum point over the Bataan Peninsula, roughly where Mount Mariveles rises to 1388 metres above sea level.

Bernard 'Bill' Enerberg of 43 Squadron claimed to see a glow in the sky to the north, suggesting it may have been A24-64 and that it had, possibly due to a radar failure, hit the mountain. Another speculation was that the aircraft was shot down at the entrance to Manila Bay. A24-64's route crossed the Bataan Peninsula between Mounts Natib and Mariveles, then turned south; after they mined the mouth of Manila Bay, they were to depart over the southern shore near Naic. Unconfirmed reports suggest that Roberts intended to fly over Corregidor, in the mouth of the bay, which had a heavy anti-aircraft battery. There are reports of an explosion in the vicinity, which suggests A24-64 may have been shot down.

In March 2019, an RAAF reconnaissance mission in the Philippines discovered the wreckage of A24-64 in bushland, south-east of Cape Calavite on the north-west end of Mindoro Island. The site is along the route A24-64 was flying to its target to mine shipping lanes in Manila Harbour when it crashed into the mountain. The RAAF has accepted that the evidence found at the crash site is of A24-64 and a full investigation is planned for 2020. Until then, an official reason why A24-64 FTR (failed to return) is still unknown.

As a direct result of that loss, after the war Ray Byfield and a friend, Jock Bellis, presented the Perth RSL with a painting of Catalina A24-64, which included a plaque to commemorate its loss. Reflecting back to that day in December 1944, Byfield said, 'My luck was in and, sadly, [that of] Jim and Roberts' crew was out'.

After the raid, some Cats returned at first light to Leyte, but others were forced to make emergency alightings in the hours of darkness due to a lack of fuel. Some arrived with less than 20 gallons (75 litres) in their tanks.

On 15 December, as planned, the US Army 24th and 19th Infantry Divisions and the 503rd Parachute Regiment made an amphibious landing on Mindoro. Once the US Forces were on the island, Filipino guerrillas assisted them to defeat the Japanese Army. The IJN were almost absent during the landings. Instead, the Japanese sent their kamikazes to batter the US Navy Task Force, which consisted of six escort carriers, three battleships, six cruisers and other supporting ships. Only two Landing Support Vessels were sunk. Mindoro was secured within three days, and Australian construction troops assisted in the building of airfields, two of which were completed by 23 December. Mindoro would serve as a base from which General MacArthur would take the main island of Luzon, and thereby the Philippines, and would assist Admiral Nimitz in his island-hopping quest to secure Formosa.

8

THE FIGHTING MEN

JANUARY TO FEBRUARY 1945

In the first week of January, the JCS gave General Douglas MacArthur a late Christmas present—he was appointed commander of all ground forces in the Pacific Theatre of war. Admiral Chester W. Nimitz was made commander of all naval forces, which now included Admiral Thomas C. Kinkaid's Seventh Fleet. This definitive separation of responsibilities meant that MacArthur and Nimitz would have to work together in their push towards Japan. The immediate task was to launch an amphibious landing on the main Philippine island of Luzon. Operations were also planned for an assault on the outer Japanese islands of Iwo Jima and Okinawa before, eventually, striking at Japan itself. Nimitz's plan to take Formosa, in the South China Sea, had been postponed.

At the end of the first Sino-Japanese War in 1895, Formosa became a Japanese colony. Any Chinese resistance had been quashed by the turn of the century, and the inhabitants were indoctrinated into Japanese culture. Part of the indoctrination included rewarding parents with increased rations if they gave their children Japanese names. Under colonial rule, particularly during the 1930s, Formosa increased its agricultural, mining and industrial output to supply food and materials to feed Japan's military. By the mid-1930s, it had become an important base for both the IJA and IJN, and was the launching pad for the invasions of British Malaya and the Philippine islands in December 1941. From 1937, over 200,000 Taiwanese were enlisted in the IJA. Some of these Taiwanese were among the invasion force that took the Philippines and had remained there as part of the occupying army.

Anticipating the Allies' move to take Formosa, as well as strategic airfields along the east coast of mainland China, Japan hurriedly reinforced its defences. Apart from building up ground forces and increasing the number of aircraft to be used in kamikaze raids, naval ships now became permanent obstacles in the harbours. After the failure at Leyte Gulf, the IJN ordered any ships that were too damaged to repair, or low on fuel and surplus to the navy's needs, to anchor in various harbours and remain there as defence platforms to repel any invasion. For the RAAF Catalinas, this meant having to face increased anti-aircraft activity when trying to reach their targets.

Former Flight Lieutenant Clem Clemesha, first engineer with 20 Squadron, recalled 'getting a surprise' when mining Surabaya, in the Netherlands East Indies, early in 1945:

> On arrival at the target area during the night, the Skipper had to fly straight and level for so many seconds at just a few hundred feet, and signal to the Navigator, who would be down in the nose of the aircraft, when to let the mines go. They were dropped so many seconds apart. This particular time, as the Navigator was just about to release them, he called over the intercom, 'Christ almighty Skipper, there's a ship right underneath us.' I don't remember what anyone else said, but all hell broke loose and without any further ado he let the mines go, while our Skipper, Kevin Hammer, turned the Cat away and climbed up at about a 90-degree angle. The lights came

The last photo taken of WOFF Reg Cleworth, Melbourne, December 1944. When asked what he would do after the war, he replied, 'I don't think I'm coming back'. (Courtesy Robert Cleworth)

LTCDR Palgrave ('Pally') Carr DFC, RAN, the architect of and brains behind the RAAF/US Navy mine-laying operations. (Courtesy Carr family)

Lt Ivor Collins, US Navy Reserve (second from left, front row), and to his left CDR Shirley L. Quimby, US Navy, part of the US Navy contingent supporting RAAF mine-laying operations. (Courtesy Ivor Collins)

Wedmore's service station in Newmarket, Brisbane, was the front for the first secret mine depot. (Courtesy Ivor Collins)

Preparing recently arrived mines inside Wedmore's service station before their shipment to Cairns. (Courtesy Ivor Collins)

Loading mines from a scow in Darwin Harbour. (Courtesy Reg Marr, DFC, QC)

Converting PBY-5As to PBY-5A(M)s at Lake Boga, Victoria. (Courtesy Reg Marr, DFC, QC)

Catalina A24-66, 43 Squadron, flying low off Rathmines FBRD, Central Coast, New South Wales, 1944. (Courtesy Reg Marr, DFC, QC)

In between mining operations, all squadrons performed other duties. Here a 20 Squadron Cat delivers supplies to Australian special forces behind enemy lines on the Sepik River, New Guinea. (Courtesy Herb Booker)

A Cat crew mixing with coastwatchers and locals on Saroea Island (now Pulau Serua), in the Banda Sea, in February 1945. *Standing (left to right):* Bob Draper, Frank Parsons, 'Pop', Jim Treagus. *Sitting (left to right):* Pat Schmidt, Wally Bishop. (Courtesy Tom Broughton)

Members of 43 Squadron taking time off to play a game of footy at Doctors Gully, Northern Territory. (Courtesy Reg Marr, DFC, QC)

Catalina crews being assisted by US Navy personnel to board launches and be taken to their aircraft, Darwin Harbour. (Courtesy Reg Marr, DFC, QC)

Catalinas on the hard stand for servicing, East Arm, Darwin. (Courtesy Herb Booker)

Cat being refuelled at East Arm, Darwin, 1944. (Source: Reg Cleworth)

The view from the expansive wing of a Catalina. (Source: Reg Cleworth)

Don Storrie (left) and Russ Jones of 20 Squadron take a break before heading off on a mining sortie. Note the mine attached to the port-side wing. (Source: Reg Cleworth)

Cyril Payne keeping watch during a return flight. He is wearing the typical uniform of Cat crews operating in the tropical heat. (Courtesy Cyril Payne)

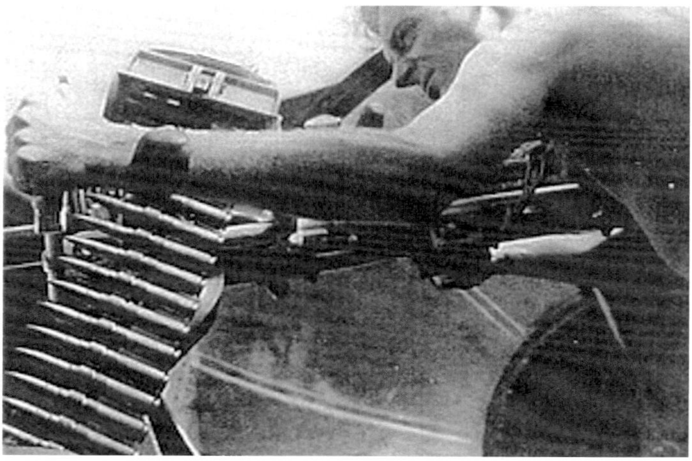

Frank Chessel checking his .50-calibre machine gun. It was not uncommon for machine guns to jam. (Courtesy Frank Chessel)

Armourer Ray Byfield at his post on an operation staged from Lingayen Gulf, Philippines. (Courtesy Ray Byfield)

Reg Cleworth at East Arm, Darwin. 'Spent the afternoon at the rifle range using rifle and Tommy gun, so apparently we are to be infantry as well as aircrew.' (Courtesy Robert Cleworth)

Cat crew being delivered by launch to home base. John Gibson (standing, second from right) and Ross Schulz (bottom right). (Courtesy John Gibson)

Inspecting a 'close call' after an explosive shell pierced the fuel tank, causing a leak but no explosion. *Top (left to right):* Don Storrie, Ron Black, Reg Cleworth, Ross Schulz (skipper), Keith Caulley. *Middle (left to right):* Bill Rowe, 'Snow' Bates and Fred Robins. *Front (left to right):* Russ Jones and Walter 'Scotty' Scott. (Source: Reg Cleworth)

The US Navy base at Jinamoc, Philippines, served as a maintenance and rest area for both RAAF and US Navy seaplanes and their crews. It was an important staging post for mining operations against Japanese shipping in the South China Sea. Pictured are PBY Catalinas and Martin PBM Mariners, with a Curtiss Seagull and a Vought Kingfisher in front of the PBY facing the camera. Another Kingfisher is obscured by the PBY at right. (Courtesy Aub Lee)

RAAF Headquarters, Jinamoc, 1944. Mine-laying crews would be billeted here for up to ten days while performing operations along the east coast of China, before returning to Darwin for rest and recreation. Persons unknown. (Courtesy Aub Lee)

42 Squadron A24-101 ground and air crew loading mines on the hard stand at Jinamoc, 1944. Each mine could weigh as much as, if not more than, 750 kg. Two mines, one under each wing, were required to keep the Cat balanced. (Courtesy Reg Marr, DFC, QC)

Back row, left to right: 'Snow' Bates, Walter 'Scotty' Scott, Bill Rowe, Russ Jones, Don Storrie. *Front row, left to right:* Reg Cleworth, Ron Black, Ross Schulz, Keith Caulley. All, except Ron Black, failed to return from a mission on A24-203 to the Pescadores in March 1945. Ron Black was replaced with PLTOFF M. Merritt on that mission. (Source: Reg Cleworth)

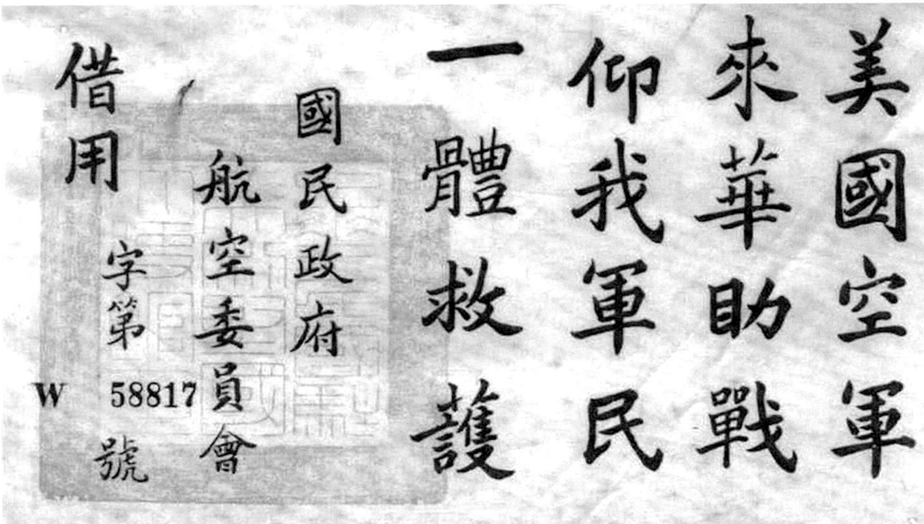

美國空軍來華助戰仰我軍民一體救護

國民政府航空委員會

借用 W 字第 58817 號

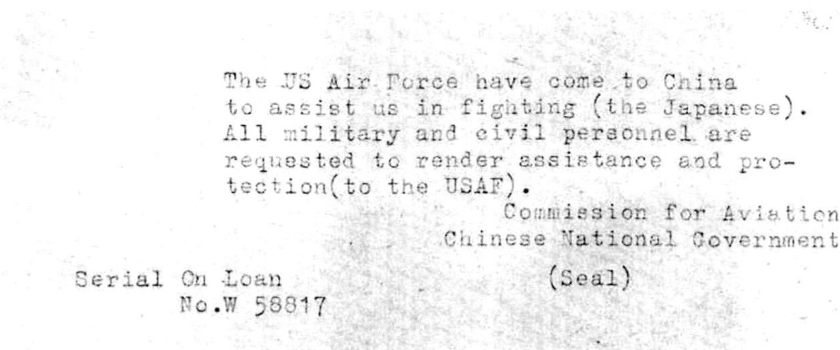

The US Air Force have come to China to assist us in fighting (the Japanese). All military and civil personnel are requested to render assistance and protection(to the USAF).

Commission for Aviation
Chinese National Government

Serial On Loan
No.W 58817

(Seal)

Top: Chinese-language instructions given to crews operating along the east coast of China, in case they were forced to ditch and seek assistance from locals.

Above: The translation explains that they are airmen with the USAAF, despite being RAAF.

Left: Chinese national emblem patches sewn onto the uniform to allow for easy identification by the Chinese militia. (Courtesy Frank Jensen)

Ray Byfield's detailed illustration of all operations performed by RAAF Catalinas in the south-west Pacific. The original is on display at the South Australian Aviation Museum. (Courtesy Ray Byfield)

USAAF B-29 Superfortresses, used by General Curtis LeMay to bomb Japan and then lay mines in the Shimonoseki Straits in Operation Starvation. (Courtesy Gordon Shrubb)

Catalina A24-1 sinking in Darwin Harbour following its crash on take-off to repatriate POWs from Singapore, 31 August 1945. (Courtesy National Archives of Australia)

A24-1, shown sinking above, was towed to the mudflats, where its remains can still be seen today. (Courtesy Robert Cleworth)

The notorious Changi Prison Camp, Singapore, seen from the air in 1945. (Courtesy National Archives of Australia)

Some of the first repatriated POWs arriving home on Sydney Harbour aboard Reg Marr's Catalina in September 1945. (Courtesy Reg Marr, DFC, QC)

20 Squadron's commanding officer, Wing Commander Athol 'Attie' Wearne DSO, DFC. (Courtesy Athol Wearne)

Former WAG with 43 Squadron, now Reverend, Dick Udy. At the time of writing, Reverend Udy is one of the last former Black Cat crew members alive. (Courtesy Robert Cleworth)

Robert Cleworth (left) with Ivor Collins, in 2003. They became good friends, with Ivor assisting Bob to uncover the secrets behind the work of the RAAF/US Navy mine-laying coalition. (Courtesy Robert Cleworth)

> on in the ship, its guns started shooting at us, all the searchlights on the mainland came alive, and the ack-ack picked us up, surrounding us with tracer. I was on the engineer's panel and brought in the emergency procedure that gave the engines more fuel for climbing power. Usually the engineer would wait for the Skipper to ask for it, but there was no time in this case. As the tracer bullets kept coming, they made you feel you must duck away from them, not that it would do any good. We were sure we would be hit, but on returning to base found that not one bullet had hit the aircraft, which seemed to be a miracle.

Having to mine the same target, Flight Lieutenant Frank Jensen, 42 and 20 Squadron, was informed by an American B-24 Liberator crew that the ship 'guarding' the harbour had been moved. The US Army Air Force had flown reconnaissance over Surabaya that morning and passed on this information upon their return. Accepting the ship was no longer near the start of their usual mine run, Jensen and his crew on A24-304

> were fairly relaxed as we flew on our own run at about a height of 80 feet [24 metres] above the water. As was the usual practice, my hand was on the mine release as I looked out to port to see the mine falling away, but to my horror there was the Flak [anti-aircraft] ship, almost, it seemed, at eye level and only 100 yards (90 metres) away. It opened up with all guns blazing and with tracer bullets, all of which seemed as though they would hit me fair between my eyes, but miraculously they passed above and below the cockpit. Never again would I believe the observation reports fed to us by the US Army Air Force Liberator crews.

A draft plan for the Allied invasion of Formosa revealed that over half a million ground troops would be needed, making it three times larger than the D-Day landings at Normandy. The reality was, however, there weren't enough ground forces available in the Pacific. The JCS agreed the operation, codenamed Causeway, would have to wait until the European conflict ended and troops could be diverted. They estimated that Causeway wouldn't take place before September. This, no doubt, pleased MacArthur and vindicated his argument for the Philippines campaign.

Nimitz wanted Formosa so that the Allies could 'strangle' Japan by cutting it off from its main supply route. The central Pacific was under Allied control, so Japan was wholly dependent on oil, rubber and other raw materials arriving via the South China Sea shipping lanes. As the Allies knew, the Japanese were desperate and would employ whatever means available to keep the lanes open. Other than some submarine and long-range aircraft incursions, as well as early sorties by RAAF Black Cats, the Allies had yet to show force in the South China Sea. As the Allies began their invasion of Luzon, US Navy Admiral William 'Bull' Halsey's Third Fleet was tasked with instigating Operation Gratitude—entering the South China Sea and testing Japan's outer defences. The main objective was to damage as much of the IJN as possible, while the secondary goal was to disrupt the supply line.

On 3 January, US Navy carrier aircraft struck airfields and shipping on and around Formosa, then Luzon, and Formosa again in preparation for MacArthur's Lingayen Gulf landings to take Luzon. Then on 10 January, as the landings were underway, fast-carrier Task Force 38 from the Third Fleet turned west, steaming through the Luzon Strait and into the South China Sea. Their destination was Cam Ranh Bay, in French Indochina. US Intelligence had informed Halsey that a large number of the enemy's warships were anchored in the deepwater bay. Halsey's ships masked their approach by following a weather front caused by a growing typhoon over Mindanao. Two days later, Task Force 38—consisting of eight fleet carriers, four light carriers and over 75 other ships in support—emerged ahead of the front, off Indochina. The reported IJN ships were not found, but the carrier aircraft did attack a number of merchant ships and their escort vessels—sinking 41 and damaging 31—as well as destroying 112 land-based aircraft, and bombing fuel depots, dockyards and other facilities. The successful raid had caught the Japanese completely by surprise. *Time* magazine journalist Robert Sherrod, who was an observer on one of the carrier aircraft, wrote that '12 January 1945 must be regarded as one of the great days of the US Navy'.

Task Force 38 then sailed north to avoid the incoming typhoon and attacked Formosa, damaging and sinking more supply vessels, and bombing land installations. From there it launched the first carrier strikes against Okinawa, before turning back and arriving at the Caroline Islands for rest and refuelling. Although the Task Force did not achieve its primary objective of engaging the IJN during its ten days in the South China Sea—simply because the Japanese warships weren't there—Operation Gratitude exceeded the expectations of its planners by delivering a blow to the Japanese supply line. The JCS considered Operation Gratitude a great success.

Around the time that the US Navy operation was about to begin, Admiral Nimitz requested that the RAAF conduct mine-laying operations in the South China Sea to support Operation Gratitude. These would be in addition to those continuing around the Netherlands East Indies. In fact, as Athol 'Attie' Wearne, CO of 20 Squadron, recalled, 'throughout Indonesia not one mineable port, harbour strait or roadstead had been left un-attacked by the RAAF as long as aircraft were available'.

Responding to Nimitz's request, sorties were planned and flown to various targets as far north as Formosa and down to the southern tip of Indochina. In between lay Hong Kong harbour, the southern Chinese island of Hainan, the Chinese coastal port of Amoy and other locations along the east coast of China, all of which were mined. The operations were designed to harass and disrupt merchant shipping, to 'bottle up' the IJN while the Luzon assault was underway and, even more importantly, to prevent the Japanese from supplying their garrisons with extra men and materials.

Around Formosa, the main targets were the approaches to the big Japanese naval base at Mako, known today as Makung, which is on an island in the Taiwan Strait that is part of the small group of islands known as the Pescadores. To reach these targets, the Catalinas would fly from Darwin to Jinamoc Island, codenamed ACORN 30, in San Pedro Bay, Leyte Gulf. Cat crews would be billeted at Jinamoc for seven to ten days while they performed their sorties, then would return to Darwin for rest and recreation. Prior to the ops, each crew member was issued with a Chinese national flag to sew onto their shirts, just in case they were forced to land in China. Flight Lieutenant Frank Jensen added: 'We were also supplied with a small document explaining our role ... that we were assisting the Chinese Forces fighting the Japanese.'

The target locations gave the RAAF Cats the distinction of being the only non-American bomber squadrons to operate north of Morotai in 1945. This accolade, however, caused some consternation among other RAAF and RAF airmen, as they had been relegated to, as Herb Booker from 11 Squadron remembered, 'looking for and sinking Jap barges around Borneo'. It was considered a menial task compared to what they had been used to and what was being asked of the Black Cats. The situation 'led to a threatened mutiny among them, and the Poms wanted to go home'. The Australian and British airmen felt sidelined because 'there were very few Jap planes flying ... it was obvious the Yanks didn't want them, only the Cats'. The China coast operations would take the RAAF Black Cats well behind enemy lines and into heavily defended territories that the Japanese, fearing invasion, were reinforcing daily. To reach their target, some sorties had to fly near Luzon, which, during the initial stages, was still being strongly defended by the Japanese. This provided yet another threat to the crews.

During the day, land-based Allied aircraft from Mindoro Island and US Navy carrier aircraft attacked shipping, IJA defence installations and enemy airfields on Luzon and Formosa in order to neutralise the kamikaze menace in the lead-up to the Luzon invasion. Inclement weather, however, grounded Allied aircraft in the days close to the landings, allowing the Japanese to repair airfields and launch their attacks against the US Navy Seventh and Third Fleets. Japanese kamikazes had improved their tactics since their failed defence of Leyte Gulf. Suicide pilots were better trained; they flew low and used deception measures to evade radar detection. After a kamikaze raid on 5 January, a communiqué from the Third and Seventh Fleets to the US Navy Commander-in-Chief, Fleet Admiral Ernest King, noted that it was the 'largest and most deadly group of suicide planes encountered during the operation'.

The kamikazes sank over twenty Allied ships and damaged a further 67, including HMAS *Arunta* and, again, HMAS *Australia*, which were part of the Seventh Fleet. After Japan had surrendered, Admiral Halsey admitted that the only thing he feared throughout the war 'were the kamikazes'.

The number of kamikaze planes eventually dwindled, and the weather improved. On 9 January, the amphibious landing began after an hour-long naval bombardment of the Lingayen Gulf area in north-western Luzon. MacArthur chose this landing location because it gave his army access to the roads and railways travelling south through Manila, MacArthur's main objective. On landing, the US Sixth Army met little resistance, mainly because day and night US raids against enemy shipping plus strategic mine laying by the RAAF Catalinas had prevented the Japanese from supplying and reinforcing their ground troops. Even though the IJA was 260,000 strong, which included IJN personnel who found themselves trapped on the island, it lacked artillery, ammunition, transport, armour and other essential equipment. Rather than face the Sixth Army head-on, the bulk of the IJA withdrew to the mountains and developed strongholds from which it planned to fight a long battle of attrition. The IJN decided to defend Manila, contrary to IJA orders to blow up all bridges and vital installations and evacuate the city.

The day after the landings, MacArthur's headquarters sent this communiqué to Washington, DC:

> Our forces have landed in Luzon. In a far-flung amphibious penetration our troops have seized four beachheads in Lingayen Gulf . . . The decisive battle for the liberation of the Philippines and the control of the Southwest Pacific is at hand . . . General MacArthur is in personal command at the front and landed with his assault troops. His ground forces of the Sixth Army are under General Krueger, his naval forces of the Seventh Fleet and Australian Squadron are under Admiral Kinkaid, and his air forces of the Far East Air Force are under General Kenney. The Third Fleet under Admiral Halsey is acting in coordinated support.

Despite the optimism, MacArthur did not declare the Philippines liberated until early July. Even then, the Japanese were still holding out—there were an estimated 115,000 soldiers spread across Luzon and some of the southern islands. As they had shown from the outset, the fanatical Japanese would not surrender and would fight to the very last man.

While the mine-laying operations were cloaked in secrecy, in February 1945 someone decided to release information to the media, specifically the British press. Not to be confused with the former Sydney tabloid of the same name, the *Daily Mirror* in London published and syndicated the following story on 8 February:

AMERICAN FLEET ASKED FOR AID

London, Thursday—The Japanese Battle Fleet, including four battleships, an aircraft carrier, six cruisers and many destroyers, was bottled-up in the S.W. Pacific after a surprise mine-laying raid by long-range Catalinas of the R.A.A.F. recently.

Another heading, believed to have appeared on the same day, stated:

JAP FLEET BOTTLED UP BY R.A.A.F.

Catalinas Block Vital Bay with Mines

It's unknown in which publication the second heading was printed, as the newspaper's name doesn't appear in the cutting handed over to Herb Booker by relatives and kept in his 11 Squadron scrapbook. The first article was short and didn't give away any details, such as a specific location or when the operation took place. Because of the timing of both pieces, it is possible that they were referring to the Manila Bay raid of the previous December. Then again, they may well have been referring to November's mine-laying operation against the IJN in Brunei Bay. Either way, both newspaper stories finally offered well-deserved public acknowledgement of the work being done by the RAAF Catalinas.

Booker is passionate about the work performed by the Catalina crews and was not happy about the lack of recognition they received after the war. He put it down to a number of factors, one of which was the lack of spectacular actions compared with the other arms of the RAAF. Booker said that the Catalinas, from early 1943, were known as the 'Splish Splash' boys, after the noise made when a mine hit the water from a low altitude. They had lost the tag of 'Boom Boom' boys, which they had had in 1942 when they were attacking enemy airfields and installations with conventional and incendiary bombs. He also blamed the secrecy attached to

RAAF/US Navy mining operations, explaining it contributed to a lack of publicity compared with that given to the bombing operations. To a large extent, the secrecy denied the Australian people knowledge of the RAAF Catalinas' more intricate work, which achieved greater results. As Booker rightly pointed out, 'no bombers closed a harbour for up to a fortnight'. Strategically placed mines in the Japanese-captured ports denied Japan the oil, minerals and food necessary for their war effort.

Booker did admit the secrecy led to fewer casualties than occurred in the more overt operations. Thanks to the intricate planning of the missions, the use of codenames and radio silence, and the small number of people who knew anything about the target, RAAF Cat crews defied the casualty rates predicted by intelligence reports. Though, on reflection, Booker said, 'Yes . . . lack of publicity reduced our losses, but even these losses are sad memories.'

At the start of 1945, between securing Mindoro and staging amphibious landings on Luzon, General Douglas MacArthur was doing the rounds of nearby installations. Naturally, Jinamoc Island was on his list. It was an important base, strategically, for the RAAF and US Navy coalition mine-laying operations, and as a general maintenance depot for both RAAF and US Navy seaplanes. Whenever MacArthur inspected a base, it was customary for all available personnel to be on parade. Consequently, according to John Gibson, former air gunner with 43 Squadron, Australian and American Catalina crewmen were lined up and standing to attention when MacArthur approached with his entourage in tow.

MacArthur walked up to the RAAF crew and addressed the senior officer, who, keeping a step behind, followed the General as he reviewed the Australian airmen. MacArthur came to the end of the line, saluted the men, turned and walked off. The American Cat crews, who were still standing at attention, seemed perplexed by MacArthur's exit. Walking briskly, their commanding officer caught up to the General and brought him to a stop. The US Navy senior officer excused himself and reminded MacArthur, 'General, you have not inspected all the men.'

General MacArthur quickly retorted, 'I've inspected the fighting men', and continued on his way.

It's not known which US Navy Catalina squadron was present during this event, but it's unlikely that it was a US Navy Black Cat squadron. The US Black Cats were given the unenviable task of hunting IJN ships during the night, to bomb and strafe the vessels. On occasion, they were also ordered to torpedo Japanese warships moored in harbours. Attacking armed ships at night was a precarious job, even though the US Catalinas had additional armour, self-sealing fuel tanks and four .50-calibre Browning M2 machine guns. As soon as the Cat's engines were given full throttle and the aircraft was put into a dive to drop an armour-piercing bomb, the enemy ship would be alerted and the US crews would come under the ship's intense anti-aircraft defences. Even the RAAF had a healthy respect for the IJN's anti-aircraft batteries, finding them more accurate than the shore batteries manned by the IJA.

The Report on Mine-laying Operations by the RAAF between 22 April 1943 and 31 July 1945 addressed the issue of the enemy's anti-aircraft defences:

> Anti-aircraft fire provided the most serious opposition encountered. This consisted of two types, shore based and ship based. The shore based fire never proved such a serious threat as encountered from shipping, which was always withheld until the critical moment and was invariably accurate and well directed. On the other hand shore-based anti-aircraft fire was, as rule, wild, uncontrolled and belated. This may have been due to the fact that the majority of shore based defences are believed to have been manned by army personnel who may have considered that the defence against minelaying aeroplanes was primarily a naval responsibility.

Like those of the RAAF, the US Navy's Catalinas were given the offensive role of hindering and harassing the enemy in support of larger operations. US pilots used the aircraft's all-over black paintwork, slow speed and low-flying abilities to 'hide' from the enemy and avoid night fighters. Regardless of the mission, the PBY Catalinas performed with high distinction throughout the SWPA.

In January 1945, nineteen-year-old Flight Lieutenant Frank Blundell had just completed his training as a navigator.

> I was posted to number 20 Squadron, based at Darwin, Northern Territory . . . But, about one week later, we were re-posted, this time to number 43 Squadron, also at Darwin, and located at Doctors Gully. There were three squadrons on the same type of operations . . . mainly mine laying from the air . . . our number 43, number 20 based at East Arm [part of Darwin Harbour] and number 42 Squadron at Melville Bay, about 400 nautical miles [740 kilometres] east of Darwin on the north-eastern tip of Arnhem land.

Although Blundell initially wanted to be a pilot, the RAAF decided he would be better suited as a navigator, and 'it turned out to be one of the best things that ever happened to me . . . I found navigating fascinating, and the long flights of 15 to 20 hours over water necessary to [reach] Catalinas' targets gave ample opportunity to use one's skills.'

Blundell's crew were all new recruits without any operational experience, except for their skipper, 22-year-old Flight Lieutenant Dick Gill. Even so,

> we developed into an efficient unit . . . completing successfully all 19 missions to which we were assigned, and flying 522 operational hours, 246 by day and 276 by night.

> We laid mines in seven different locations, all at night and usually carrying out two or three missions to each place. On our forward journey to Laout Strait . . . off the southeast tip of Borneo . . . we refuelled at West Bay on the northwest coast of WA, and again on the return trip. Total flying time, about 23 hours. Elapsed time, Darwin to Darwin, 29 hours. When on a mission to Surabaya, a busy port on the island of Java in the Dutch East Indies, we also stopped for refuelling at West Bay, but on the return flight, when aided by a strong tail wind, we could fly direct to Darwin. Total flying time, about 25 hours. Elapsed time, 30 to 32 hours.

The realities of war struck home early for Blundell when, on one of his first operational sorties, one of the six participating aircraft was lost. 'We had encountered very severe cyclonic conditions over the Timor Sea during our return flight [and] at one stage our Catalina dropped suddenly by about 1000 to 2000 feet [300 to 600 metres], it was scary, but we survived. It seemed likely that the lost aircraft went down while struggling through that same cyclone.'

Blundell gave a very dramatic example of what he and his crew were dealing with during the storm. Above the navigation table, there were exposed cables leading from the pilot's compartment to the rudder and ailerons. In normal flight, these cables moved gently, but when Blundell's Cat was being tossed about, 'the cables were continually looping down almost to the table and then snapping back into place [a drop of about 1 metre]. It was disturbing to say the least, and was due to the whole aircraft flexing. I experienced the same phenomenon on two other occasions during extremely bad storms.'

When Admiral Nimitz requested strategic mine laying along the South China Sea, specifically targeting the Hainan Strait, Pescadores, Amoy, Hong Kong and Bangka Strait, all three Darwin-based squadrons of 76 Wing were involved. As Blundell remembered,

> we flew overnight from Darwin, taking a route west of Irian Jaya and east of the Halmahera Islands, to Jinamoc Island . . . For our three Hainan operations, the flight from Leyte to Lingayen Gulf took about five hours. There, we topped up our fuel and the mines were armed. Then, continuing on the track to the datum, a straight run of about 600 nautical miles [1100 kilometres] in a north-western direction across the China Sea. Our main problem was mist or low cloud in the target area, a constant plague during all our operations along the China coast.

Ray Byfield, of 43 Squadron, echoed Frank Blundell's recollections of bad weather. The conditions made Swatow, now Shantou, and its harbour on the China coast another difficult port to approach:

> [I]n the hours of darkness the Navigator would continually check our position to keep on track to the target. In these circumstances navigation by the stars was essential. The navigators would follow the coast to the target area and then visually identify the planned datum point. At this point, course, height and speed would be set to drop their mines . . . this may seem mundane, but when flying China coastal missions the weather was always unpredictable and flying low over the China Sea was scary. At times you could see through the breaks in the clouds the white-capped sea in the moonlight. It was . . . very rough, indeed. It was hard to imagine anything surviving if one had to put down in that sea. There was only one situation worse, and that was to fly through a severe electrical storm or inter-tropic front.

In January 1945, 42 Squadron Catalina A24-96 did have to ditch in the rough seas while on route to Surabaya, in the Netherlands East Indies. Skippering the aircraft was Ron Harrigan, with Herb Hough as his second and Keith Stevens as his navigator. The other crew members were

Air Gunner Tom Blight, Armourer Ron 'Bombo' Gray, First Engineer Jack McDonald, Wireless Air Gunner Fred Pearce, Second Engineer Leo Lock and second Air Gunner Fred Barry. They were about fifteen hours into their journey when they encountered a tropical storm front, a monsoonal band reaching from the equator down over the Netherlands East Indies archipelago. As the weather deteriorated, Harrigan decided he needed to set an alternative course to avoid the brewing storm. He and Stevens discussed the issue at the navigator's table, leaving Hough at the controls.

As a new course was being plotted, Hough banged frantically on the interconnecting door between the cockpit and the navigator's compartment. Stevens recalled:

> Ron departed at the double, flung himself into the left hand seat, and realised the starboard engine had failed. He and Herb fought to control the aircraft, dump the mines and fuel, and [he was] forced to make a highly dangerous alighting on the sea [rough-water alighting] ... with only the light of the planet Venus shining through the murk of rain and cloud ... and alight he did, with a huge bounce followed by a series of smaller ones. Of course ... nobody knew what had happened ... then came the first enormous thump as the aircraft hit ... the crew were thrown in all directions ...

The Cat had alighted so hard onto the cross swell that the hull had ruptured; it began filling with water. Stevens was thrown against the radio, putting it 'out of action'. He noted that, once on the water, 'eventually the aircraft stopped and began to corkscrew, roll from side to side, thump from float to float, bounce with the waves, and generally behave in a way which had everyone on board, except Bombo and me, very seasick indeed'.

Quickly, someone switched on the auxiliary power unit (APU) so that water could be pumped out of the fuselage. Jack McDonald and

Leo Lock slung a catwalk to the starboard engine to 'attempt repairs, but to no avail'. It was discovered the problem was the carburettor, and not the weather. As unusual as it was, the Cat had suffered a mechanical failure. This could have been fixed at an AOB or back at base, but unfortunately the hard alighting in rough seas had now disabled the aircraft—and they were floating in enemy-held territory. They were drifting about 28 kilometres from the island of Soemba, a Japanese patrol-boat base, and just over five hours from their target.

Keith Stevens recalled that 'Soemba was becoming ominously closer with the drift of the near westerly wind . . . Ron eventually re-started the port engine in an effort to take us further out to sea, away from [the] Japanese PT boat base . . . This taxiing proved too dangerous in the sea conditions, and we went back to wallowing and drifting.'

Stevens and Ron Gray took up positions at the blisters, keeping an eye out for the Japanese, 'which realistically we had no hope of repelling', and checking on the level of water inside the fuselage. Two hours after their alighting, Fred Pearce got the radio repaired and sent a mayday, which was 'picked up by RAAF Fenton in the Northern Territory. Then nothing to do but wait and hope . . . firstly, that the aircraft would stay afloat, and the Japs stay at home, also, that the calculated position was good enough for the rescue team to find us, and the seas permit a Catalina to land to take us off.'

As they waited, they heard the drone of the other Catalinas flying overhead, returning from their mission to Surabaya. Stevens noted that Pearce 'shone an Aldis lamp vertically in the hope of its beam being seen by their crews through what had become a more broken cloud cover'.

Nine hours after the mayday had been sent, a RAAF B-24 Liberator bomber was heard approaching. Scrambling to look up, the crew saw that the Liberator 'was followed by the enormously welcome sight of A24-60, a 43 Squadron Cat'. The rescue aircraft was skippered by Brian Ortlepp, who also performed a rough-water alighting to reach the troubled crew. According to Stevens, Ortlepp

> set down nearby, but not without incident . . . the landing punched quite a large hole in 60's hull. However, the transfer of Harrigan's crew was carried out without a hitch, and a very relieved, though somewhat bedraggled lot, sat on anything we could find to cover the hole in Brian Ortlepp's Catalina.

Even though A24-96 was filling with water, there was still a risk that the Japanese may be able to retrieve the aircraft before it naturally sank. The standard order for such situations was to render the plane unusable to the enemy. In this instance, once A24-60 was airborne, it circled the area so the blister gunners could take turns shooting at the stranded Cat. Unfortunately, their aim was less than perfect. Stevens remembered that

> Tommy Blight brushed the Ortlepp gunners aside, and with his first burst hit the partially full fuel tanks up in the stricken aircraft's wing. What a spectacular sight! The port wing was hurled a couple of hundred metres, the aircraft blew up, and A24-96 ceased to be.

In memory of the event, Stevens wrote a short poem to commemorate the last hours of being with his aircraft:

> She'll take no more to fight the war
> To ditch in darkest pitch
> We left her 'light and sinking fast
> She's had it—Ninety Six!

Weather was, indeed, as much an enemy to the RAAF Catalinas as any anti-aircraft battery or Japanese fighter, as Flying Officer Ivan Clempson, engineer with 20 and 43 Squadrons, explained:

> [O]n mine laying operations we visited targets at both ends of Borneo, Surabaya, Hainan Island, Sumatra, Burma and so on . . . our first Squadron set-back was the tragic loss of Jim Seage and his whole crew during a tropical storm. We were on a similar trip another night, and on the same type of mine drop target area. On our return we encountered this severe tropical storm. After discussion with our Navigator, and assessing the situation, the Skipper [Flight Lieutenant Jack Hill] decided that the best action was to climb over the storm. This was a very wise decision and we did it successfully, I might add, not without some considerable discomfort, as we climbed to an altitude in excess of 10,000 feet [3000 metres], and the Catalina was not equipped with oxygen.

The oxygen bottles were one of the many things removed from the aircraft to keep its weight down. The mine-laying planners never envisaged the Cat flying at altitudes requiring oxygen, as to do so would expose the aircraft to radar and enemy fighters. Keeping low and staying in the shadows were its best defence. However, no one considered that the Cats would encounter such horrific storms and have to fly above them for safety reasons. Clempson continued:

> Firstly, we were only dressed in shorts and shirt, so we nearly perished with the excessive and prolonged cold . . . the water in the bilge of the aircraft was all ice. Secondly, and I would say the major concern, was the lack of oxygen. This affected our normal function, or at best, slowed us all down to the extent it was difficult to even carry out the simplest of calculations and movements. Still, we at least survived and got back to base. The accompanying crews . . . also went around the storm satisfactorily. But Jim Seage was not so lucky the night they disappeared. No doubt they would have made every effort, but sadly to no avail. To my knowledge they were never ever traced. The thought is, the Japs must have got 'em.

Official records attribute the loss of A24-204, Flight Lieutenant Seage's aircraft, to bad weather.

On another sortie, a tropical rainstorm broke as Clempson's plane was nearing the target area. It had been an uncomfortable flight for Clempson, not because of the storm, but because he was suffering from sunburn—a condition that, if it prevented the person from doing their job, was considered a self-inflicted wound and would result in disciplinary action. Clempson, rightly, ignored his pain and made himself available for the op. Shifting in his seat to get some relief from the burning agony, he looked out of his window and noticed that the protective perspex cap, which should have been covering the arming bolt of the mine, was missing. This meant that the salt washer was exposed to the rain—when it dissolved, the mine would be activated. If the mine sensed a magnetic field and/or vibration from an engine, it would explode. Clempson was sure that the Cat was magnetic and noisy enough to set off the mine. His sunburn was quickly forgotten, and 'flashes of my early days kept passing before my eyes'.

Clempson informed his skipper, Jack Hill, who calmly told him to 'keep an eye on it'. Clempson realised the skipper 'had less of an idea how to deal with the situation than I did'. His next thought was that the armourer would know what to do. The advice from the armourer, Sergeant Max 'Blue' Craig, proved to be less helpful than Clempson had hoped: '[D]on't look at it and it may not happen.' Clempson then 'spent the next anxious eight hours squirting a torchlight out onto the problem mine . . . we were all relieved to feel the mine leave the bomb rack over the target'.

As Clempson would find out on his return, the mine would not have exploded, even if the salt washer had dissolved in the rain. For the mine to fully activate, it needed water pressure, which is greater than air pressure. With this knowledge in hand, the sense of mortality left and the discomfort of blistered skin returned.

If the Japanese defences and severe tropical weather weren't enough to contend with, incursions into the South China Sea also saw the RAAF Catalinas coming under 'friendly fire'. From September 1944, the US Army Air Force had a new weapon, the twin-engine Northrop P-61 Black Widow. It had a crew of three, and its firepower was deadlier than that of most other fighters at the time, certainly in the Pacific. Mounted in a traversing turret on top of the aircraft were four .50-calibre M2 Browning machine guns, with 560 rounds per gun; four 20-millimetre cannons were located in the belly, with 200 rounds per cannon. A purpose-built night fighter, the P-61 was used by the United States as protection against Japanese night raids, and to patrol deep into enemy territory. Like the RAAF Catalinas, the Black Widows prowled around the South China Sea. They took notes on ship movements and attacked any enemy aircraft they came upon.

During a sortie deep into the South China Sea, Warrant Officer Bob Walker, the radio operator on Ivan Clempson's plane, picked up some chatter. Then suddenly, according to Clempson, 'a couple of short, sharp bursts of tracer came across our bow . . . two very fast Black Widows flashed through, across our flight-path'. To avoid such an incident, all Allied aircraft were fitted with Identification Friend or Foe, or IFF, which emitted a coded radio signal that identified the aircraft as an ally. However, someone had forgotten to flick the appropriate switch. As Clempson noted, 'it was rectified in almost "nothing flat" . . . There are two switches to activate this transmitter, one in the pilot's cockpit area and the other in the navigator/radio operator's compartment . . . this was never a problem again.'

Ray Byfield also had what he referred to as 'a scary incident' on his return from a sortie, when his crew was just out of Manila. It was normal for all Catalina navigators returning from China to use Manila as their location for fixes. On this occasion, however, a US Army Air Force night fighter picked them up on his radar. Although the Cat was observing strict radio silence, the Cat's wireless operator overheard the American night fighter talking to his base: 'I've picked up an aircraft not having his IFF on . . . I think it's a Catalina.'

Realising the pilot had probably seen the Cat's silhouette in the light reflected off the moonlit sea, the wireless operator quickly switched on the IFF. He then heard the pilot report back: 'He has switched on his IFF.'

As Ray Byfield remembered, 'thankfully the American reputation of shooting first and then asking questions did not apply to this Black Widow pilot, and the crew were thankful for that. All night fighter pilots from Manila were warned of our Cats coming from China . . . We hoped!'

During earlier mining operations, the RAAF Catalinas had really only faced opposition from ground or ship defences. Occasionally, in the early morning hours as they flew back to base, they were vulnerable to Japanese fighters. While the Allies had used radar from the beginning of the war, the Japanese didn't adopt the technology until very late. Eventually, in 1945, the Japanese developed their own radar-equipped night fighters. For the Catalina crews, this meant that they could no longer hide in the clouds or blend into the landscape at night to avoid their foe, but had to fly low and slow. Japanese pilots weren't comfortable with flying at low altitudes at night. They may have mistrusted the new radar equipment, or believed it was not accurate enough to keep them safe from ditching in the water. The Cat's slow speed, which many perceived to be a weakness, turned out to be its strength and saviour.

Ken Chessell, former armourer and air gunner with 43 Squadron, recalled an earlier time when his aircraft was set upon by two fighters while making its way home during daylight hours. The first was a 'Rufe', a version of the Zero, which had floats for operating off the water:

> [I]t attacked the Cat from underneath, curled up in front and flew back upside down over the top of us while firing. Fortunately the pilot's aim was poor, but his manner of attack made it very difficult for

> us to get a hit. A Dinah, a twin-engine Jap plane, appeared suddenly on the port side, had a quick look and broke away to the rear . . . I fired at it but couldn't be sure if I hit it or not, but it didn't come back.
>
> To shake off the Jap fighters, the Skipper, Flight Sergeant Don Abbey, put the Catalina immediately into a very steep dive and pulled out just above the ocean. He was virtually skimming the water. The Japs didn't attempt to follow at that altitude . . . the Cat was never intended for that type of flying . . . it got us home safely . . . it did suffer structural damage and was only used as an instructional air frame afterwards.

Ivan Clempson recounted a time when his crew was attacked, illustrating the defensive manoeuvre:

> [W]e were on our way to Hainan Island . . . later we discovered it was one of the worse [sic] Japanese Prisoner-of-War camps in the area . . . when we were jumped by a Jap night fighter . . . our exhaust flames gave us away, that's how he located us. He made a few passes, until he ran out of ammunition, or got bored, and went off home . . . our great protection in a situation like that was to get down as close to the water as possible . . . perhaps as low as 20 or 30 feet [6 or 9 metres] . . . while we, being black, low, slow and in the dark . . . he was so much faster that he was unable to dive, or get down low enough to aim his aircraft to fire his guns.

In mid-February 1945, as General MacArthur's ground forces were making their way south from Lingayen Gulf to the Philippine capital, Manila, Admiral Nimitz, commanding the Fifth Fleet, was steaming towards Iwo Jima. During Operation Detachment, three Marine Divisions—the Third, Fourth and Fifth—would land on the ash-covered island to secure the three airfields, which would provide a staging area for air attacks on the main Japanese islands.

Although B-29 Superfortresses had begun bombing Japan, they did so without fighter escort. The US Army Air Force bombers were also targets for Japanese suicide pilots determined to ram the big aircraft out of the sky. Iwo Jima would, therefore, be a base for the US Army Air Force fighters, P51 Mustangs, and also provide an emergency landing area for any damaged bombers returning from the raids.

Prior to the landings on 19 February, the US Navy conducted a three-day bombardment of the entire sulphurous atoll, though it was not continuous due to spells of bad weather on each day. According to author Derrick Wright in his book *The Battle for Iwo Jima 1945*, this action prompted Nimitz to say, 'Well, this will be easy. The Japanese will surrender Iwo Jima without a fight.'

The Americans didn't know that the Japanese commander of Iwo Jima, General Tadamichi Kuribayashi, had ordered his troops to dig an elaborate underground defence system. The IJA would fight unseen by the Marines. This tactic wasn't designed to help the IJA survive; indeed, Kuribayashi did not expect any of his soldiers, including himself, to live. Rather, the tactic was designed to prolong the battle and allow the IJA time to inflict as much damage as they could. Each Japanese soldier was expected to kill ten Marines before he himself was killed. Iwo Jima was an island of Japan and, for over 5000 years, no foreign army had ever successfully stood on Japanese soil. Kuribayashi believed, as the Army High Command had told him, that if the Americans suffered high casualties, 'Washington will think twice before launching another invasion against Japanese territory'.

When the three Marine Divisions first landed, all seemed quiet as they disembarked. They quickly found that they couldn't 'dig in' because of the soft volcanic ash. As the first groups assembled at the beachhead, heavy and accurate defensive fire began. The Japanese had been ordered to hold their fire until the Marines had gathered in numbers. From then on, the Japanese made it near impossible for the remaining Marines to land in an orderly manner. They were exposed and suffered high casualties. According to the US Navy Department Library website, 'the 36-day assault resulted in more than 26,000 American casualties, including 6800 dead'. It was the first time American casualties had outnumbered those of the Japanese, although three times as many Japanese died, with just over 200 being taken prisoner.

9

END GAME

MARCH TO AUGUST 1945

As the Battle of Iwo Jima was being fought, early March saw General MacArthur's ground forces getting a foothold on Luzon. They had moved south and were engaged in fierce street-to-street fighting in Manila alongside Filipino militia. Defending the city were elements of the Japanese Navy, known as the Manila Naval Defence Force. They did not have the training or tactics of their army cousins, but were well armed and determined. Their commander, Rear Admiral Sanji Iwabuchi, had vowed to 'fight to the last man'. As one US Airborne commander reportedly quipped, 'Tell Halsey to stop looking for the Jap Fleet . . . it's dying on Nichols Field [a nearby airfield].' Although the IJN commander had rejected orders to blow up bridges and evacuate the city, the local army commander, General Yokoyama Shizuo, committed three of his battalions to support the naval force. During the battle, MacArthur restricted the use of artillery and aerial bombing to try to save Manila and its people, but the intense fighting would, inevitably, cause great destruction.

While Manila was under siege, MacArthur's supply line from Lingayen Gulf was becoming strained. It was important, then, to secure Manila Bay to ease this logistical problem. After airborne and ground-force invasions of the Bataan Peninsula and the island of Corregidor, at the mouth of the harbour, Manila Bay was secured by 2 March. MacArthur announced that Manila had been 'liberated' on 4 March. Addressing prominent Filipinos, MacArthur told them, 'My country kept the faith . . . Your capital city, cruelly punished though it be, has regained its rightful place—citadel of democracy in the East.' Although the city of Manila and its bay were in Allied hands, skirmishes continued close by as pockets of Japanese resistance launched counterattacks. The battle for Luzon had not yet been won.

American military intelligence services monitored all Japanese communications. Not just those relating to operations, but also those sent between government departments, giving the United States an understanding of the 'home' situation. US Intelligence colour-coded their intercepts, depending on the origin. One transcript, known as an ORANGE decrypt, is a message from the Imperial Military Headquarters to general staff dated 8 March 1945. In this communication, the Japanese had accepted the loss of the Philippines and were preparing for an Allied invasion of the main Japanese islands, given the assault on Iwo Jima.

More importantly, from the RAAF's mine-laying perspective, the Japanese believed that they could no longer rely on resources from the SWPA, and had begun producing alternative fuels and using what materials were available to them in their homeland and parts of China under their control. As noted in the decrypt, 'the transportation crisis, occasioned by the increase in the rate of shipping losses, is, even now when our lines have been contracted, our severest difficulty in the maintenance of imperial war strength'. The decrypt, therefore, shows that RAAF mining was successful in neutralising important oil and mineral ports in the SWPA, leaving Japanese vessels vulnerable to submarine and air attacks.

The decryption also reveals the Japanese resolve to 'annihilate the enemy' and bring about victory. The Japanese Government had civilians—both males and females of appropriate ages—trained in the use of firearms, close combat and basic military tactics. Should the Allies set foot on the Japanese homeland, they would be forced to fight both military personnel and armed civilians.

As indicated by the ORANGE decrypt, the Japanese had given up on the Netherlands East Indies and now relied on the materials they could extract elsewhere. The RAAF Black Cats had been laying mines in the South China Sea for a little over a month before the date of the intercepted communication. While the Black Cats continued to mine the East Indies, their new targets along the east coast of China would add to Japan's woes.

The primary targets were Hong Kong harbour, the sea lanes approaching the Pescadores (now known as P'eng-Hu Ch'un-Tao), Formosa and the harbour of Amoy (today's Xiamen). Because the east coast of China was so far behind Japan's line of defence, little action had been seen by the Chinese locals since the 1937 invasion. This meant that, as the Cats began their sorties, lights from villages, open fires and fishing boats could be seen along the route. As the crews had experienced back in 1943, some Japanese military personnel believed the approaching planes were their own and turned on landing lights. The Japanese did not realise that the modifications done by the RAAF and the use of AOBs had extended the range of the Cats. Of course, as before, the Japanese wised up after the first few raids, and the east coast of China was blacked out.

Hong Kong harbour was problematic from a geographical standpoint. Due to the terrain and the fact the water was so deep, in some places right to the mountainous shoreline, laying mines in appropriate depths to ensure their effectiveness demanded nerves of steel. As Ray Byfield recalled,

> the Skipper had to get the mine as close to the mountain as possible. Great trust was placed in his ability and also the mathematicians who

> calculated the actual mine drop. The technique was, as soon as the last mine was released, but before it entered the water, the aircraft had to bank sharply either hard to port or starboard as the case may be . . . the sensation was as if somebody held the wing tip, while at the same time was putting on power to get maximum lift and performance to complete a sharp turn . . . it was very nervy.

Flight Lieutenant Ralph Bruce, 11 and 42 Squadrons, remembered coming across a different problem during the initial stages of mining Hong Kong: 'An alarming situation occurred there when we commenced our mining run, with stop watches running, to find we were over a huge fishing fleet . . . we had to drop our mines amongst them. I'm pleased to say we did that without any accidents.'

There were few, if any, maps of the Pescadores in 1945, so the RAAF crews relied on latitude and longitude coordinates as well as surveillance photos of the datum and the area to be mined. The datum, as it turned out, was a very small island that was uninhabited, low-lying and virtually invisible to radar. It measured no more than about 188 by 457 metres in area. The tiny landmass had to be visually identified, which was not an easy task in complete darkness, and even more difficult in bad weather. It was, however, uniquely shaped like a horseshoe, which made it stand out in clear and calm conditions.

On 7 March, three Catalinas set off to mine the Pescadores. One was from 20 Squadron, A24-203, piloted by Ross Schulz and with Reg Cleworth as navigator. This would be their last operation. Flight Lieutenant Frank Blundell was the navigator on 43 Squadron's A24-65, with John Gibson manning the starboard-side blister gun. Blundell remembered:

> We flew one of the few missions to that target . . . it is worthy of comment since it illustrates the extent to which crews were left free to decide on their route to a target and the method they used to

locate the datum point. It illustrates, also, the problem caused by mist and/or low cloud, which was prevalent in the South China Sea ... In case the island could not be found, we were given an alternate target on the coast of Formosa ... The Captain [Richard 'Dick' Gill] and I decided the best way to locate the island was to set course just before dusk from the north-west tip of Luzon in the Philippines, which would give us a northerly run of about 350 nautical miles [650 kilometres] over open sea to the target. When my dead reckoning position was 5 miles [8 kilometres] short of the target, we would commence a 'creeping line ahead' search. This type of search involved flying a series of 'legs', two visibilities apart and 10 miles [16 kilometres] long, at right angles to the track we had been flying ... When we commenced the search for the island, we posted one crewman in the bow compartment and three in the blister compartment. The two pilots were in their normal positions, thus giving us six lookouts. I remained in the navigation compartment, plotting and calling the courses we had to fly.

Our strategy proved successful as we sighted the island on the second or third leg of the search. I gave the Captain the course for the mine-laying run and he said he was turning off to starboard and would return to the island flying the required course. I replaced the crewman in the bow compartment to carry out my usual duties for the mining run. The turn to starboard was completed, and we were set to commence the run. The only problem was we could not see the island, and about an hour later we were still searching for it. After about [a further] 15 minutes, I returned to the navigation compartment and plotted a 'square search', which was the appropriate search in the circumstances, gave times and courses to the second pilot and returned to the bow compartment. Throughout the search, I knew we were in the general vicinity of the island we were seeking since there was constant searchlight activity from the main islands of the group to our north, and our position relative to the searchlights remained reasonably constant.

After another hour of searching, the weather turned for the worse and visibility was hampered by low cloud. Blundell had set a course for the alternate target of Formosa, when 'unbelievably, we flew directly over the island for which we had been searching. This was pure luck aided by a break in the low cloud. This time we did not lose the island and completed the mine-laying run successfully.' He added:

> Three aircraft flew to the Pescadores that night [and] all were to use the same island as datum . . . a second aircraft found it by flying to Formosa and setting off from a point [that] gave it a run of only about 100 nautical miles [185 kilometres] to the target. The technique used by the third aircraft [A24-203] is not known, as it did not return from the mission. It is possible that [this] plane failed to find the island datum, flew to the alternate target and crashed on the coast of Formosa due to the very poor visibility.

The official records state A24-203 was lost to bad weather and that 'searches were made of the area South East of Formosa, but with nil results'. Former radar mechanic Walt Smith had fitted a new type of radar to A24-203 just prior to the mission:

> I arrived at Darwin about the same time as the replacement radar sets arrived and was the only radar mechanic trained in the later gear. The earlier radar required Yagi Antennas out in the slipstream, and the VMU [the radar screen or monitor] showed only a vertical trace in centre screen [and] all the information was obtained by watching for blips on the sides of this vertical green line. A radar operator was carried to interpret information on the VMU. Eventually, all aircraft

> were fitted with ASD 1 that had a parabolic antenna enclosed in a teardrop shaped cover above the cockpit, and projected an amber map on the screen . . . I remember we worked seven days a week and much more than eight hours a day, sometimes well into the night to get the changeover finished. I don't recall the sequence the ASD 1 sets were fitted, but A24-203 had the new gear fitted because I don't remember them carrying a radar operator on that last fateful operation.

While the radar set was the latest and best technology, Smith admitted that he was concerned because it was prone to malfunctioning at times in tropical weather. He questioned the wisdom of not having a radar operator accompanying the flights as a precaution. However, he didn't know what impact a failed radar set would have had on A24-203.

Bryan Monkton, who also flew this operation, recalled seeing that night what he believed was an aircraft, a Cat, downed in the waters off the coast of Formosa. John Gibson, the air gunner on A24-65, had an alternative theory about the fate of A24-203. He recalled there was anti-aircraft fire in the area and believed the Catalina was shot down on its approach to the drop point. Gibson remembered that his radio operator received a signal from A24-203. No message was sent, but their transmitter had been turned on. All ops observed strict radio silence, so if A24-203 had turned on their transmitter, it meant that they were in trouble and about to ditch. For Gibson, it was evidence that the crew had lost control of the aircraft, and they had tried to send a mayday before hitting the water. Because the Cats flew at such low altitudes, it wouldn't have given the crew much time to send a message. As Gibson recounted, 'their radio came on, then nothing'.

The crew of A24-203 were Pilot Officer Ross William Schulz (skipper), Warrant Officer Malcolm Oswald Merritt (second pilot), Warrant Officer James Reginald Cleworth (navigator), Warrant Officer Walter

Voss 'Snowy' Bates (wireless air gunner), Flying Officer Keith McClement Caulley (wireless air gunner), Sergeant Donald Kelway Storrie (first engineer), Flight Sergeant William Alan Rowe (second engineer), Flight Sergeant Alfred Russell Jones (first crew) and Sergeant Walter Douglas 'Scotty' Scott (second crew).

The Americans decided to begin their own mine laying in late March, using big B-29 Superfortresses for the job. At the insistence of Admiral Chester W. Nimitz, the B-29s would lay mines in the Shimonoseki Straits—on Japan's doorstep—between the islands of Kyushu and Honshu. The Superfortress was chosen because it was the only Allied bomber with the range to reach the targets.

Codenamed Operation Starvation, the plan was to sever the mercantile sea lanes between Japan and both China and Korea, and prevent Japan from sending men and materials to the island of Okinawa, where an amphibious assault was planned for 1 April. In addition, sorties would also be flown to mine ports in China and Korea that were well outside the range of the RAAF Catalinas. Nimitz believed Operation Starvation would deprive Japan of materials and food, which would have a detrimental effect on its people and, ultimately, lead them to surrender. This, Nimitz hoped, would avoid the need to invade Japan—a prospect that neither Nimitz nor General Douglas MacArthur now wanted, particularly given the casualty rates experienced on Iwo Jima.

Interestingly, RAAF Air Vice-Marshal William Bostock had proposed a similar plan to General George Kenney, Fifth US Army Air Force, earlier in 1945. The plan, however, was conditional on the Americans securing a forward base for the target to be within range of the Catalinas. The most northern staging area at the time was Leyte Gulf in the Philippines, which wasn't forward enough. Codenamed Operation Amazon, the plan involved RAAF Catalinas accurately laying sixteen mines at strategic points to block this sea corridor that was essential for Japanese heavy industry. Kenney rejected the proposal. In his 1992 thesis *Mines Away!*, US Air Force Major John S. Chilstrom wrote that Kenney, 'had a poor opinion of mining and [was] unwilling to spare planes for mining if bombing was at all possible'.

Unbeknown to both men, US Navy Lieutenant Commander Ellis Johnson, a mine expert working with Admiral Nimitz, had earlier briefed US Army Air Force XXI Bomber Command leadership on the idea of mining the Shimonoseki Straits. The briefing took place in Hawaii in July 1944, but was not received with enthusiasm. Nimitz then went directly to General Henry Harley 'Hap' Arnold, Chief of the Army Air Force; he outlined the benefits of the plan and requested the use of the B-29s. General Arnold agreed with Nimitz and Johnson, and Operation Starvation was given the green light.

Assigned to head Operation Starvation was General Curtis E. LeMay, who provided over 150 B-29s from the 313th the Bombardment Group, XXI Bomber Command. The US Army Air Force pilots and crews trained for five days prior to the first sortie, making practice runs and, on the last day, dropping dummy mines. Helping the American airmen were RAAF Catalina navigators, seconded to share their experience and skill. Such was the respect given by the American airmen that, on the first day of Operation Starvation—27 March—RAAF navigators were in the leading aircraft, guiding the group to the target in the darkened hours. An estimated 1000 mines were dropped in the straits that night. Operation Starvation would continue through to the end of the war and be responsible for laying over 12,000 mines.

While the B-29 Superfortress was capable of altitudes of over 31,000 feet (9500 metres), pilots flew at a lower height so the mines could be laid as accurately as possible. How low they flew, though, varies depending on the source, ranging from 5000 feet (1500 metres) and 8000 feet (2500 metres) to 13,000 feet (4000 metres). It was hardly the precision mine laying conducted by the RAAF Catalinas at an average altitude of 100 feet (30 metres).

It was no secret that LeMay preferred height to accuracy. He himself said: 'As to worrying about [the] precision of what we were doing . . . nuts. I was a soldier, soldiers fight. If we made it through the day without exterminating too many of our own people, we thought we'd had a pretty good day.'

When Lieutenant Ivor Collins, US Navy Reserve, completed his time with the RAAF mine-laying operations in December 1944, he was promoted to Executive Officer at the Mine Assembly Base, Pearl Harbor, and placed in charge of about 600 men working to prepare mines for Operation Starvation. Given his firsthand experience with both operational methods, Collins said that the accuracy obtained by the RAAF Catalinas was unmatched; '[Operation Starvation] was hardly precision mining'. Because of the speed and altitudes at which B-29s released their mines, Operation Starvation could not compare in accuracy with the lower altitude and slower speed adopted by the RAAF.

Nonetheless, Operation Starvation was a success. Thanks to the sheer volume of mines laid—regardless of accuracy—shipping to and from Japan was severely disrupted. According to an article written in *World War II Magazine* (2008), 'Ship passage through the Shimonoseki Straits decreased from 70,000 tons [64,000 tonnes] per day in March to 35,000 tons [32,000 tonnes] in April, plummeted to 7500 tons [6800 tonnes] in May and 1750 tons [1590 tonnes] in June.'

The article also notes that Operation Starvation may have been responsible for the sinking of the IJN flagship, *Yamato*, as it steamed to Okinawa in a suicidal bid to defend the island in April. Its mission was to sail into the US Landing Fleet, to cause as much damage as possible to the invading armada, and/or beach itself and become a coastal fortress, whereupon its crew would join the Japanese Army land forces. Because the Shimonoseki Straits were closed, *Yamato*—the largest battleship ever built—had to use Bungo Strait, between the Japanese islands of Kyushu and Shikoku. This forced the battleship into the deeper waters of the Pacific, where it was within range of US Navy carrier fighter-bombers. As *Yamato* left the strait, it was shadowed by a US submarine and spied upon by reconnaissance aircraft. On 7 April, US Navy and Marine carrier aircraft attacked the giant battleship and pride of the IJN; it took just two hours to sink. *Yamato* and most of its supporting vessels were lost just south of Japan, well before reaching their destination.

As with the earlier sorties conducted in 1943, the RAAF relied on whatever maps were available to hit selected targets along the east coast of China. With regard to Amoy, the RAAF used British naval charts dating back to 1880 and 1890. As Frank Blundell explained:

> The only large-scale map of the datum . . . showed contour lines, but not heights, starting about 2 nautical miles [3.7 kilometres] inland and culminating in a peak a few miles further inland. Reading the chart, it gave the impression that the datum point was low-lying and, therefore, would be a suitable starting position for the mine-laying run, planned to be at a height of 200 feet [60 metres].

At the briefing for the operation on 4 April, the three crews taking part were told that it was 'essential' for the job 'to be successful'. There were no secondary targets given, and no explanation was forthcoming as to why this operation was so important. Even at the time that Blundell recounted this story, he still didn't know why the laying of the mines in Amoy harbour was imperative. He only knew that 'it had to be done'.

Amoy is situated just over 555 kilometres north-east of Hong Kong and to the west of Formosa, on the Taiwan Strait. To reach the target, the three Cats left ACORN 30 and took a similar route to the one they had used in their approach to the Pescadores a month earlier. As with most of the ops in the area, overcast conditions inevitably hampered visibility. Blundell noted:

> We made a satisfactory landfall, turned to starboard and, despite poor visibility, were able to fly towards the datum by visual observation. But as we drew closer to the target area, the mist or low cloud thickened and all I could see were the waves breaking on the shoreline. However, we decided to commence the run feeling confident that we had the datum 'pegged', and had in mind our briefing instruction, 'essential to be successful'.

As they approached the datum to begin their mine run, the second pilot, Keith Carlisle, and Blundell relayed information to the skipper, Dick Gill. Blundell gave the course, while Carlisle checked the altimeter and relayed the readings to Gill so that he could correct if necessary. Blundell gave an insight into how the 'chatter' went during that particular run over the datum to Amoy:

> Carlisle: 200 feet [60 metres].
> Blundell: Turn to port.
> Carlisle: [14 seconds later] 200 feet [60 metres].
> Blundell: Keep turning port.
> Carlisle: [15 seconds later] 100 feet [30 metres].
> Blundell: Hard to port.
> Carlisle: [5 seconds later] 50 feet [15 metres].
> Blundell: Hard to port.
> Carlisle: [5 seconds later] 100 feet [30 metres].
> Blundell: Keep turning port.
> Carlisle: [10 seconds later] 200 feet [60 metres].
> Blundell: Fly course 138 degrees. Okay now.

According to Blundell, when the radio altimeter read 50 feet (15 metres),

> we were in a steep turn, so the reading probably did not indicate our height above the water, but rather our distance from the ground at an angle of about 45 degrees. Since the wingspan of a Catalina was 104 feet (32 metres), we must have been desperately close to crashing. Later, the Captain said he was surprised I had not sounded more worried. My reply was that, throughout the episode, I could always see waves breaking to starboard even though it was impossible to see land . . . I recalculated the mining run from a position off-shore from the datum, navigated to that point, and we dropped the mines without further drama.

The flight from Leyte to Amoy and return took 22 hours. The day after, Blundell celebrated his twentieth birthday at the US Navy recreation island, San Antone, in Leyte Gulf. It was a double celebration, as Blundell's crew was the only one to successfully lay its mines. The other two crews had returned with their payload, unable to find the target because of the 'ridiculous datum point', as Blundell called it. He continued his story:

> Six weeks later we flew another mission to Amoy, but with a different datum. On that occasion the night was crystal clear, so we diverted to take a look at the datum we had used in April. There was no flat land at the datum point, only steep cliffs rising 300 feet [90 metres] from the water, and the wingtip of our Catalina must have missed those cliffs by a cat's whisker! We had been extremely lucky. So much for 50-year-old naval charts!

After Amoy, Blundell's crew was tasked with mining Bangka Strait, which separates the relatively small island of Bangka from the large island of Sumatra, in the Netherlands East Indies. Blundell noted:

> Because all intervening territory was in enemy hands, laying mines in Bangka Strait involved a circuitous journey of about 3200 nautical miles [5900 kilometres] staging through Jinamoc, as on the previous mission. From there, we made a daylight flight of about eight hours across the Mindanao and Sulu seas, to stay overnight at Labuan in Brunei Bay. Although the port was in Australian hands by then, there were still enemy snipers in the hills. Officers in Catalina crews were advised not to wear their caps (or give or accept salutes to indicate seniority) when ashore, so heeding the caution, some of the crew elected to sleep on board. Nobody fancied being a target.

These sorties around the Netherlands East Indies would be some of the last mine-laying operations conducted by the RAAF.

On 22 May, Air Vice-Marshal Bostock received an operational message from General Kenney, informing him that the RAAF Cats were no longer required to perform any mine-laying duties above eighteen degrees north—basically, nothing north of the Philippines. It also stated that US Navy Catalinas would take over the role of mine laying along the coast of China and those targets closer to Japan. Even though the battle for Okinawa was still ongoing, Kenney believed it would be soon be won and the island could be used to stage the US Navy Cats. The RAAF Cats were relegated to continuing their operations in the SWPA, under instruction from the Seventh Fleet. Fundamentally, they were sidelined and out of the war. The message read:

OPERATIONAL PRIORITY 22 May 1945
AX-90663

UNCLE SUGAR NAVY CATALINAS NOW PREPARED TO ASSUME COMMITMENT OF CONDUCTING MINING OPERATIONS IN CENTRAL AND NORTHERN CHINA WATERS PD IN VIEW OF THIS CMA THE REDUCTION OF LUCRATIVE MINING AREAS CENTRAL CHINA AND DEVELOPMENT OF OKINAWA BASES FOR LAND BASED AIRPLANES WHICH CAN OPERATE AGAINST ENEMY SHIPPING AND HARBOURS NORTHERN CHINA CMA RAAF CATALINAS WILL BE WITHDRAWN FROM THESE OPERATIONS FD EFFECTIVE JUNE ONE RAAF MINING OPERATIONS WILL BE CONDUCTED TO DESTROY AND INTERRUPT ENEMY SHIPPING IN ENEMY HARBOURS OF SWPA OR ADJACENT THERETO SOUTH OF ONE EIGHT DEGREES NORTH PD RAAF COMMAND WILL SUBMIT TO COMMAND SEVENTH FLEET FOR APPROVAL AND TO THIS HEADQUARTERS FOR INFORMATION PROGRAM FOR MINING OPERATIONS BEGINNING IN JUNE AND BASED ON ABOVE INSTRUCTIONS.

COMAAF SWPA

How Bostock reacted to the news is unknown, but he replied to General Kenney three days later and asked for an extension so his crews could complete their planned operations. He wrote:

FOR GENERAL KENNEY FROM BOSTOCK
FROM RAAF COMMAND
NR A-50 25 MAY 1945

REFERENCE YOUR AX 90663 of 22 MAY COM 7TH FLEET HAS NOW ADVISED THAT NO WORTH WHILE MINING TARGETS EXIST SOUTH OF LATITUDE 11° NORTH AT PRESENT WITHIN

RANGE OF RAAF CATALINAS REQUEST YOU PERMIT RAAF CATALINAS TO CONTINUE WITH MINING OF CHINA COAST PORTS UNTIL COMPLETION OF PRESENT PROGRAMME ON 1 JULY THIS WILL ENSURE USEFUL EMPLOYMENT OF CATALINAS ON MINELAYING UNTIL ANTICIPATED MOVE INTO BRUNEY AREA WHEN MINELAYING PROGRAMME AGAINST PORTS IN MALAYA AND SUMATRA CAN PROBABLY BE COMMENCED.

Kenney accepted Bostock's request for an extension. Despite what Kenney told Bostock, it appears that the remainder of the mine laying along the coasts of China, Korea and Japan was done by B-29 Superfortresses. There is no evidence US Navy Catalinas began mine laying in place of the RAAF Cats.

Some insight into why this order was made may be gleaned from Jack Gallaway's book written in 2000, *The Odd Couple*, which examined the wartime relationship between General Douglas MacArthur and Australia's Commander-in-Chief, General Thomas Blamey. Their relationship was strained, with Blamey being kept on the outer by MacArthur from the beginning. MacArthur had promised Blamey 'that one Australian division would be used in the landing at Leyte in 1944 in the Philippines and another in an operation to take Lingayen Gulf the following year'. But he did not keep his promise.

MacArthur's broken promise may have been due to the backlash he received when he decided that the Australian divisions attacking the Philippines would be under American command. In 1942, he had accepted that the United States and other Allied forces should operate independently, as their supply systems were very different. Consequently, throughout the Pacific War, Australian commanders had always directed Australian infantrymen. Now, however, MacArthur had seemingly changed his mind—but Blamey saw no reason why the attack on the Philippines should be an exception. This caused Blamey to write to Prime Minister John Curtin, complaining about MacArthur's request:

> Gen MacArthur has always insisted that the difficulties of two different systems of supply made it necessary to ensure that the American and the Australian commands should, as far as possible, work independently . . . there is no adequate reason why the Australian corps should not be employed [in the Philippines] as a corps under its own commander.

Flight Lieutenant Doug Nolan, 20 Squadron, remembered his brothers, who had joined the army, training 'incessantly' for amphibious landings. They never undertook such action. In fact, according to Gallaway, 'three divisions of crack Australian infantry were training for an amphibious assault in North Queensland'.

Like the RAAF in mid-1945, the AIF had been sidelined a year earlier. And, again like the RAAF, the efforts of the AIF in New Guinea and in securing the Bismarck Sea—allowing MacArthur's push north to his beloved Philippines—would be lost to the publicity machine that was MacArthur. Gallaway stated:

> By mid-1944 there was very little action that involved Australia in the conflict . . . the achievements of the AIF and the Australian Militia in 1942 and 1943 would carry little weight in any discussions . . . Their victories had been damned with faint praise by MacArthur when they were achieved; they would be long forgotten by the time the victorious Allies sat down to divide the spoils of war. Indeed, American newsmen had quickly forgotten them.

As Bostock was dictating his reply to Kenney, the JCS in Washington, DC, were approving Operation Downfall, the land invasion of Japan.

Planned for 1 November, it would start with Operation Olympic—the invasion of the southernmost island, Kyushu. Meanwhile, the European Axis powers had been defeated and officially surrendered on 8 May. Sadly, President Roosevelt died just one month before the Allies celebrated victory in Europe; and Vice President Harry S. Truman had taken office. Even though the JCS had approved the invasion of Japan, there was great concern among the commanders in the Pacific and the politicians in Washington, DC, about the potential cost of the invasion in American lives. The bloody battles of Iwo Jima and Okinawa were weighing heavily on the minds of the military planners. Intercepted Japanese communiqués alerted the United States to Japan's preparations for the invasion. Some referred to these intercepts as 'previews of hell'.

Those concerns were heightened in June when Japanese prime minister Baron Kantarō Suzuki, a former IJN admiral, announced that Japan 'would fight to the very end' rather than accept unconditional surrender. In fact, the Japanese had been withdrawing troops from China since 20 May in order to defend their home islands.

To avoid mass casualties, which some estimate would have been in the hundreds of thousands, President Truman approved the dropping of the atomic bomb as a means of forcing Japan to surrender. The first atomic bomb was dropped on Hiroshima on 6 August. Three days later, a second bomb was dropped on Nagasaki. At the same time, Soviet leader Joseph Stalin fulfilled the promise he had made to President Roosevelt at their last meeting and sent Russian forces to fight the Japanese in Manchuria (north-eastern China). The Russians also planned amphibious assaults to take Japan's northern islands.

With two cities devastated by atomic blasts, Russia entering the Pacific conflict, and the homeland starved of food and basic supplies, Emperor Hirohito announced 'the end of hostilities' on 14 August. When Japanese representatives signed the official declaration on 2 September, the war in the Pacific was over. The unconditional surrender of Japan meant that World War II had officially ended.

In his 1997 book *Storm Landings*, author Joseph H. Alexander quotes a former Japanese soldier recalling his reaction to the news: '[W]hen word got around that the bombs had forced the Japanese to surrender, we knelt in the sand and cried. For all our manhood, we cried. We were going to live. We were going to grow up to adulthood after all.'

Lieutenant Ivor Collins, US Navy Reserve, gave an insight into how the Japanese changed when hostilities ceased. In August, not long after the surrender, Collins was posted on board the USS *Adams*, a former destroyer that had been converted to a minesweeper after being severely damaged in a kamikaze attack. His duties included the preparation and laying of modified Mark VI mines to be used as marker buoys for mine clearance in Tokyo Bay. He described how the Japanese reacted to their new situation:

> [W]e had the assistance of Japanese mine officers to show us where the minefields were located . . . they were very cooperative, and the proof is I am still here. When they came aboard, they approached in a small boat. They were only allowed a small ensign that they flew for recognition purposes with the red dot on it . . . no rising sun. We flew our largest ensign and posted our biggest and meanest looking ratings [sailors] with Tommy guns on the gangway and also to escort them to the forecastle. As I mentioned, they did their job. I have never ceased to be amazed how subservient the Japs became when the order came from their Emperor. It was as if, with the flick of a finger, the war was all over. The Japs we had helping us with the mines were pretty undernourished. We invited them into our canteen. The Japs could not believe what they saw, food everywhere, and they hoed into it eating as they had not done for a while, and drinking coffee as if it was going out of fashion.

10

BRINGIN' 'EM HOME

SEPTEMBER 1945

When the war ended, it was time to bring back all those Australian airmen, soldiers, sailors, nurses and civilians who had been kept as POWs by the Japanese. All Catalina squadrons—mine laying and rescue, seaplane and amphibious—were quickly put into service. Crews were reduced so there would be as much room as possible for the number, and comfort, of returning prisoners. This was a relatively easy task, as armourers and gunners were no longer required.

According to Australian War Memorial records, 22,376 Australians—military and civilian—were POWs in south-east Asia. Most were army personnel, and the majority of those were from the AIF 8th Division, which was captured during the fall of Singapore; the largest civilian internment, of around 2400 people, was also in Singapore. The RAN accounted for 354 prisoners, and the RAAF had 373 in camps. There were also nearly 40 nurses imprisoned. Of the total number of prisoners, over 8000 died in captivity. The Australian War Memorial stated:

> By September 1945, Australian prisoners of war were scattered widely across south-east Asia. The largest group was congregated on

> Singapore Island and Johore (5549); but 4830 were distributed in several camps and in a number of working parties in Thailand and remote areas of Burma. In addition, 265 were in French Indo-China; about 750 were distributed throughout the islands of the Netherlands East Indies, with 385 in Java and 243 in Sumatra; about 100 were on Ambon; two were at Macassar; seven on Bali; another 150 were at Kuching in British North Borneo. About 2700 were distributed between Japan, Korea and Manchuria, while about 200 remained on Hainan Island.

One RAAF Catalina crewman incarcerated by the Japanese was Flight Lieutenant Brian Stacey of 9 and 11 Squadrons. He was the second pilot in Catalina A24-34 when it went down off the coast of New Britain on 7 February 1944. After the crew had completed a bombing raid, the skipper, Jack Todd, had decided to make a reconnaissance run over Rabaul harbour. Being night-time, the armourer got ready to drop a flare to 'light up' the scene, but heavy anti-aircraft fire caused Todd to take evasive action, putting an end to the effort. The flare was never dropped. Todd then told Stacey: 'Go back and have a rest Stace . . . I'll set a course for base . . . On your way back, tell the armourer to set that recco flare back to safe.'

As Stacey explained:

> [I]t is of immense importance to know, in the light of subsequent events, that recco flares have a bad habit of pre-detonating when being set back to safe, after being prepared for action. As a consequence, there is an order that such action must be done in the blister compartment by torchlight. Should pre-detonation occur, there is plenty of time to jettison the flare out of the blister, for it takes some seconds for the nose fuse to burn down to explosion. Regrettably, the armourer chose to defuse in the bunk compartment under diffused light. You can guess what happened.

The flare ignited under the bunks, and Stacey was pulled back into the blister area by one of the crewmen. The door between the bunk quarters and rear area, similar to a bulkhead on a ship, was quickly closed. Stacey continued:

> There we were, five of us in the rear of the aircraft whilst five-thousand candlepower burnt in the next compartment. Ammunition exploded and a second flare ignited. Flames and heat blew back, and the only thing that we could do was to open the blister and put our heads out into the air rushing past. I could see the aluminium skin on the bunk compartment glowing red hot from the heat and had visions of the aircraft breaking up. To say I was scared is no exaggeration, but I knew our only chance was to reach the south coast of New Britain. I guessed what was going on in the pilots' compartment . . . Jack was losing height gradually . . . I later heard that efforts to control the fire failed when the extinguisher ran out of foam, and that our only chance was to reach the ocean before the fuel tanks blew up.

Todd alighted the Catalina without incident. The crew bailed out and waded to shore, finding themselves in enemy territory. They believed that the chances of at least some of them surviving were better if they separated, so they split up into groups. Four crew members found friendly natives and were delivered safely into the hands of Allied coastwatchers. The remainder, including Stacey and Todd, were captured. According to Stacey,

> we commenced a trek along the coast, being handed over from one section of Jap marines to another. At each handover, the new section leader would demonstrate his authority by slapping our Skipper, mainly because he was the largest of us, being six feet tall. Although

we were not in the mood to be amused, it was nevertheless laughable to see small Japanese having to jump in the air to reach and slap Jack's face.

They eventually arrived at Rabaul for their grilling. As Stacey remembered, 'An interpreter soon began interrogations. He was a Japanese Hawaiian with an American accent, and each interview was filmed for propaganda purposes ... Any information I could give them was minimal ... However, one operation on which we kept silent was that of mine laying on harbours occupied by Japanese outposts.'

Because they did not say anything about their mine-laying mission, they were thankfully spared from being beheaded. In time, Stacey was separated from the group because of his rank. As he was the skipper, Todd was held in Rabaul for further questioning. After being shuffled along the islands to different camps, Stacey ended up in Japan. His final destination was a camp on Shikoku, the smallest of Japan's major islands. Stacey described the conditions there:

> This was the show camp of the Japanese, open to Red Cross inspection and to which Red Cross parcels were sent for distribution. Officers and enlisted men were segregated, the latter worked in agriculture and consequently were fed better. We officers received very meagre rations of seaweed and a jam-sized tin of soggy rice, barley, millet and corry seed three times a day. It was amazing that to fill our stomachs, it was common practice to trade off meals to be returned on a certain day. With this extra food supplement, and with a small quantity of rations from our Red Cross parcels, we were able to finish up with the sensation of feeling full. Needless to say, this practice resulted in severe reactions from the bowel, creating periods of constipation or diarrhoea.

The commandant of the camp eventually issued a decree offering extra rations for the officers if they worked in the fields. Stacey admitted that

> it was not a very tempting offer, as it entailed distributing human offal into rows between the vegetables. After consideration we agreed to give it a try, but it did not last for long, for when the vegetables were ready to be harvested, we were informed that, regrettably, the Japanese Army had confiscated the produce. So much for our efforts to improve conditions, foodwise.

It wasn't only the lack of food with which Stacey and his fellow prisoners had to contend:

> [W]eather conditions changed dramatically with the change of season. We were very short of warm clothing, and when the winter arrived the only way to keep warm was to hop into our beds with whatever rugs we had. We slept on grass mats on a wooden floor with small pillows filled with sand, but it was amazing how the body can adjust to severe conditions when it has to. In our condition, it was possible to rest or sleep, so in one way we were fortunate compared to other POWs in Japanese hands.

Stacey was lucky. The Japanese used most POWs as slave labour, ordering them to lay railways, build bridges, cut through mountains and serve in heavy industry. Australian War Memorial records show that 45 Australian army officers were sent to work in the Hokkaido coalmines. The majority of prisoners across the Pacific were given less food and lived in poorer conditions than Stacey described; they were severely punished for the smallest of offences, or just worked to death. In fact, after the war, trials were held to investigate reports of atrocities, massacres and other causes of Australian deaths at the hands of the Japanese.

The Catalinas weren't just repatriating prisoners—they were also delivering medical personnel, stores and other supplies necessary for prisoners' comfort. While the Cats were put into service in September, planning for these 'missions' had begun as early as late July. By then, everyone—possibly even the Japanese—knew that the war would soon be over.

One of the first Cats to be sent to 'bring our boys home' was A24-351, with Flight Lieutenant Bernie Parker as skipper and Flying Officer Gordon Wicks as his navigator. This was somewhat of a reunion for the two, because they had flown together in 20 and 43 Squadrons before Wicks had been posted to Rathmines as a navigation instructor the previous April. They had a mutual confidence in one another's skills and enjoyed each other's company. So much so, they continued their friendship for years after the war.

A24-351 was one of eight Catalinas chosen to fly to Singapore, where the majority of Australian prisoners had been held. It was given the honour of bringing home the first POW group. There were meant to be nine Cats headed to Singapore, including A24-1, the first Catalina received by the RAAF and placed into service. It was to act as the 'flagship', a beacon of pride for the RAAF. However, not all would go to plan.

On 27 August, the nine Cats flew from Rathmines to Rose Bay on Sydney Harbour and collected medical supplies, as well as medical and records personnel, fondly referred to as the 'Prisoners of War Reception Group'. They returned to Rathmines, where they loaded with fuel. On 31 August, the nine Cats took off for Singapore, travelling via Darwin and Labuan, near Brunei. As Gordon Wicks remembered, 'disaster struck' when leaving Darwin:

> Our Flight Commander, in the old original Catalina A24-1, crashed on take-off, so Number One had to be towed to the mud flats ... Nobody was injured ... the stores and records were taken off, and later transferred to other aircraft ... all [eight] aircraft were greatly overloaded with fuel supplies, personnel and stores, so that take-off was extremely difficult.

Catalina A24-1 can still be seen today, embedded in the mud at East Arm, Darwin Harbour.

Midway through the next leg of the journey, a distress signal was received from one of the Catalinas. It had encountered severe icing, which caused the flying surfaces to stiffen up in level flight and could detrimentally affect lift by building up on the leading edges of the wings. Wicks noted that

> this was brought about because of some problems with navigation instruments, which forced the Skipper to endeavour to cut across North Borneo direct to Labuan. The thermal currents over the mountains of Borneo had pushed the Cat ever upwards [into freezing temperatures] ... finally, when across the mountains, the aircraft gradually descended as the ice melted, controls were restored, and we were all relieved to hear another radio message that they were proceeding to Labuan as planned.

The eight Catalinas arrived at Brunei Bay, near Labuan, on 1 September. They were, however, not given immediate clearance to fly on to Singapore. Bureaucratic machinations stranded all crews and the reception group for eight days. Although the crews were impatient to get to Singapore, Wicks recalled that they managed to entertain themselves:

> [N]ow 48 young fit airmen, caged up in the tropics in the metal hulls of the Cats, needed some diversions. Each afternoon, when the heavy

> rain squalls appeared, we climbed up on the wing and had a good shower. A cold beer could have been a problem, but our Skipper was a very thoughtful and innovative person, as well as being an excellent pilot. He instructed that the canvas drogues carried on the aircraft be tied in the form of a bag, and then suspended beneath the drain valve of the fuel tank under the wing, with six bottles of beer inside. Then the valve was allowed to drip steadily into the bag, and you would be amazed at how the evaporation cooled that beer, so as to make it quite suitable for drinking.

The crews received clearance to fly on the morning of 9 September, and they set off for Singapore, arriving at around 5.30 p.m. As Wicks noted: 'We landed in the straits adjoining Singapore Island and proceeded to inflate our rubber dinghy, so that we could go ashore and find the Changi Prison to rendezvous with Brigadier Galleghan.'

Brigadier Frederick Galleghan, later Sir Frederick, was the commander of the AIF prisoners in Changi, having been taken prisoner in 1942 after the fall of Singapore. His biography, in the *Australian Dictionary of Biography*, states:

> He was given the name 'Black Jack' for his complexion, dark hair, and brown eyes. He was a stern figure with a natural air of authority that brooked no dissent. Some officers claimed to have feared Galleghan more than they did the Japanese. Nevertheless, he is said to have been a respected leader who understood that his men's survival depended on their morale, which he maintained through the imposition of military discipline. After liberation, he told his men that they were returning home as soldiers not prisoners.

Three of the A24-351's crew remained on the Cat, while Wicks, Bernie Parker and one of the engineers went ashore. According to Wicks, they '"acquired", for want of a better word, a motor vehicle which had been abandoned by the Japanese, and quickly proceeded to Changi'.

The state of the prisoners shocked the crews and members of the reception group. All were malnourished, a few to the point where they were almost unrecognisable. Some were little more than skeletons, with loose skin sagging across their bones; they were unable to hold themselves up or even speak. Wicks recalled that 'we were all instructed not to give them food, as the richness of even plain biscuits could prove fatal or at least make them seriously ill'.

That evening, as crews and medical personnel attended to the prisoners of war, Wicks, amazingly, found an old friend from Sydney 'who really only wanted to know about his family back at home, and indicated he would like some "clean dry clothes". A pair of shorts and a short-sleeved khaki shirt from my own kit brought about the first smile.'

Three days later, those prisoners deemed fit enough to endure the long, slow and uncomfortable flight back home were selected. Seventeen men from Changi boarded A24-351, with a similar number joining each of the other seven Cats. Each plane had four bunks, one small toilet and a small electric stove with a cooktop that measured about 30 centimetres by 60 centimetres. Including the crew, provisions and care had to be provided for an average of 23 people for periods of up to fifteen hours in the air. Wicks admitted that 'hygiene was not our first objective'.

All eight Catalinas departed Singapore on the morning of 12 September, arriving in Labuan just over six hours later. Wicks noted:

> It was designed to test the effect on our passengers because of the long flights ahead. Whatever their sufferings, they did not complain. They were just so glad to be going home. There was a rest period in Labuan for about 24 hours, before we began what we knew would be their longest 'haul', if we were to make Sydney as desired

on the Sunday afternoon of 16 September and get our first POWs back home.

The next day, the Cats flew direct to Darwin. The flight took fifteen hours and was flown mostly during the night. Again, the crews and prisoners of war were taken ashore, where they slept while the aircraft were serviced and cleaned. The following morning, 15 September, they flew a short leg to Cairns in Far North Queensland, and were then billeted overnight before the last leg to Rose Bay, Sydney.

The media were anxious to hear from the returning soldiers. Being in Cairns, the *Townsville Daily Bulletin* reported on the arrival:

> Prisoners of war who arrived in Cairns by eight Catalinas on Saturday afternoon, told of hardships experienced during their three and a half years in Changi prison camp, and on building the railway on the Burma border. They stated that it seemed just like lingering death. Words could not explain it.
>
> One prisoner told of the joy that prevailed among the prisoners when they were informed of the Jap surrender.
>
> Large crowds assembled on the Cairns wharves to meet the prisoners, who were conveyed from the Catalinas in the inlet to the wharves in launches, where representatives of the ACF, Red Cross, Army, Navy and RAAF leaders met them. Tea was served to them.
>
> Many prisoners showed signs of the trials and tribulations they had experienced, but, generally, they were mostly in fairly good health. The prisoners talked enthusiastically to the gathering, and expressed their keen enthusiasm to again be returning to their homes.
>
> Changi camp was designed for 560 natives and 120 white people, but a maximum of 6800 had been confined in the prison. During the whole time they were in the prison, they slept on bare concrete.

> Their ration was eight ounces [225 grams] of rice daily, and a small piece of dried fish, and two leaves of vegetable . . . they were forced to build roads, working from early in the morning until late at night. Any refusal to work or lagging would bring a thrashing from the Japanese, who kept a watchful eye on them all . . . One got his head opened up with a bayonet because of his refusal to work while on road building. If there were not sufficient men, malaria patients were secured from the hospital to make up the balance required . . . [a] South Australian prisoner of war said that he received a belting in Singapore from the Japanese for waving to natives. He was struck over the head several times with a crank handle.

Not all the soldiers were eager to share their prison experiences. When asked by reporters, Private R.W. Clark responded that he 'would rather not talk of what he had seen'. Regarding the flight home, the *Townsville Daily Bulletin* noted:

> They described the flight as grand, in fact, everything had been marvellous, since their arrival in Labuan. In Darwin, an Army General came in to talk to them, and had refused to allow them to salute when they left to board the Catalinas. In Singapore, one boy said, he patted a wharf pile and said, 'Goodbye Malaya'.
>
> They found it hard to realise that what they had dreamed about for years had come true—home, and good food.

Between 6.00 a.m. and 7.00 a.m. on 16 September, the eight Catalinas staggered their departure from Cairns for the direct flight to Sydney. Gordon Wicks remembered that

> this flight was as uneventful as we could hope, but flying quite low over the coastal strips most of the way, or not far out to sea, our 'returning

> survivors' were able to watch the east coast of Australia slowly passing by. We touched down at Rose Bay at 16.25 hours, about nine hours 30 minutes after leaving Cairns . . . The sight of Rose Bay on our arrival was, and always will be, unforgettable. I doubt whether there has ever been more small boats, ferries, yachts, and anything that would stay on top of the water, out on the Harbour . . . Each of the eight Catalinas, one after another, landed down a narrow corridor between the pleasure craft . . . which were well controlled by the Navy and Water Police. All of the passengers were disembarked onto launches . . . the launches then passed slowly through what amounted to a guard of honour to the wharf at Rose Bay.

The arrival in Sydney was big news, as *The Canberra Times* reported:

> People in Sydney went delirious with joy late this afternoon when the first batch of returned prisoners of war to arrive was driven through the city on their way from Rose Bay flying base . . . The route was lined with cheering, happy people . . . 'Good old Sydney,' cried one man as he stepped onto the jetty to the accompaniment of cheers from the crowds which lined the wharf and stretched along the foreshore.

Gordon Wicks remained in Sydney to see his wife and six-week-old baby girl, while the rest of the crews returned to Rathmines. He admitted he often thinks about what happened to those first seventeen men brought back on A24-351, how they settled and the reactions of their families. For Wicks, it wasn't long before he returned to Rathmines himself, and the crews were, once again, off to repatriate more POWs.

This was the routine for all the Catalinas during September and beyond. They were sent to all former Japanese-held territories across the

SWPA, taking medical supplies, personnel and special envoys to discuss terms and conditions with local Japanese commanders. For the crews, these were 'special missions'. Of all the jobs they were given throughout the war, 'bringin' 'em home' was the most satisfying.

11

CORRECTING HISTORY

POST-WAR PERIOD

As the Allies began reclaiming occupied territories, they took the opportunity to interview IJA and IJN commanders to get their points of view on the strategies employed against them. What worked, what didn't and why? The Allies, particularly the United States, were very keen to know how effective their campaigns were, how the Japanese reacted, what countermeasures they employed, and if the two sides agreed on the results. Did the Allies achieve their desired operational objectives? At the same time, Allied reports on operations were also reviewed and analysed, so an accurate picture of the conduct of the war in the Pacific could be obtained.

Regarding mine-laying operations, three official reports were published within two years of the war's end. The first came from the RAAF in June 1946. Based on interrogations and captured documents, RAAF Headquarters concluded that the success of the mine-laying operations was 'far ahead of expectations and . . . repaid the effort expended and the losses sustained'. This report is not complete, however, as it doesn't include numbers and results from the operations along the coast of China, and it was awaiting information from US interrogations. The report reads in part:

SECRET REPORT ON RESULTS OF R.A.A.F. MINE-LAYING OPERATIONS . . .

EFFECTS OF R.A.A.F. MINE-LAYING CAMPAIGN

3. The effect of the mine-laying operations on the enemy has been:
   - (a) The sinking of, and damage to, shipping.
   - (b) Disruption and delay in the movement of shipping.
   - (c) Time lost by ships due to delays in harbour awaiting the completion of minesweeping operations and to the re-routing of shipping to avoid mined areas.
   - (d) The use of vessels for minesweeping operations which would otherwise be employed for carrying supplies or as escort vessels for convoys.
   - (e) The employment of vessels to salvage ships damaged by mines and to tow these to port, thereby exposing the salvage vessels to the dangers of a mined area and to air and submarine attack during the slow haul back to port.
   - (f) The forcing of shipping away from shallow water passages, which had been mined, and compelling the use of open sea passages where submarines could operate.
   - (g) The holding up or loss of vital supplies such as oil and other raw materials due to the mining of strategic harbours in the enemy's conquered territory.

The first of the American reports was *The United States Strategic Bombing Survey* (*USSBS*)—*The Offensive Mine-laying Campaign against Japan*, published by the US Naval Analysis Division on 1 November 1946. It would be reprinted in 1969 by the US Department of the Navy. The second was from the US Joint Army–Navy Assessment Committee (JANAC). This 1947 report used data from *USSBS*, on the *Japanese Naval and Merchant Shipping Loss during World War II by All Causes*. Both reports gave little, if any, acknowledgement to the RAAF/US Navy coalition mine-laying operations.

Searching through the Australian military archives, there is an extract from the US Seventh Fleet's *Mine Warfare Report—Top Secret Summary*. It is a summation of aerial mining for the first eighteen months of the campaign in the SWPA. The report stated that

> between 22 April 1943 and 31 October 1944, Catalinas of the RAAF made 568 successful sorties on 132 nights and laid a total of 1142 mines in Kavieng, Lorengau, Woleai, Palau and 36 locations in the Netherlands East Indies. The four targets first named were in support of military operations elsewhere. The mining campaign against the Netherlands East Indies was designed to disorganise the enemy maritime supply systems, to deprive him of essential war materials, to enforce upon him the diversion of men, materials and shipping necessary for the establishment and maintenance of the defence, and incidentally to sink as many of his ships as possible.

The Seventh Fleet's report confirms that the RAAF was very active laying mines and fulfilling its charter. However, it seems that this US Navy report was overlooked or ignored by the *USSBS*. Worse still, the *USSBS* report doesn't accept there was such an action against Japan 'until well into 1945' (referring to Operation Starvation)—this totally disregards the efforts of the RAAF/US Navy coalition:

> Frequently the effect of such an attack is the imposition of a blockade, in which case the threat of loss of shipping is of as great concern as the actual loss of shipping. Such a condition of blockade . . . [means] the enemy no longer maintains the initiative in determining the direction of the impact. Except for the unlikely possibility that numerous widespread sources of equally high quality raw materials are at the enemy's

> disposal, by selective blockade he can be made to bear the impact where it hurts most. Restriction of the area in which the fleet can operate may be just as effective as the physical disabling or destruction of the fleet. However, it must be emphasized that in this war the conditions of blockade were not attained until well into 1945.

Furthermore, the *USSBS* report gives the impression that the RAAF efforts were of little importance. This is especially true of the chapter called 'The Beginning of the Mine Campaign', which implies it was a completely American affair:

> The final phase of the attack on shipping began with the undertaking by the Twentieth [other references credit the Twenty-first] Air Force on 27 March of the laying of mines in Japanese coastal waters by B-29s. This effort increased through May, June, and July, and eventually included all important Japanese and Korean seaports on the Japan Sea and Korean Straits. In April the campaign really began to get underway. The most important target was the Shimonoseki Straits: the western entrance to the Inland Sea, western terminus of the Honshu railroads, northern terminus of the Kyushu railroads, and the most important area of shipping concentration in Japan. In April in these areas, 18 ships totalling 30,917 tons [28,047 tonnes] were sunk or damaged and put out of action for the rest of the war by mines.

A significant aspect of the mine-laying campaign in the SWPA—the importance of the selected targets—is included in the US Seventh Fleet's *Mine Warfare Report*. It also reveals the cooperation between the Australian mine-laying planners and the US Navy submarines. The planners notified submariners about when and where mines would be laid, so the latter knew that enemy ships blocked from entering harbours would be wading in deep waters and vulnerable to attack. A number of the submarine 'kills' recorded, against both military and mercantile shipping, were the result of this cooperation, as were those of Allied bomber raids.

Notable among the harbours mined exclusively by the RAAF are Balikpapan, the site of a large oil refinery and from which some 2 million barrels of bunker fuel and aviation fuel were shipped monthly; Tarakan, the centre of a high-grade bunker fuel oil district, with a storage capacity of 7.5 million barrels; Surabaya, the site of excellent docking and ship-repair facilities that served 216,000 tons [196,000 tonnes] of shipping monthly; Pomalaa, which supplied over 90 per cent of the total Japanese nickel consumption; Macassar (Makassar), the chief port of the Celebes (Sulawesi); and Kendari, at which an important aircraft engine-repair base was located.

Successful joint operations between submarines and Australian aircraft were conducted, in which aircraft laid mines that denied enemy shipping the sanctuary of inland and inshore waterways. Convoy assembly points, harbours of refuge and new bases under development were then subject to timely attack by Allied submarines; ships that were driven from defended harbours to undefended emergency anchorages became easy prey for Australian and American bombers.

In commenting on the effort of the RAAF mine-laying Catalina squadrons during the critical early 'holding' period of the Pacific War, the US Navy Seventh Fleet's *Mine Warfare Report* said that

> the resources available for the conduct of the campaign during the first twelve months consisted solely of the part-time services of two Catalina SQNs which completed, on the average, fifteen minelaying sorties per month. Other tasks assigned to these SQNs were convoy protection of the waters between AUSTRALIA and NEW GUINEA, air-sea rescue, [and] supply dropping to Coastwatchers who behind enemy lines played a very valuable role of assistance to the allies.

Sent to the JCS in Washington, DC, the *Mine Warfare Report* covered the RAAF mining of the heavily defended Japanese-held harbours, illustrated the effectiveness of operations during and around the nights of a new moon, and highlighted the strategy of laying mines from low altitudes. The report acknowledged that the enormous distances involved to reach these targets—such as the 2000-mile (3200-kilometre) sortie to Balikpapan—were without peer, and emphasised that the average distance per single sortie for the entire campaign was in excess of 2600 miles (4200 kilometres).

The Vice Chief of US Naval Operations, Admiral Frederick J. Horne, responded to the Seventh Fleet's *Mine Warfare Report* and stated that

> the primary objectives of the campaign have been achieved on a scale disproportionately large in comparison with that of the effort put forth. There have been 25 ships credited as sunk or damaged by aerial mines, not including 18 reported by the RAAF, but for which records are not complete in WASHINGTON. It is noteworthy in this connection that an operational research report prepared by the RAAF at the end of the first year of the campaign indicated our aerial mining operations in this area had been in the order of 100 times as destructive to the enemy as an equal number of bombing missions against land targets would have been.

This final statement is certainly not overenthusiastic. Conventional bombing during World War II was not an exact science and could be very inaccurate. To obtain a direct hit on a moving target, such as a ship, was virtually impossible. Consequently, bombers attacking from higher altitudes achieved a low success rate. In contrast, the offensive mining carried out by RAAF Catalinas was highly selective and performed with great precision.

IJN Rear Admiral Akira Matsuzaki, Chief of Staff of the Second Southern Expeditionary Fleet from April 1943 to February 1945, gave credit to RAAF Catalina mine-laying operations in the Netherlands East Indies when interrogated after the war. In the transcript, which is used as a source in the RAAF's 1946 report, Matsuzaki detailed the disruption caused by the RAAF operations:

> [T]he Second Expeditionary Force at SOERABAJA [Surabaya] was responsible for mine countermeasures in the BORNEO, CELEBES, and JAVA areas. In these areas mine sweeping was a continuous process. During the first part of 1943, the magnetic mine was difficult to sweep but the problem was solved when magnetic bars were procured from SINGAPORE in September and October, 1943. By the end of 1943, mines became of serious consequence. A radar warning net was established, as well as a system of watchers. By tracking planes with radar, an effort was made to establish dropping points. Night fighters were also used but proved ineffective.
>
> Beginning in 1944, mining had considerable effect on the exploitation of the vast resources of the NETHERLANDS EAST INDIES. Not only were ships and cargoes destroyed but convoys were delayed and unloading areas were jammed at SOERABAJA and BALIKPAPAN pending sweeping operations. The destruction of tankers and delay in oil shipments was particularly serious.
>
> Due to the use of small wooden ships, mining had little effect on the supply to garrisons.
>
> Mining countermeasures involved the use of 1,500 men and 30 ships in the CELEBES, BORNEO and JAVA areas. Nevertheless, about 40 per cent of all vessels over 1,000 tons [900 tonnes] which sailed into the BALIKPAPAN–SOERABAJA area were sunk or damaged by mines. In many cases ships were salvaged only to be sunk a second time.
>
> Even before the capture of the PHILIPPINES, the traffic to the NETHERLANDS EAST INDIES was reduced to a trickle. After

February 1945, no attempt was made to use large ships and only small schooners and wooden barges were employed.

The Japanese admiral also gave his assessment of the cause of the total sinkings of all vessels in the East Indies area. He stated that 50 per cent of all tonnage sunk was due to submarine attack, 40 per cent due to mines and 10 per cent due to aerial attack.

It is well known General Douglas MacArthur refused Admiral Chester W. Nimitz's request to continue using the TBF Avengers for mine laying in the central Pacific. Air Vice-Marshal William Bostock's offer of RAAF Catalinas was accepted, and the RAAF campaign was initiated; it ran from April 1943 to July 1945.

The RAAF was virtually the sole protagonist in the SWPA. The US Army Air Force performed some aerial mining in the Rangoon River, Myanmar (Burma), Sumatra, Indochina (Vietnam) and Singapore, from bases in India and China, but with B-24 Liberators, B-25 Mitchells and, later, B-29 Superfortress bombers. These sorties were conducted at high altitudes, with questionable accuracy and without precision. Lieutenant Ivor Collins, US Navy Reserve, who had experience with both the RAAF and US Army Air Force operations, admitted that 'the RAAF did the "real" mining in the Pacific'.

Even Admiral Thomas C. Kinkaid, Commander of the US Navy Seventh Fleet, is recorded as recognising that the RAAF essentially had the monopoly on the mining operations in the SWPA. Before the US Army Air Force relieved the RAAF of the mine-laying role in 1945, Australian Catalinas had mined Chinese coastal ports; there were plans (codenamed Operation Amazon) to mine the Shimonoseki Straits in Japan. The straits were eventually 'pattern' mined by US bombers during Operation Starvation.

In 1974, the Deputy Chief of Research and Development for the US Air Force commissioned a report into the effectiveness of aerial mining as an alternate offensive weapon when other military action is not available, be it for political or other reasons. In the report, *Lessons from an Aerial Mining Campaign (Operation Starvation),* author Frederick M. Sallagar wrote:

> The B-29 mining campaign against Japan's Inner Zone, which started at the end of March 1945, was preceded by a two-year mining effort directed mainly against conquered territories in Japan's Outer Zone. A brief review of this effort shows that aerial mines, whose first use in the Pacific was in early 1943, accounted for the major portion of this activity.

Just like the official reports, Sallagar fails to credit or mention the RAAF/US Navy mine-laying coalition being responsible for the earlier operations.

The problem with the JANAC and *USSBS* reports is that they focus on using 'ships sunk' as a measure of the effectiveness of mine laying, which has influenced the opinions of historians. Some historical viewpoints cite the work of the RAAF/US Navy mine-laying coalition as important but insignificant when compared to the work of other units. Not surprisingly, this hasn't been well received by personnel, both US and Australian, who were engaged in these missions, and who deserve much more than a few throwaway lines or—as has occurred in some reports—being completely ignored.

In his publication *Air War Against Japan 1943–1945*, military historian George Odgers wrote:

> Allowing that the RAAF minelaying Catalinas did sink more tonnage than is admitted by the JANAC, and this seems likely, it will be seen

> that results in terms of total shipping losses were relatively small. The total number of Japanese vessels sunk during the war was 3032 with a tonnage of 10,583,755. Of this total, American submarines sank 1314 vessels totalling 5,320,094 tons [4,826,308 tonnes]. The RAAF however laid mines on only a very small scale and, when measured against the efforts made, the results were satisfactory, and in addition, the laying of mines was often an important factor in impeding operations.

To report that the RAAF laid mines on 'a very small scale' ignores the time and the import of the tactics employed, the expanse of the area mined and the complexity of the operations. It also disregards the austerity imposed by the JCS due to the Germany First policy.

Looking at the results of ships sunk and other effects of mine laying, the *USSBS* report concludes, as quoted by Odgers: 'It is believed that this campaign, begun earlier and laid with greater weight, would have reduced effective shipping nearly to the vanishing point. It would, thus, have produced a condition of crisis in Japan sooner than actually occurred.'

The laying of mines in the Shimonoseki Straits by the B-29 Superfortresses during the closing months of the war did render this important shipping route virtually impassable and throw the administration of Japan into chaos. Of the 266 ships sunk by mines during the Pacific War, the mines laid by the Superfortresses during Operation Starvation—headed by General Curtis E. LeMay—accounted for the majority. However, Odgers has erred in his book by placing great emphasis on LeMay's mine laying in March 1945. The operations conducted by LeMay are not comparable to those of the RAAF.

In comparing RAAF results to the total for the duration of the war in the Pacific, Odgers ignored the fact that from April 1943 to July 1945—a period of just over 24 months—RAAF mining employed just four squadrons at the most, and usually only three. As other reports have done, his analysis also overlooked the main purpose of the RAAF campaign—to harass and disrupt supply lines, and to compel the enemy to devote manpower to clearing mines, rather than fighting. History shows Japan was almost wholly dependent on its merchant fleet to import raw materials to keep its industries going. In fact, it was the pursuit of those raw materials that saw Japan enter the war. The RAAF/US Navy coalition's ability to sever Japan's supply lines had a vital impact on the outcome of the war.

Sir Arthur 'Bomber' Harris, well-known head of bomber command, inadvertently gave further weight to the effectiveness of the RAAF mine-laying missions. In the European campaign, both the British and the Germans used mines offensively and defensively. Harris formulated a theory that 'for every known ship lost, at least one unknown had probably been sunk'. Harris's experience confirmed that mining diverted at least 40 per cent of naval personnel into a countermining operation. The Japanese, like the Germans, had to build wooden minesweepers and divert fighting men to minesweeping duties. The Japanese went one step further than the Germans by sacrificing expendable vessels and crews to keep ports open, particularly after the acoustic and pressure mine had been introduced.

The RAAF Headquarters' report of June 1946 summarised what the IJN personnel thought of the effects of the coalition's mine laying:

> [A]ll Japanese naval officers interrogated were convinced of the value of mine laying and considered that mines contributed largely to their defeat. It was impossible, however, for them to convince the Army authorities of the dangers of mines or of the difficulties in sweeping them . . . the exploitation of occupied territories was seriously affected by minefields. This was especially the case in JAVA and BORNEO where the effect on the shipments of raw materials,

> especially oil, was considered to have been particularly serious ... If traffic to or from a mined harbour was considered essential, the harbour was only closed for one day and was swept three times only. Any subsequent shipping losses were accepted. If traffic could be delayed, however, an attempt to carry out a thorough sweep was made. Thus, ships were deliberately passed through minefields known to be dangerous in order to expedite the shipment of vitally needed cargoes.

In his 1974 report, *Lessons from an Aerial Mining Campaign (Operation Starvation)*, Frederick M. Sallagar explains why the sinking of ships was important to US accounts of the war:

> Whether the goal of a mining campaign should include ship sinkings as well as blockade will therefore depend on the opponent's situation and on the manner in which he reacts to mining ... the results of blockade 'cannot be evolved directly' and their impact is delayed. Ship sinkings, on the other hand, can be observed immediately and reported in concrete and material terms.
>
> It should not be surprising that 'the effectiveness of Operation Starvation' is universally demonstrated by ship loss statistics. Wartime commanders are expected to show tangible results that are easily understood and can be used to satisfy the hunger for good news. This is why the number of enemy troops killed or captured is so often accepted as the measure of success in ground battles, and why the number and tonnage of enemy ships sunk played a similar role in the mining campaign. If the campaign planners were tempted, or were under pressure, to produce a high 'body count' of ship losses, it would not have been the first time, nor was it the last, that this familiar syndrome influenced the goal as well as the reporting of military operations.

The JANAC report included a tally of all ships that were sunk, based on information in the *USSBS*:

Australian Forces:	13 vessels totalling 31,802 tons [28,850 tonnes];
US and Australian Forces:	11 vessels totalling 44,000 tons [40,000 tonnes];
US, Australian and the Netherlands:	2 vessels totalling 16,362 tons [14,843 tonnes];
Unknown forces:	33 vessels totalling 107,117 tons [97,174 tonnes].

These statistics do not reveal the true effect of the offensive mine laying in isolation from other operations. It is also virtually impossible to discover the results of the RAAF effort, as distinct from that of the US Navy and Army Air services, within the JANAC report. The RAAF results had been embedded within those of the US Seventh Fleet and Fifth Air Force, without even a cursory acknowledgement.

In his 1958 book *Australia in the War of 1939–1945: The role of science and industry,* Professor David P. Mellor stated that to fully appreciate the effect the RAAF/US Navy mine-laying operations had during the Pacific War, 'ships sunk could be completely ignored if the object is imposing a blockade'.

Professor Mellor decided the best way to equate the effectiveness and success of the mine laying to other operations was to look at the proportion of aircraft used in comparison to other operations, the number lost, and what effect mine laying had on the enemy. In doing so, Mellor concluded:

> The task of the RAAF was to prevent the Japanese from using the sea-lanes of the Pacific. This they did by cooping up their ships in the harbours . . . the proportion devoted to sea mining was roughly

> 20 per cent of the total . . . distribution of effort for 11 SQN, 20 SQN and 43 SQN . . . 230 sorties against 18 harbours had resulted in the closing of 10 harbours for periods of up to five weeks, the sinking of about 60,000 tons [54,000 tonnes] of shipping, and the damaging of about 75,000 tons [68,000 tonnes]. It was estimated that if the cargoes of these sunken ships had been dispersed among airfields and dumps, their destruction would have required about 12,000 sorties from 20 SQN. Since these results were achieved with what was equivalent with half a SQN [sic] occupied full time, it meant that minelaying was 40 times as effective as the bombing of land targets. Moreover, this estimate took no account of enemy losses due to damaged shipping, or to the diversion effect of minesweeping, or the loss of war production resulting from dislocation of sea communications . . . Not only was sea-mining a highly effective method of harassing the enemy, it was also one that achieved results with relatively small loss to the attacking force . . . Fewer aircraft were lost for each ship sunk or seriously damaged on these minelaying operations than on any other operation, and the results achieved were out of proportion to the efforts in manpower and materials put into them.

While the *USSBS* and JANAC figures show an increase in vessels sunk from July 1943 to March 1945, attributed to 'All Causes', they also reveal a drop in quarterly oil imports to Japan from April 1943. This corresponds to the RAAF/US Navy coalition's mining period.

Former RAAF wing commander Athol 'Attie' Wearne gave a succinct summary of the work of the mine-laying Catalinas, and a reason why its effectiveness is hard to measure:

> [C]onsidering that the maximum effort available for the aerial mine laying throughout the campaign [was] the resources of only three Squadrons, each of ten or less aircraft, and that over 2500 mines were

> successfully laid, it must be accepted that the campaign was a very economical one. This is the reason why it is hard to estimate the real value of their mining, or any mining for that matter, as the results are not always immediately visible . . . they are like the beaters in a fox hunt or partridge shoot, they never catch a bird or a fox but, without them, the tally of kills would be considerably less.

Encyclopaedia Britannica was a trusted source of information for many years before the internet. However, on page 524 of volume 15 of the 1962 edition, it was also 'selective' in its review of the RAAF mine-laying operations:

> In the Pacific, aerial mine-laying was carried out by the US Army Air Force, the Royal Air Force and the Royal Australian Air Force. The first mine-laying missions by US B-29 bombers, and also the longest combat missions of any kind during the war, took place on Aug. 10 1944, when Superforts based in Ceylon flew 3800 mi. [over 6100 kilometres] round trip to Palembang in Sumatra, where 16 mines sank three Japanese ships and damaged four more . . . The first mining of a harbour by planes flying from aircraft carriers was conducted in April 1944 when US carrier forces raided Palau in the Caroline Islands . . . only a few mines had been laid in Japanese waters until the last few months of the war. In late 1944 and early 1945, the capture of air bases within practical bomber range of Japan gave every prospect of success for an aerial mine-laying designed to cut Japanese lifelines to the Asian mainland and the Indies. Submarine attacks on Japanese shipping had already forced most ocean-going traffic into a few crowded mineable channels opening into the inland sea.

Encyclopaedia Britannica ignored the earlier efforts of the US Avengers, as well as the period when RAAF Catalina flying boats, without the need for established land bases, mined the 'back streets' to Japan prior to August 1944. In the fifteenth edition (1982) of the *Encyclopaedia Britannica Macropaedia*, the editors omitted any reference to the RAAF altogether, only finding sufficient space to give credit to the US Army Air Force and submarines.

Careful research can winkle out mining results from the reports on Allied actions, by cross-referencing the material absorbed into the reports with the operational histories of each squadron. This bolsters the information that is barely acknowledged in American or Australian histories.

In American maritime historian Samuel Eliot Morison's *History of United States Naval Operations in World War II: Breaking the Bismarcks Barrier 22 July 1942–1 May 1944*, the presence of the RAAF is briefly acknowledged:

> General Kenney's bombers of the MacArthur command frequently helped the New Georgia campaign by striking shipping or raiding Rabaul airfields. On 15 July a mine planted by Australian Catalinas damaged light cruiser *Nagara* in Kavieng Harbour. On 28 July, near Cape Gloucester, several skip-bombing B-25s sank destroyers *Ariake* and *Mikazuki*. On 3 August, south of Rabaul, Southwest Pacific Fliers mashed the topsides of destroyer *Akikaze*. Kenney's raids on Rabaul, about every three days, further relieved pressure down the Slot.

In his book *Black Cat Raiders of WWII*, American author Richard C. Knott pays tribute to the experienced RAAF Catalina crews who provided familiarisation flights to fast-track American pilots in 1942 and 1943. While the book is about the US Black Cats, Knott quotes Captain Donald H. Hartwig, US Navy Reserve (Retired), who described his experiences as an American Catalina pilot flying with the RAAF crews:

> They [RAAF] loaded ammo and flares on the catwalk so high . . . that you could not move around. We were so heavy; we ran three or four miles to get off. Then we stayed at about 500 feet [150 metres] in a nose-up attitude and remained constantly at 95 knots [175 kilometres per hour]. When fuel burnt off and speed increased, the skipper reached up and pulled the power back a bit. All hands flew in khaki shorts. We slept until nightfall when we got into the enemy area and then began looking for targets. I do not recall what we did that night but do recall we were empty and nose down on the way back. Back at Cairns we had been in the air for 24 hours and 10 minutes.

The RAAF Catalinas flew 1210 mine-laying sorties over 240 nights and, of those, 1130 were successful. Just 7 per cent of the 80 unsuccessful sorties were due to mechanical or radar breakdowns. However, only 10 per cent of the unsuccessful sorties were not eventually completed. Of the 2512 mines laid, 1851 were American and 661 were British. The results are impressive, as many of the operations exceeded 15 flying hours, and some were 24 hours or longer. The end of the *USSBS* report acknowledges, albeit indirectly, the impact of these flights: 'Greater economy of effort could have been attained by the strangulation of the Japanese economy already taking place as a result of prior attacks on shipping. This could have been done by an earlier commencement of the aerial mining program.'

Major John S. Chilstrom's 1992 thesis, *Mines Away!*, specifically notes the RAAF aerial mine laying in the Pacific, and acknowledges that the mining operations by the RAAF and US Navy were a real coalition effort. The US Navy elected the target and supplied mine experts, while the planning and execution were controlled exclusively by the RAAF. Major Chilstrom also recognises the influence of the European experience on RAAF mining, which underpinned the successful mine-laying campaign from its inception. Lieutenant Commander Palgrave 'Pally' E. Carr RAN brought this expertise to the coalition, thanks to his period of secondment to the Royal Navy's Fleet Air Arm.

In his book *Air Force Australia,* George Odgers states that the RAAF was not given a direct role in the invasion of the Philippines; its participation was reduced to the construction of an airfield at Mindoro, and the few sorties carried out by RAAF bomber squadrons operating from Morotai. How could Odgers overlook the contributions that the RAAF made through mine laying prior to MacArthur's landings and to protect his Seventh Fleet?

Four RAAF squadrons were called upon to 'mine-in' the IJN fleet at Brunei Bay. They were used to block the Balabac Straits, north of Borneo, to prevent a possible early return to Leyte by the IJN via the shorter route, while the Seventh Fleet was being resupplied. Then they were tasked with 'mining-in' units of the IJN at Manila Bay. All of these operations were carried out in a minimum time frame, and they contributed to the success of MacArthur's return to the Philippines.

Some 65 years after the Manila Bay operation, the squadrons involved finally received recognition for their actions. Following a review in 2008 and approval by the Australian governor-general, Michael Jeffery, on 10 August 2009 the Chief of the Air Force notified 11 Squadron that it had the right to display the Philippines Campaign as a battle honour. The citation also included 43 Squadron; however, it did not include 20 and 42 Squadrons, which also participated. Perhaps this occurred because those squadrons had been disbanded—20 Squadron on 27 March 1946, and 42 Squadron on 30 November 1945. But why was 43 Squadron mentioned, when it was disbanded on 11 March 1946? The air-force researcher may have gone no further than George Odgers' *Air War Against Japan 1943–1945*, as Odgers' summary of the Manila sortie noted the involvement of 11 and 43 Squadrons only; there was no reference to 20 and 42 Squadrons. If the researcher had crosschecked against squadron records, or even the work of David Vincent (author of *Catalina*

Chronicle), they would have readily discovered the names of all the squadrons involved.

While it is not possible to describe every aspect of a campaign in a military history book like *Air War Against Japan 1943–1945*, these glaring omissions devalue the RAAF/US Navy coalition effort. The involvement of the RAAF Catalinas in the Philippines and, particularly, the assistance given to MacArthur by stemming the IJN's last-ditch stand in the Battle of Leyte Gulf—the world's largest sea battle—definitely deserved recognition.

Other historians overlooked the critical time at Guadalcanal, just after the Battle of Midway had turned the tide of the Pacific War against Japan. The Allies could not afford to become complacent and bask in a single victory—it was important to keep applying pressure to the enemy. This was done by the RAAF/US Navy mine-laying coalition, which was called upon to disrupt the 'jugular vein' of the Greater East Asia Co-Prosperity Sphere. The crews performed their duties both efficiently and effectively.

The omissions of earlier historians were not intentional, as the 'body count' approach was an accepted policy. Secrecy surrounding the mine-laying operations, as well as the thirty-year rule—the period of time before official documents are released publicly—also had an impact on the information available to historians. During the intervening period, however, historians have tended to rely heavily on the US interpretation of statistics, particularly the assessment of shipping losses. They may have been of the opinion that their job was already done by the *USSBS* and JANAC.

This downgrades the effort and dedication of RAAF Catalina crews, as well as the US personnel who worked with them. Both the US and Australian citizen soldiers deserve a better reward for their unstinting efforts in the harsh tropical conditions of the Pacific. A revision of earlier 'official' histories is required to put the RAAF/US Navy mine laying into perspective. There is always a danger that, without due diligence, the real value of the RAAF/US Navy coalition's work may fade from view in the future.

The Japanese failed in the Pacific War not because they did not have good soldiers or commanders. They were, in fact, a formidable enemy of experienced, battle-hardened troops who had been at war since 1937, four years before the Pacific conflict. At the outset of hostilities, Japanese pilots were better trained than their Allied counterparts. No military force, however, can maintain the upper hand without food, ammunition and adequate fuel. It was the strangling of fuel and supplies around the Pacific Ocean that, in the end, contributed to Japan's defeat.

The RAAF Catalina offensive mine laying was an unexpected bonus for the Allies. It took the war to the Japanese, with what was incorrectly described after the war as a 'handful of obsolete aircraft and make-shift crews', according to LTCDR Shirley L. Quimby, US Navy, which is surprising, given Quimby was one of the architects of the coalition and would have been aware of the extensive training of the crews and the suitability of the aircraft. Working together with the US Navy, the RAAF methodically deprived the enemy of the resources it needed to feed its war machine.

The RAAF Catalina crews played a larger part in the effort to win the war in the Pacific than is currently portrayed. At the very least, evidence has revealed that the RAAF Catalina mining operation became a psychological strategy. Every battle has a pivotal moment that can lead to success or otherwise for a side. It cannot be denied that the use of offensive mines was the hinge that made it easier to swing the door open for the Allies in the Pacific.

By blockading the shipping lanes to enemy ports at crucial times, the RAAF Black Cats assisted the United States when the JCS in Europe could not spare the equipment needed to push the Japanese back. The tide was turned at Midway, but Allied supremacy would have been washed away had Guadalcanal been lost. Unfortunately, the secret classification of the

Catalina operations, and the fact they were part of the Fifth Air Force and the US Navy Seventh Fleet strategies, has led to many of their exploits being absorbed into the American history of the war. This situation is not helped by the sparseness of information from Japanese sources, and the doubtful statistics that detract from the full effect of the RAAF aerial mining campaign.

EPILOGUE

REVEREND RICHARD 'DICK' UDY, 43 SQN: LEST WE FORGET

At the time of writing this book, Reverend Richard 'Dick' Udy, former Flight Lieutenant and wireless air gunner with 43 Squadron, is one of the last surviving veterans from the mine-laying operations. During his time in service and after, Udy put pen to paper to write of his experiences, mostly in poetry. It is only fitting he has the last words to remember those 'very special' volunteer airmen who died in action.

In April 1944, Udy was a crew member in one of six Catalinas sent to mine Balikpapan. Only five Cats returned. He remembered that operation and those lost—one of whom was a good friend—in a poem, 'Lest We Forget'.

The six crews began their op at the USS *Childs*, the AOB moored off Yampi Sound in Western Australia, where they prepared for the twenty-hour round flight. They were briefed in the morning, and then relaxed before leaving. Udy recalled:

> The waiting time for the next couple of hours in the heat of the day pressed hard upon us. One Skipper, Flight Sergeant Don Abbey,

> said laconically, 'This is worse than waiting for the dentist!' He had only recently joined the Squadron after training down south, and a close friend of mine, Flying Officer Frank Robinson, had been seconded to fly as an experienced second pilot with this new crew.

Early in the afternoon on 20 April, the Cats took off for their destination. Just after 11 p.m., according to Udy, 'the coast of Borneo began to show up on the radar screen and action stations [were] manned. We were fortunate in being early on the target and easily identifying our datum point. Already searchlights were sweeping the sky and quite intensive anti-aircraft fire [was] developing.'

Despite the fracas, Udy's navigator and skipper were able to drop their mines in the required location. Udy noted that, as the skipper began to pull away,

> the other side of the harbour burst into light and fire. Don Abbey, Frank Robinson and crew had been hit directly by a naval shell, their altitude being so low the aircraft, with its explosive load, disintegrated. We learned later that Flight Lieutenant Ivor Righetti had come in over the same datum point as Don a little earlier and had been shocked to see a heavy collection of warships unexpectedly on their track. He tried to contact Don by wireless to abort his run, but it was too late to warn them and they had no hope.

On the same night, another Catalina skippered by Flight Lieutenant Fred Robins was holed badly by shrapnel. On his return to Yampi Sound, Robins had to beach the aircraft to prevent it from sinking, which was 'a remarkable flying feat'. Udy and his crew attacked Balikpapan again on 24 April, but 'strangely, there was little determined opposition from the datum point we were assigned for that night. There was erratic and heavy gunfire, but not the same degree of naval gunfire.'

For veterans, the memory of a lost comrade remains. They do not require the nightly call to 'remember them' at an RSL Club, or to wait for Anzac or Armistice commemorations. Those lost are never forgotten. Reverend Udy wrote the following poem 'so that something of the movement and the lifelong emotion of this event is captured'.

Lest We Forget

Not for us so-called 'First & Furthest' Catalina crews
Can the familiar words of Binyon's ode suffice, which say
'At going down of the sun and in the morning. We will remember them'
Those words still cling to 'surly bonds of earth' we've stripped away,
They try to keep our thoughts and memories strictly marshalled
At regimented hours and under earthbound, disciplined parade,
Where those who have not known the threat and thrill of flying
Dutifully remember, on command, their valiant dead.

No! Far more often, memory ravishes us in that quiet time
When our free spirits notice it's just midnight hour,
And, as if struck, remember for a moment, previous 'action stations'
When there, just up ahead, the dark night sky suddenly devoured
Friends who had gone ahead, on track through harbour installations . . .
Now like the ancient mariner we are gripped with vivid video frames
Which in slow motion gyrate round us once again
With tracers, searchlights and volcanic flames.
Or sometimes our wild summer storms with vicious lightning flashes
And thunderous howl of rasping, ripping rain
Jolt us into remembering the impenetrable, tropic fronts
That tossed us round the sky, wrestling the epileptic controls
And trying vainly to keep dry the precious radar and wireless gear.
That's when we best remember them and silent, shout the
  accustomed greeting
To Frank and Don, Angus, Billy and the rest.

Maybe it's when we hear the labouring piston-driven engines
Of an old DC-3 go lumbering past aloft,
Still claiming its rights to fly though, like us, past their prime . . .
That's when we cannot stop the thoughts and the emotions once again
Break into remembrance of our friends gone on.

Or maybe as we look out over wild white caps on windy days
And see the swell rise higher and the waters churn,
We try to judge the wind and current for a rescue bid.
'On such a day as this' we say . . . again we can't help reminiscing
That is when memory is jolted for us by white foam before us,
Not by the bugled sound of disciplined reveille
And marshalled orders on parade ground barked on cue,
But by the uncontrolled and clamouring memory
That cries out aloud, 'Remember them! Remember then!'
And silently we frame those words, 'Lest we forget!'

NOTE FROM THE AUTHORS

When Bob Cleworth began his research into the work done by Catalinas during World War II, he just wanted to know what his brother, Reg, did during the war and how he died. Yet Bob's hunger for knowledge, his appreciation of the mechanical and his inherent gregarious nature took him on a far greater journey than he ever imagined. Listening and recording the stories of veterans, befriending many of them and sharing their passion for the PBY Catalina remains a large part of Bob's life to this day.

Of all the veterans Bob has met, Ivor Collins—the former US Navy lieutenant from the Mine Warfare Office—became one of his closest friends. With Ivor, Bob visited most of the locations in which Reg and his squadron had operated. They travelled to Darwin in the Northern Territory, and to the various staging locations in the Philippines. The only location Bob has yet to visit is the Pescadores (now known as P'eng-Hu Ch'un-Tao), where Reg and the crew of A24-203 lost their lives.

Bob and his wife, Gwen, visited Ivor for the last time in 2010. In 2012, 'sadly Ivor passed away 18 days short of his 92nd birthday'. Bob feels privileged to have known Ivor and owes much to author David Vincent for the introduction. Ivor Collins will always be remembered with affection.

Bob's research into the full story of the RAAF mine-laying operations had its frustrations. The secret classification of the Catalina missions, and the fact that they were part of a coalition with the US, meant that their achievements became part of the Seventh Fleet's history. The material Bob discovered at the National Archives and Records Administration (NARA) was fragmented and not held in a single dossier. The gaps in the US Seventh Fleet's secret monthly reports were also found in the copies of those reports held at the National Archives of Australia in Canberra. It is possible some files were culled or misfiled elsewhere. Because of this, any additional research was limited.

Bob believed he would find further information in the personal logbooks of the veterans themselves. However, this was no easy task. Apart from the fading recollections of those who served in the mine-laying campaign, the secrecy limitations imposed at the time upon entries in personal logbooks did not help. It was also obvious to Bob that not all crews knew the real purpose of every sortie.

Regarding logbooks, former 11 Squadron engineer Keith Hamilton told Bob: 'The clinical figures of a logbook tell little of what happens during an operation, or of the hours spent on the water and land in the time before actual take off, or the time spent at the end of the operation before the tired crews finally fall into bed.'

Bob's time at NARA in 2003 was not a complete waste—he did come across secret communiqués between MacArthur's Seventh Fleet and Washington, DC, and between the Seventh Fleet and the RAAF. He also found deciphered Japanese communications, which revealed their response to the mine laying. Bob requested and was successful in having these documents declassified. He used them, along with his other research, as supporting evidence in a thesis he wrote on the Catalina mine-laying operations, *'Beware this Harbor is Mined': Aspects of the history of the Catalina with special reference to its role as a minelayer with the RAAF in the Pacific War*. In 2011, Bob was awarded a Master of Philosophy, based on his thesis, from Macquarie University. Then, in 2015, Bob rewrote his thesis into a book, *The Night Shift*. Even with these two publications, few people were aware of the important role the Catalina played during the Pacific campaign.

In 2010, Bob visited the Australian War Memorial in London. Located in Hyde Park, it commemorates the Australian servicemen and women who fought in defence of freedom alongside Britons in both World Wars. What astounded Bob was that, among the 47 battle sites commemorated, there is no mention of the actions against the coastal ports of China in 1945. Bob noted:

> Darwin, Lingayen Gulf in the Philippines and Borneo, where the Catalinas had bases, are inscribed, but the Chinese coast ports are not. Such a quirk of history can only be corrected by an accurate historiography. It also affects the RAN minesweepers who swept these ports after the hostilities . . . the omission overlooks that RAAF Catalinas penetrated further into enemy-occupied territory than any other Australian (air) unit during the Pacific War.

Although Bob is an advocate for the Catalina crews involved in the RAAF mine-laying operations and believes they should receive the credit which is due to them, he is the first to admit that their operations—although more important than has been acknowledged—were just one element of a whole plan. Bob explained:

> [I]t is important to recognise that the reason for winning a war, not least a World War, and a war on the scale fought in the Pacific, is never going to be about one event, one group of people, or one decision.

Victory, if one can call it that, is the composite of many actions and events, some seemingly small, yet without doubt instrumental.

The men who served in the RAAF Black Cats played a vital role in tactically thwarting Japan's material gains by cutting supply lines and limiting ship movements, thereby strategically putting a stranglehold on the Imperial war machine.

ACKNOWLEDGEMENTS

It takes many people to research material for a book of this nature, and it is virtually impossible to measure the contributions made by each individual, many of whom were Catalina veterans and have now passed on. If they are not mentioned here, then they have been acknowledged in *The Night Shift*, on which most of the material in this book is based.

Special thanks go to Reverend Richard 'Dick' Udy, former wireless air gunner with 43 Squadron, who gave valuable assistance with the proofreading of *The Night Shift*; the late Ivor Winston Collins, former lieutenant of the US Navy Reserve, who was posted to Australia in November 1942 to become part of the RAAF/US Navy coalition mining team until August 1945; Captain Brett Hilder, a Master Mariner who was Chief Engineer Officer of the MV *Sariba* when we sailed together on that ship. During World War II, Brett was a Wing Commander in the RAAF and flew a number of mine-laying missions as a pilot with 20 Squadron.

I'd also like to acknowledge David Vincent, the author of *Catalina Chronicle*, who provided access to material that served as a jumping-off point for the deeper research that culminated in much of this work. Relevant files relating to the RAAF Catalina operations were viewed at the National Archives of Australia, the Australian War Memorial

(RAAF Historical Section), the Office of Australian War Graves and the National Archives and Record Administration (NARA) at College Park, Maryland, United States.

Bob Cleworth

I'd like to thank Selwa Anthony for introducing me to Bob Cleworth and believing that the story of the RAAF Black Cats needed to be told to a wider audience. To Bob and his wife, Gwen, for their generosity and warmth, and to Bob specifically for allowing me to share the exhaustive research from his thesis and book *The Night Shift*, letters from his brother, Reg, and recorded recollections from veterans to complete this book. I'd also like to thank my wife and son for giving me the time to write.

John Suter Linton

Appendix A

RAAF CREWS KILLED-IN-ACTION (KIA) AND AIRCRAFT LOST OR DAMAGED IN THE MINING CAMPAIGN 1943–45

Date	Location	Aircraft	Squadron	Remarks
2 Sept 1943	Sorong, Irian Jaya	A24-50 PBY-5 BU 08264	11 SQN	Missing believed crashed into a mountain. FLGOFF J.W.B. Amess FLGOFF J.P. Oliver FLGOFF E.C. Smith PLTOFF A.S. Boyd PLTOFF E.M. Howe FLTSGT R.G. Hobbs SGT M.B. Tyrrel CPL A. Burns CPL I.L. Penrose LAC A.H. Crouch

Date	Location	Aircraft	Squadron	Remarks
20 Apr 1944	Balikpapan, Indonesia (Borneo)	A24-53 PBY-5 BU 08334	43 SQN	Shot down by enemy A/A fire. Seen to crash in flames. FLGOFF F.K. Robinson WOFF R.A. Swan FLTSGT D.A. Abbey FLTSGT A.M. Belshaw FLTSGT D.G. Hoffman FLTSGT L.K. Winterbon SGT W.D. Reece SGT K.E. Thompson SGT N.D. Woodhouse
28 Apr 1944	Manokwari, Halmahera Islands	A24-49 PBY-5 BU 08285	11 SQN	Missing believed shot down by A/A fire. FLGOFF A.R. Meakin PLTOFF W.N. Rose FLTSGT A.J. Hine FLTSGT J.B. Miller FLTSGT L.W. Stringer FLTSGT J.W. Willesden SGT P.C. Carter SGT H.J.A. Coates SGT A.H.B. Wadham CPL G.W. Whitley
20 May 1944	Surabaya, Java	A24-73 PBY-5A(M) BU 48300	20 SQN	Holed in both petrol tanks by A/A fire. Remained airborne for approximately two hours. Believed lost while attempting to ditch. WGCDR H.G. Havyatt FLTLT F.W. Jeffrey FLGOFF N.B. Gill FLGOFF L.A.G. Maslin FLGOFF C.R. Whincup FLTSGT L. Dellitt FLTSGT F.H. Russell SGT K.H.J. Clarke SGT J.D. Cowley SGT H.W. Hall

Date	Location	Aircraft	Squadron	Remarks
23 Sept 1944	Tiworo Strait, Indonesia	A24-94 PBY-5A(M) BU 46489	42 SQN	Pilot FLGOFF Kane. The aircraft was destroyed by MG fire after ditching en route. All crew rescued. The aircraft developed engine trouble in the starboard motor in position 0758S—12846 E. The two small British mines were jettisoned, and the aircraft turned for base. Owing to low altitude and the strain on the port motor, it was impossible to continue the flight and a landing was made near Pulau Sermata (east of Timor, Indonesia). The aircraft was found by FLTLT Clarke of 43 SQN and destroyed after the crew was rescued.
14 Oct 1944	Macassar, Sulawesi	A24-90 PBY-5A(M) BU 48355	42 SQN	Shot down by A/A fire. No crew members survived the war. Five crew members were never recovered, and their names are commemorated on the Ambon Memorial to the Missing. SGT Ernst is buried at Ambon CWGC, and the three others were taken prisoner and are buried at Jakarta, Indonesia, in Ancol Netherlands Field of Honour. FLTLT Williams WOFF McMullin FLGOFF Bodie WOFF Billington FLGOFF Sloman SGT Vetter SGT Ernst SGT Brown SGT Ryan

Date	Location	Aircraft	Squadron	Remarks
23 Oct 1944	Macassar, Sulawesi	A24-100 PBY-5A(M) BU 46576	42 SQN	Severely damaged by A/A fire. Remained airborne for approximately one hour then ditched. Crew rescued.
14 Dec 1944	Manila, Philippines	A24-64 PBY-5 BU 08405	43 SQN	Missing believed crashed into a mountain. FLTLT J.H. Cox FLTLT H.C. Roberts FLGOFF R.C. Barbour FLGOFF R.H. Bradstreet FLGOFF F.W. Silvester SGT D.J. Albert SGT H.S. Goodchild SGT J.C. MacDonald SGT J.R. Robinson
15 Jan 1945	Surabaya, Java	A24-96 PBY-5A(M) BU 46532	43 SQN	Pilot FLTLT Harrigan. The aircraft was destroyed by MG fire after ditching en route. All crew rescued. The aircraft was en route to Surabaya and experienced engine failure, the mines were jettisoned, and it alighted south of Soemba. The aircraft was rescued next morning by FLTLT Brian Ortlepp, who, upon alighting in a heavy swell in A24-60, dumped ammunition and other items to enable take-off. He destroyed A24-96 by MG fire before setting course for Darwin. The operation was covered by 24 SQN.

Date	Location	Aircraft	Squadron	Remarks
27 Jan 1945	Laut Strait, Indonesia (south-east Borneo)	A24-204 PB2B-1 BU 44219	20 SQN	Missing believed due to bad weather. FLTLT J.A. Seage FLGOFF P. Laney PLTOFF J.H. Brown WOFF M.V.M. Bowness WOFF H.R. Wickham FLTSGT R.L. Warne SGT A.S.R. Martin SGT R.C. Preston SGT J.K. Thompson
7 Mar 1945	Mako (Makung), Pescadores, Taiwan	A24-203 PB2B-1 BU 4425	20 SQN	Missing. Unconfirmed, believed possible loss due to weather, shot down by A/A or premature mine explosion. PLTOFF R.W. Schulz FLGOFF K.M. Caulley WOFF M.O. Merritt WOFF W.V. Bates WOFF J.R. Cleworth FLTSGT A.R. Jones FLTSGT W.A. Rowe SGT W.D. Scott SGT D.K. Storrie

Seventy-five airmen lost their lives during the mine-laying campaign, and a total of eleven Catalinas were destroyed by the enemy or because of mechanical failure or misadventure. The table does not include the nine crew members of A24-67 from 20 Squadron, because although it was accompanying a mining mission, the aircraft was technically on a torpedo mission to Pomalaa in Sulawesi. If A24-67 had been included in the total number of killed-in-action during mine laying, the total loss during the two-year campaign would have been 84 crew members.

During A24-67's mission on 30 September 1943, Lieutenant Commander Palgrave 'Pally' Carr RAN was onboard the aircraft, observing the torpedo attack. Two members of A24-67's crew were on secondment with the RAAF: Wing Commander Stanley Stilling, an Australian who had joined the Royal Air Force, and Flight Lieutenant John Barnes, an officer with the Royal Canadian Air Force.

List of A24-67 Crew and Casualties:

39579 WGCDR Stanley Gordon Stilling DFC RAF KIA
AUS260445 FLTLT Jack Robert Hyde RAAF KIA
AUS411876 FLGOFF Ronald Frank Dickinson RAAF KIA
AUS402648 PLTOFF Norman Falkner Dwyer RAAF KIA
AUS400562 FLTOFF Douglas Graham McDiarmed RAAF Died as POW
AUS15916 SGT Thomas McMahon RAAF KIA
AUS34362 SGT Frank Haydock Thomson RAAF KIA
AUS40274 CPL Samuel James Carnell RAAF KIA
CANJ/5310 FLTLT John Malcolm Barnes RCAF KIA
LTCDR Palgrave Ebden Carr RAN Survived as POW

Appendix B

PROPOSAL FOR AERIAL MINE LAYING 1942

Bob Cleworth uncovered the mailgram during his research at the National Archives and Record Administration (NARA) in Maryland in 2003. The letter was declassified on 13 February 2003 by authority NND755036 US Archives:

United States Pacific Fleet
AIR FORCE SOUTH PACIFIC
Serial 0052 of 3 October 1942
From: Commander Aircraft, South Pacific Force
To: Commander South Pacific Force
Subject: Offensive Mining Operations Using Ground Induction Type Aircraft Mines—Proposals regarding
Reference: (a) ComSoPac Secret Mailgram 202237 of September 1942

1. In accordance with reference (a) which requested proposals regarding offensive minelaying operations with aircraft, mines particularly at Gizo and in the Buin–Faisi area, the following is submitted:
   (a) According to advice received from the two officer mine experts recently arrived from WHITE POPPY [codename for Noumea,

New Caledonia], the Mark 12-1 mine and the Mark 13 mine are effective only at depths not exceeding twenty and ten fathoms [36 and 18 metres], respectively. These limitations are highly restrictive, especially in waters of the Solomon's [sic] area where the bottom tends to fall off rapidly from the shore line. The Mark 12-1 can be carried only by planes carrying aircraft torpedoes. The Mark 13 mine can be carried by any plane capable of carrying 1000-pound [450-kilogram] bombs.

(b) Recent reports indicate the Japs have evacuated Gizo [Island, located between Bougainville Island and Guadalcanal]; hence mining operations there would appear to be uneconomical.

(c) It would be possible using Mark 12-1 mines, to mine the Northern end of Tonolei Harbor where Jap ships have been frequently observed. This is not considered desirable for the reason that ships here are within bombing range of B-17 aircraft basing at BUTTON [codename for New Hebrides (Vanuatu)]. Ships within the Harbor are grouped closely together and are not free to manoeuvre, hence offer excellent bombing targets. After discovery that the Harbor had been mined, Jap ships would probably avoid entering and would remain in the open roadsteads, widely dispersed and free to manoeuvre to Faisi. The B-17s have not done badly there and are eager to do more.

2. To lay mines along the shoreline [off Buin, for example] and parallel to it, would involve extensive operations, which in the view of the present employment of aircraft in this area and their limited number, would be very uneconomical and is not recommended. The accuracy of positioning mines from aircraft at night is debatable. Rabaul appears to offer possibilities for profitable offensive mining operations. H.O. Chart No 2972 indicates that aircraft mines could be laid along the range, bearing 351.5° [true] through the two markers at the north end of Simpson Harbor, in the area between Dawapia Rocks and bridges

Point or in the general area at the north and east end of the Harbor between the twenty-fathom [36-metre] curve and the various wharves. At present it would be necessary to stage PBY-5 type aircraft [Catalinas] at RINGBOLT [codename for Tulagi Island, Solomon Islands] in order to lay Mark 12-1 mines at Rabaul inasmuch as this type is the only one available that has the range and can carry torpedoes. Mark 13 mines could be laid by type B-17 aircraft but in this case only within the ten-fathom [18-metre] curve. One disadvantage would seem to be in the hope of using Simpson Harbor ourselves one of these days. The mine experts are very vague as to how these mines are swept in such case. In view of the foregoing and of the shortage of aircraft of range necessary to these operations, which would entail cessation for the time of other employment for the purpose of placing what is really an insignificant number of mines, Commander Aircraft South Pacific recommends against such operations until and unless the situation worsens to the extent that this 'offensive' type of defensive operation appears necessary.

Signed AUBREY W. FITCH
Drafted by M.B. Gardner, Capt. USN. Typed by Steveley, Y2c. 10/2/43

Appendix C

MEMO FROM BOSTOCK TO KENNEY SUPPORTING A CHANGE OF PLANS FROM WEWAK TO KAVIENG

Australian Archives A 11093/373/21A/3A

Brisbane, Q.
29 MAR 1943

The Commander,

ALLIED AIR FORCES

MINE-LAYING OPERATIONS BY CATALINA AIRCRAFT

1. With refer to R.A.A.F. Command's letter, Number 898 / encl 1A, of 22nd March, 1943 and proposed plan for the planting of ground mines at WEWAK, a number of factors have arisen since which make it desirable to modify the original plan and perhaps postpone it.

2. These factors are:-
   (a) Performance trials with a Catalina loaded with mines indicate that these aircraft will not be able to cross New Guinea to reach WEWAK. This will entail using MILNE BAY as the advanced base for the operation, instead of HORN ISLAND. A copy of the preliminary report on the trials attached.
   (b) A harbour more suitable for mining than WEWAK, within easy reach by Catalinas out of MILNE BAY, is now suggested for the initial mine dropping operation by these aircraft. This target is SILVER SOUND, an anchorage between NEW IRELAND and NEW HANOVER some ten miles [16 kilometres] S.W. of KAVIENG, which is very suitable for ground mines.
   (c) U.S. Naval Authorities believe that this anchorage is about to be developed by the enemy and suggest that it would be wise to have it mined before defences are built up.
3. A plan has been prepared for the mining of SILVER SOUND with Mark XII Mod. 1 mines and can be put into operation as soon as mines are shipped to MILNE BAY and moon conditions are suitable.
4. Owing to the limited enemy defences at SILVER SOUND it is unnecessary to obtain co-operation of 5th Air Force to provide diversionary bombing attacks.
5. Approval is requested to conduct this operation.

Signed Bostock

Air Vice-Marshal,
Air Officer Commanding,
R.A.A.F. COMMAND, A. A. F.

Encl.

Appendix D

SECRET CODENAMES FOR TARGETS

The following is a chronological list of targets and their codenames, compiled from material available from the National Archives of Australia and documents discovered at the National Archives and Record Administration (NARA) in Maryland in 2003.

RAAF targets, 1943–45	Location	Nights mined	Successful sorties	Mines laid	Codename
Kavieng area	New Ireland	20	47	104	POPSY 1 (Silver Sound) POPSY 2 (Ysabel, Santa, Alexandra Passages, Planet Channel and Byron Strait)
Lorengau	Admiralty Islands	4	16	35	FAIRY 1 (Seeadler Harbour) FAIRY 2 (Lorengau Anchorage)

RAAF targets, 1943–45	Location	Nights mined	Successful sorties	Mines laid	Codename
Babo	Irian Jaya (Dutch New Guinea)	5	6	17	FILLY
Geser	Ceram	1	3	10	
Boela	Ceram	3	6	12	
Macassar (Ujung Pandang)	Sulawesi (Celebes)	21	69	142	LOVELY?
Sorong	Irian Jaya	8	15	29	CUTIE
Surabaya	Jawa (Java)	48	200	399	VIRAGO
Kokas	West Irian (Dutch New Guinea)	3	4	8	
Kendari	Sulawesi (Celebes)	9	22	44	SMIGGET
Pomalaa	Sulawesi (Celebes)	9	26	51	SPINSTER
Kolaka	Sulawesi (Celebes)	3	6	12	
Manokwari	West Irian (Dutch New Guinea)	9	9	17	MILKMAID
Kaimana	West Irian (Dutch New Guinea)	8	10	19	BLONDIE
Baubau (Baoe)	Pulau Mona, Sulawesi (Celebes)	2	2	4	
Waingapu	Sumba (Soemba)	1	3	4	MAIDEN
Kau Bay	Halmahera Islands	7	29	62	DARLING
Balikpapan	Kalimantan (Borneo)	14	59	118	TROLLOP

RAAF targets, 1943–45	Location	Nights mined	Successful sorties	Mines laid	Codename
Woleai Atoll	Caroline Islands	3	18	36	DUCKIE
Tioro Strait (Selat Tioro)	Sulawesi (Celebes)	11	36	76	GRUMMET
Vesuvius Bay	Soela (Kepulauan Sula)	1	2	8	AUNTIE
Palau	Caroline Islands	6	11	23	SCHOOLGIRL
Selat Butung (Buton Strait)	Pulau Butung, Sulawesi (Celebes)	9	21	42	FRUMP
Bima (near Raba)	Sumbawa (Soembawa)	1	4	8	WENCH
Banka Strait	Sulawesi (Celebes)	6	14	28	LASSY
Lembeh Strait	Sulawesi (Celebes)	2	2	4	
Selat Tanakeke (Tana Keke Strait)	Sulawesi (Celebes)	8	22	43	MATRON
Wowoni Strait	Sulawesi (Celebes)	6	12	24	COURTESAN
Pasuruan	Jawa (Java)	2	4	8	
Probolinggo	Jawa (Java)	3	4	8	
Panarukan	Jawa (Java)	3	5	10	MILLGIRL
Laikang Bay	Sulawesi (Celebes)	2	4	8	
Malosoro Bay	Sulawesi (Celebes)	3	7	15	LOVELY?
Selat Laut (Laut Strait)	Kalimantan (Borneo)	28	5 or10*	209	CHORINE?
Parepare (Pare Pare)	Sulawesi (Celebes)	3	7	14	COCOTTE

RAAF targets, 1943–45	Location	Nights mined	Successful sorties	Mines laid	Codename
Telak Brunei (Brunei Bay)	Brunei, Sarawak & Sabah (Borneo)	2	10	20	COWGIRL
Tarakan	Kalimantan (Borneo)	6	15	30	SKIRT
Sandakan	Sabah (Borneo)	3	6	12	JEWESS
Samarinda	Kalimantan (Borneo)	2	6	12	TIGRESS
Tanjung Selatan (Cape Selatan)	Kalimantan (Borneo)	6	14	28	MOTHER
Cape Bulu Bulu (Nr Bulukumba)	Sulawesi (Celebes)	3	6	12	
Balabac Straits	Philippines/ Sabah	3	22	60	SQUAW
Manila Bay	Luzon, Philippines	1	20	54	GRANNY
Takao	Taiwan	4	8	18	STARLET
Makung (Mako)	P'eng-Hu Ch'un-Tao (Pescadores), Taiwan	3	4	10	LANDLADY
Hong Kong	China	19	59	152	ANGEL
Xiamen (Amoy)	China	12	31	114	SHOWGIRL
Shantou (Swatow)	China	6	8	31	FISHWIFE
Qiongzhou Haixia (Hainan Strait)	China	18	49	131	GIRLIE
Yulinkan bay	Hainandao (Hainan Island), China	6	17	52	HARLOT

RAAF targets, 1943–45	Location	Nights mined	Successful sorties	Mines laid	Codename
Wenzhou (Wenchow)	China	1	4	8	WAHINE
Bangka Strait	Sumatra	10	41	117	CZARINA
Total targets 52		**Total nights mined** 377	**Total sorties** 1030 or 1035*	**Total mines laid** 2512	

* Discrepancies exist between the RAAF records and crews' logbooks.

The secret coding system adopted to deceive the enemy was so effective that matching codenames to targets or vice versa using the available reports is not a simple task. Bob Cleworth had to sift through many documents, which were fragmented over different files in the various archives. It was a time-consuming process, and is still a work in progress.

Of the 52 main target locations, Bob has only been able to link 42 to codenames. However, he found that the records held at the National Archives of Australia in Canberra listed 56 possible codenames. This means that at least fourteen locations are left unaccounted for. Bob believes that nine of those fourteen possible targets were given codenames but were not mined, perhaps due to cancellation of the operations. These nine codenames are:

AMAZON—Kammon tunnels under Shimonoseki Straits. The RAAF planned to mine the tunnels, but this did not happen. They are listed in the National Archives of Australia (A11093 373/212N). The location may have been mined by the USAAF on 24/7/45.

BRIDE—Bone (Watampone), Sulawesi. Located on the Bone Peninsula, en route to the nickel ports of Pomalaa. This location is not listed as being mined.

DUCHESS—Jesselton (Kota Kinabalu). The site of a Japanese airfield and other installations. This port and its approaches are not listed as being mined.

HUSSY—unknown location at present. It is listed in the National Archives of Australia (A11093 373/21S) as 'Operation HUSSY' and noted 'N.D.'

LULUA—unknown location at present. It is listed in the National Archives of Australia (A11093 373/212L) with the date 6/6/45.

POETESS—unknown location at present. It is listed in the National Archives of Australia (A11093 373/21S) as 'Operation POETESS' and noted 'N.D.' (no date).

SKIVVY—unknown location at present. It is listed in the National Archives of Australia (A11093 373/21V) as 'Operation SKIVVY' and initiated on 7/9/43.

WIDOW—Miri, Sarawak, Malaysia. A major port that loaded tankers with crude oil via an undersea pipeline from the Sierra oil fields in Brunei. There is no record of it being mined.

WITCH—unknown location at present. It is listed in the National Archives of Australia (A11093 373/212A) with the date 17/2/45.

In addition, Bob has not been able to link the following eight codenames to any target so far, but they are listed as operations performed by the Catalinas in the National Archives of Australia:

BARMAID (A11093 373/21Q)—mined in the period 24/8/43–13/10/43
COLLEEN (A11093 373/21R)—mined in the period 2/10/43–23/11/43
GAMINA (A11093 373/M)—mined in the period 6/6/45–30/7/45
LADY (A11093 373/21S)—mined in the period 18/12/43–14/10/44
NIECE (A11093 373/212E)—mined in the period 15/4/45–20/5/45
SENORITA (A11093 373/21G)—mined in the period 16/7/43–29/7/44
SISTER (A11093 373/21J)—mined in the period 16/7/43–4/11/43
SOPRANO (A11093 373/21N)—mined in the period 13/8/43–23/9/43

Appendix E

THE JAPANESE ORANGE DECRYPT OF 8 MARCH 1945 (USNARA)

From: Tokyo (Vice Chief, General #208 Circular 08 March)
To: Staff

1. General Summary 8 MAR 1945
   To meet the new developments in the military situation The Empire is putting herself into a state of firm preparedness for the decisive phase of the war, basing her plan on Japan, Manchukuo, and China. We are making the most thorough preparations, and hastening all measures required for this critical stage of the war so that we shall be able to muster the total war strength of our national army to smash the enemy's attacks, and so that, even though the enemy invades our homeland, we shall be able to arouse the whole people to such a spirit of fanatical valour as will utterly annihilate the enemy.

2. The general situation. (Popular morale and the political situation.)
   The development of the Philippine situation to its present phase, together with the situation on IWO Island, has had a wide and rather

serious effect on the homeland. We must admit that elements of the population have given way to a spirit of unrest. Further certain political circles are launching a movement for a new party, with a program of national solidarity. However, the people evince no great interest in such questions as this of the formation of a new party.

The people as a whole regard the war as their war, as a matter of life and death to themselves. They confess to themselves that the present urgently critical war situation is due to their failure to utilize efficiently the total national strength, and now, roused to action, realising that it lies with them to open the way to victory, they are devoting themselves with increasing fervour and self-sacrifice to the war effort.

3. National strength and War strength.

Foreseeing, ever since last summer, the developments of the military situation, we have been freeing ourselves from dependence on resources from the south, and been taking all measures for enabling Japan to wage a modern war with such resources as are available in Japan, Manchuko, and China. This is well exemplified in the case of oil and that of aluminium. We are rendering ourselves self-sufficient in these commodities, by increasing production, and in one case liquid fuel (alcohol, etc.) from vegetable resources in Japan, Manchuria, and China; and by use of alumina shale, in the other.

Bending the full strength of our nation to the maintenance of national strength and war capacity, keeping up production at all costs, we are doing everything possible to make sure that, even now when we are cut off from the south, there is no essential diminution in our war strength such as it would make it impossible for us to meet the needs of war. However the transportation crisis, occasioned by the increase in the rate of shipping losses, is, even now when our lines have been contracted, our severest difficulty in the maintenance of Imperial war strength. Hereafter, together with the intensification of our counter measures against air attacks, we shall plan counter measures, and continue our efforts to maintain national strength and war capacity.

4. Manpower resources and food Supply.
The armed forces in line with their preparation for repelling any attack on the homeland are making great efforts for large-scale re-enforcement of military strength in Japan proper. Nevertheless at the same time, manpower for other needs is being maintained at the necessary level, and we even find it possible to increase personnel used in agriculture and communications.

As for the food supply, considerable increase in production and greater shipments from the two nations on the continent are matters of vital importance in the conduct of the war, and we are devising measures which will provide for their complete realisation.

5. Effect of the air raids
The air raids against the homeland are being steadily intensified. Civilian casualties, up to the end of February were, dead 4,400, wounded 5,600. The effect of the air raids is not so great as enemy propaganda claims it is, but such factors of the loss of IWO, our impotence in the Philippines, the activity of enemy task forces, and advance of enemy air bases, will, hereafter permit even greater intensification of air raids. We are planning all necessary measures for countering these raids, and are also hastening the accomplishment, in accordance with the lessons taught by the European war, of all necessary steps for the maintenance of production and of land and sea communications, such as the dispersion and transfer underground of Great East Asia installations and equipment.

6. Conclusion

Briefly, then, henceforth the war will rage with over increasing intensity, particularly about the homeland. Throughout the homeland there are elements which we will have to watch carefully lest they endanger the conduct of the war, but the Army, the Navy and the Air Force, closely united round the solid core of the Imperial headquarters directing tactics and overall strategy, strive forward to the completion of military preparations such as will satisfy the demands of any military situation and ensure victory, while all other preparatory measures for the decisive phase of the war in the homeland are being accomplished. At this moment, firmly persuaded of inevitable victory, we await in readiness the moment of decision when we are confident, we shall most certainly repel and successfully defend the Empire.

(JAP MILITARY ATTACHE #D-9787-D1) (SUM: 1413 Mar/NVK)

Appendix F

RAAF POST-WAR REPORT ON THE EFFECTS OF MINE LAYING IN THE SWPA

SECRET REPORT ON RESULTS OF R.A.A.F. MINE-LAYING OPERATIONS

INTRODUCTION

1. This report on the results of aerial mine-laying operations undertaken by the R.A.A.F. should be read in conjunction with the 'Report on Mine-laying Operations by the R.A.A.F. between the 22 April, 1943 and the 31st July, 1945'.
2. The results given in this report are by no means final as the United States Navy have yet to complete the interrogation of Japanese personnel and the translation of Japanese documents, some of which can be expected to provide further information.

EFFECTS OF R.A.A.F. MINE-LAYING CAMPAIGN

3. The effect of the mine-laying operations on the enemy has been:–

   (a) The sinking of, and damage to, shipping.

(b) Disruption and delay in the movement of shipping.

(c) Time lost by ships due to delays in harbour awaiting the completion of minesweeping operations and to the re-routing of shipping to avoid mined areas.

(d) The use of vessels for minesweeping operations which would otherwise be employed for carrying supplies or as escort vessels for convoys.

(e) The employment of vessels to salvage ships damaged by mines and to tow these to port, thereby exposing the salvage vessels to the dangers of a mined area and to air and submarine attack during the slow haul back to port.

(f) The forcing of shipping away from shallow water passages, which had been mined, and compelling the use of open sea passages where submarines could operate.

(g) The holding up or loss of, vital supplies such as oil and other raw materials due to the mining of strategic harbours in the enemy's conquered territory.

SOURCES OF INFORMATION

4. The results enumerated in this report have been obtained from a number of sources, viz:—Aerial Reconnaissance, Interrogation of enemy prisoners of war, captured enemy documents, and Interrogation of enemy service personnel in Japan after the cessation of hostilities.

5. Although all enemy service personnel interrogated in Japan appeared to be the most cooperative and willing to divulge all possible information, the majority of these personnel had to rely entirely on memory, as all relevant official documents had been destroyed by the enemy before the Allied occupation of Japan. So far as it proved possible to check, the information given by the Japanese has proved reliable.

DIFFICULTIES IN ASSESSING MINE-LAYING RESULTS

6. Great difficulty has been experienced in determining when a ship has been sunk by mines. This has been due to the extensive Allied submarine campaign against Japanese shipping, coupled with the fact that the electric submarine torpedo leaves no tell tale wake. There has been no way of telling, therefore, whether an underwater explosion beneath a ship has been due to a mine or a torpedo, and the Japanese were prone to credit the loss of a ship to a torpedo rather than a mine even in shallow and confined waters. The Japanese Naval Authorities have themselves admitted that they consider that a substantial amount of merchant shipping reported to have been sunk by submarine torpedo was, in reality, sunk by mines.

SINKING OF AND DAMAGE TO SHIPPING

7. Throughout the campaign the proportion of ships sunk has approximately equalled that damaged by mines, and this has been borne out by the U.S. naval authorities in assessing their mine-laying results in Japanese home waters where more detailed figures have been available.

SUMMARY OF SINKING AND DAMAGE TO SHIPPING

8. So far as can be assessed at present the direct results obtained have been as follows–

KAVIENG:	6 ships, mined, of which 3 are known to have been sunk and 3 damaged (2 cruisers are thought to have been amongst those damaged).
BABO:	1 M.V. sunk.
MACASSAR:	1 M.V. damaged.
SOERABAYA:	At least 10 ships sunk and a further 10 damaged.
POMALAA:	1 M.V. seriously damaged.
BALIKPAPAN:	2 ships sunk and a further 6 damaged.
LAUT STRAIT:	1 M.V. sunk and 2 M.V.'s damaged.

BANGKA STRAIT:	1 M.V. sunk and 2 M.V.'s damaged.
TIORO STRAIT:	1 M.V. sunk
SORONG:	1 M.V. damaged.
KIAMANA:	1 M.V. sunk and 1 M.V. damaged.
KAU BAY:	2 M.V.'s and 2 minesweepers sunk. 1 M.V. damaged.
TOTAL:	23 vessels sunk and 27 damaged = 50

9. In addition to the above, at least 5 ships are known to have been sunk by Allied submarines as a direct result of mine-laying operations which forced shipping from sheltered into open waters.
10. It will be noted that no mention has been made of the CHINA COAST ports where no less than 516 mines were laid. It is understood, however, from the Japanese that 'one or two vessels were sunk by mines at each of the main Chinese ports' (exclusive of Shanghai and the Yangtze River).
11. It will be seen, therefore, that the results enumerated in para.8 are those achieved for the laying of 1,996 mines (2,412 mines less 516 laid on the CHINA COAST). This gives a figure of one ship sunk or damaged for every 40 mines laid.

<u>OTHER RESULTS</u>

12. No definite figures can be given of the periods that ports were closed and traffic disrupted due to mine-laying, but the following extract from interrogation of Rear Admiral MATSIKAZI [sic], IJN Navy (Chief of Staff, Second Southern Expeditionary Force at Surabaya, from April, 1943 to February, 1945), gives a clear idea of the disruption caused in the NETHERLANDS EAST INDIES.
    (a) In reply to a question on the effect of Allied aerial-laid mine fields in JAVA, CELEBES and BORNEO areas, the Admiral stated–

    'The Second Expeditionary Force at SOERABAJA [Surabaya] was responsible for mine countermeasures in the BORNEO, CELEBES,

and JAVA areas. In these areas mine sweeping was a continuous process. During the first part of 1943 the magnetic mine was difficult to sweep but the problem was solved when magnetic bars were procured from SINGAPORE in September and October, 1943.

By the end of 1943, mines became of serious consequence. A radar warning net was established, as well as a system of watchers. By tracking planes with radar, an effort was made to establish dropping points. Night fighters were also used but proved ineffective.

Beginning in 1944, mining had considerable effect on the exploitation of the vast resources of the NETHERLANDS EAST INDIES. Not only were ships and cargoes destroyed but convoys were delayed and unloading areas were jammed at SOERABAJA and BALIKPAPAN pending sweeping operations. The destruction of tankers and delay in oil shipments was particularly serious.

Due to the use of small wooden ships, mining had little effect on the supply to garrisons.

Mining countermeasures involved the use of 1,500 men and 30 ships in the CELEBES, BORNEO and JAVA areas. Nevertheless, about 40 per cent of all vessels over 1,000 tons [900 tonnes] which sailed into the BALIKPAPAN–SOERABAJA area were sunk or damaged by mines. In many cases ships were salvaged only to be sunk a second time.

Even before the capture of the PHILIPPINES, the traffic to the NETHERLANDS EAST INDIES was reduced to a trickle. After February 1945, no attempt was made to use large ships and only small schooners and wooden barges were employed.'

13. The Admiral also assessed the total sinkings of all vessels in the NETHERLANDS EAST INDIES area as follows: 50% of all tonnage sunk was due to submarine attack. 40% due to mines and 10% due to aerial attack.

14. Further information of interest obtained from interrogation of other enemy service personnel is as follows:-
   (a) Allied aerial mine-laying in the S.W.P.A. had no effect on Japanese strategy or on the supply of outgoing garrisons, but in all cases the exploitation of occupied territories was seriously affected by minefields. This was especially the case in JAVA and BORNEO where the effect on the shipments of raw materials, especially oil, was considered to have been particularly serious.
   (b) If traffic to or from a mined harbour was considered essential, the harbour was only closed for one day and was swept three times only. Any subsequent shipping losses were accepted. If traffic could be delayed, however, an attempt to carry out a thorough sweep was made. Thus, ships were deliberately passed through minefields known to be dangerous in order to expedite the shipment of vitally needed cargoes.
   (c) Although both British and American mines were recovered by the enemy these proved to be of little value, as mines of these types had previously been recovered and analysed. British sweeping gear was recovered at SINGAPORE early in 1942 and some complete British mines were found at SINGAPORE in June or July in 1942.
   (d) The tactics used by the R.A.A.F. aeroplanes were most effective, particularly at BALIKPAPAN and SOERABAYA, and attempts to track aeroplanes by radar were completely unsuccessful. Towards the latter part of the campaign the presence of low flying aeroplanes was always associated with minelaying activities.
   (e) At no time throughout the campaign were there sufficient minesweeping vessels, equipment or personnel.

(f) The Japanese evinced considerable surprise that our mines were not fitted with either anti-handling device or fuse to explode if they fell on land.

(g) The Japanese had learned from the Germans of the use by the British of a combined magnetic or acoustic mine. They expressed surprise that we had never used this type of mine in the S.W.P.A. as they consider it would have been particularly effective.

(h) The co-operation between the Germans and the Japanese on the exchange of information on mine-laying matters was very poor.

(i) Convoys entering port always did so in single line ahead formation, usually preceded by an escort. No minesweeper was ever used to precede a convoy into port.

(j) All Japanese naval officers interrogated were convinced of the value of mine-laying and considered that mines contributed largely to their defeat. It was impossible, however, for them to convince the Army authorities of the dangers of mines or of the difficulties in sweeping them. One Army Officer interviewed disclosed that at SOERABAYA there was an Army minesweeping unit which was used there on frequent occasions whenever the Army authorities considered that naval minesweeping was too slow.

CONCLUSION

15. In conclusion it is considered that the results of the R.A.A.F. mine-laying campaign, though still incomplete, are far ahead of expectations and have repaid the effort expended and the losses sustained.

R.A.A.F. Headquarters,
Victoria Barracks,
Melbourne, C.2. 12 June 1946.

GLOSSARY

ACORN A US Navy codename for an airfield assembly designed to construct, operate and maintain an advanced landplane and seaplane base and provide facilities for operations. The RAAF Catalinas used ACORN 30 at Jinamoc.

AG Air gunner

AIF Australian Imperial Force, formed in World War I in 1914. In World War II, they were known as the Second AIF.

AOB Advanced operational base—it could be on land, a Seaplane Tender or a submarine.

AORC Air Officer RAAF Command

APS 3 Latest centimetric radar—similar to that fitted on A24-203

B-17 The Flying Fortress was a four-engine heavy bomber developed in the 1930s by Boeing. It was used widely during World War II. There were several variants; the B-17E was the type mainly used in the Pacific Theatre.

B-24 The Consolidated Liberator was a four-engine heavy bomber that replaced the B-17 later in the Pacific War. It flew in all combat theatres, but was especially useful in the Pacific on long-range missions. The B-24 served as a bomber, tanker and transport.

B-25 The North American Mitchell was a twin-engine medium bomber. It was one of the US Army Air Force's best medium bombers. The RAAF also operated a relatively small number of the type.

B-29 The Boeing Superfortress was a long-range, four-engine heavy bomber operated by the US Army Air Force for mine laying late in the Pacific War. It was also used for conventional bombing missions against Japan and, later, to drop the two atomic bombs in 1945.

Beaufighter The Bristol Beaufighter was a fast, low-altitude, long-range, heavy fighter operated by the RAAF. Although it was of British origin, 329 were built in Australia under licence.

Canso Originally the RCAF used the name Convoy for the PBYs that they ordered direct from the United States. Later, when Canada built its own PBY-5s at Vancouver and Quebec, the name Convoy was changed to Canso (after the Strait of Canso between Cape Breton Island and Nova Scotia) to avoid confusion with the shipping use of the term Convoy. The name has become synonymous with Canadian-built Catalinas.

Catalina An island off San Diego, California, close to where PBYs were originally built. The RAF named the PBY after the island. Other names were suggested, including Plymouth and Manchester.

CINCPAC Commander-in-Chief Pacific Fleet

COMINCH US Navy Commander-in-Chief

DAM Delayed Arming Mechanism. Salt washers attached to mines dissolved when immersed in the sea, arming the mines after a predetermined period.

DFC Distinguished Flying Cross

DSO Distinguished Service Order

FBRD Flying Boat Repair Depot

Fitter 2A Fitter airframe classification—for air gunners on Catalinas or fitter 2As (airframe and control technicians)

Fitter 2E Fitter engine classification—for air gunners on Catalinas or fitter 2Es (engine mechanics)

FLGOFF Flying Officer

FLTLT Flight Lieutenant

FSGT Flight Sergeant

GPCAPT Group Captain

HMAS His Majesty's Australian Ship (Royal Australian Navy)

IFF Identification Friend or Foe. This was a special radar-detection device. The modern equivalent is the transponder (often called the 'squawk').

IJA Imperial Japanese Army

IJAAS Imperial Japanese Army Air Service

IJN Imperial Japanese Navy

IO Intelligence Officer. They often accompanied Catalina crews to gather information on enemy movements and build-ups.

Iron Bottom Sound The stretch of water between Guadalcanal and Savo and Florida Islands in the Solomon Islands, named for the number of ships sunk there in World War II.

JANAC The US Joint Army–Navy Assessment Committee produced the *Japanese Naval and Merchant Shipping Loss during World War II by All Causes* report in 1947.

JCS US Joint Chiefs of Staff in Washington, DC.

Kamikaze Translating to 'divine wind', kamikaze was officially known as Tokubetsu Kōgekitai (Special Attack Unit). It involved suicide attacks by military aviators from the Empire of Japan on Allied naval vessels in the closing stages of the Pacific campaign of World War II. They were designed to destroy warships more effectively than was possible with conventional attacks. The first attack is believed to have been on HMAS *Australia* on 21 October 1944 during the Battle of Leyte Gulf. Kamikazes were also used against US Army Air Force bombers.

LTCDR Lieutenant Commander

MIT Massachusetts Institute of Technology

PB2B-1 Catalinas built for the US Navy by Boeing Aircraft Corporation at their Vancouver plant under licence from Consolidated. They were essentially PBY-5s equipped with an eyeball turret and a radome (a dome cover for the radio equipment).

PB2B-2 Catalinas built for the US Navy by Boeing Aircraft Corporation at their Vancouver plant under licence from Consolidated. They had an eyeball turret, a radome and a modified larger tailfin similar to the PBN built by the Naval Aircraft factory in Philadelphia.

PBY The designation used to classify the Catalina by the US Navy: P=Patrol, B=Bomber, Y=Maker, in this case Consolidated Aircraft Corporation. 'C' had been given to another manufacturer, Curtiss, years before.

PBY-5 The most produced of all the Catalina models. An improved model with more powerful engines (Pratt & Whitney Twin Wasp R1830-82), it was the first to use 100-octane fuel; about half of those built were amphibious.

PBY-5A The amphibious version of the PBY-5 (the 'A' is for amphibious). Some 200 were delivered to the US Navy by the end of 1939. Later models were the first to be fitted with armour plating to protect the pilots and the waist (blister) and tunnel gunners; self-sealing material in the fuel tanks; and dump valves to unload fuel quickly. The RAAF removed these items to extend the range and/or mine loads for mine-laying operations.

PBY-5A(M) Modified Catalina amphibians were converted into seaplanes by the removal of the tricycle landing gear, self-sealing insulation on the fuel tanks and armour plating. The designation 'M' identified the aircraft as PBYs specifically modified by the RAAF for mine laying; records show that 45 were modified between December 1943 and March 1945. The modifications were performed at the Flying Boat Repair Depots at

Lake Boga in Victoria and Rathmines in New South Wales. The purpose was to achieve deeper penetration behind enemy lines for mine-laying operations.

PDM Period Delay Mechanism. A device attached to a mine that could be set to identify a certain number of ships passing above it before triggering the mine to explode.

PLTOFF Pilot Officer

Port (side) Left-hand side looking forward, and right-hand side looking aft (towards the rear of the craft)

QANTAS Queensland and Northern Territory Aerial Services

RAAF Royal Australian Air Force

RAF Royal Air Force (United Kingdom)

RAN Royal Australian Navy

RCAF Royal Canadian Air Force

RN Royal Navy (United Kingdom)

RNAS Royal Naval Air Service (United Kingdom)

RSL Returned and Services League. It was established in 1916 to support former and current members of the Defence Force, and the families of those who lost their lives in service. It also operates various licensed clubs across Australia that offer recreational facilities. In every club at 6.00 p.m., 'The Ode' is read and a minute's silence is observed to remember the fallen.

SGT Sergeant

Shecat US codename for the AOB at Yampi Sound, Western Australia

Sortie An attack from a defensive position made against an enemy

SQNLDR Squadron Leader

Starboard Right-hand side looking forward, and left-hand side looking aft (towards the rear of the craft)

SWPA South West Pacific Area

The Slot Officially known as New Georgia Sound, this is the sea passage between Santa Isabel Island and New Georgia Island in the Solomon Islands.

Tokyo Express The name given by the Allies to the route from Bougainville Island to Guadalcanal in the Solomon Islands that the Japanese used in the hours of darkness to transport reinforcements and supplies, and to bombard American positions.

US United States

USAAF United States Army Air Force

USSBS *The United States Strategic Bombing Survey—The Offensive Mine-laying Campaign against Japan*. Published by the US Naval Analysis Division on 1 November 1946, it was reprinted in 1969 by the US Department of the Navy, Washington, DC.

Very pistol A special handgun or pistol designed to fire coloured signalling flares

WAAC Women's Auxiliary Army Corps (Australia)

WAG Wireless air gunner

WGCDR Wing Commander

WOFF Warrant Officer

Z Special Unit Special covert operations unit that included Australian, British, Dutch and New Zealand soldiers in World War II. It operated behind enemy lines and used guerrilla tactics to harass the Japanese. Also referred to as Z Force.

Z Time Zulu time or Greenwich Mean Time. For example, 071419Z is code for the 7th of the month at 1419 hrs or 2.19 p.m. Greenwich Mean Time or 04.19 hrs or 4.19 a.m. Sydney Eastern Standard Time.

NOTES

With regard to the quotes attributed to Catalina Black Cat veterans, except for those from Bryan Monkton (Chapter 4) and Michael Nugent (Chapter 5), all are from recorded interviews conducted by Robert Cleworth between 1998 and 2014. While Cleworth had befriended many of the veterans and become a member of the Catalina Association as he sought to discover what his brother, Reg, did during the war, it took ten years before any of the former flyers and ground crew agreed to tell their stories. Cleworth then always carried his tape recorder, capturing candid conversations to chronicle the history of the RAAF/US Navy mine-laying coalition.

As well as giving a recorded interview, Bryan Monkton allowed Robert Cleworth to quote from an article he wrote for *Blackwood's Magazine*, a quarterly periodical in the United Kingdom that ceased publication in 1980. This appears in Chapter 4. Michael Nugent, former fitter and engineer with 113 Air Sea Rescue, recounted his story to John Suter Linton. This is quoted in Chapter 5.

All quotes attributed to General Douglas MacArthur are from *American Caesar: Douglas MacArthur 1880–1964*, a biography written by American historian William Manchester and published in 1978. Quotes attributed to Fleet Admiral Ernest King, US Navy Commander-in-Chief, are from *Master of Sea Power: A Biography of Fleet Admiral Ernest J. King*, written by Thomas B. Buell and published in 1980.

Ivor Collins, formerly a lieutenant in the US Navy Reserve, was interviewed by Robert Cleworth in 2003 and provided various written documents and updated information through to 2010, which are referred to within the text.

Sources for all other persons quoted are included within the text, and a full list of sources is supplied in the Bibliography.

BIBLIOGRAPHY

Records from the Australian War Memorial and National Archives of Australia

Australian War Memorial, Logbook of J.R. Cleworth for November 1944 (cat. no. PR00094)

Australian War Memorial, RAAF Operations Record Book and Narratives for 11, 20, 42 and 43 SQNs, 1943–5

Australian War Memorial, *RAF Command Report on RAAF Mining Operations*

National Archives of Australia, *Report on Mine-laying Operations by the RAAF between 22 April 1943 and 31 July 1945* (cat. no. A 85/12/2, Series AWM54)

National Archives of Australia, *Summary of Aircraft Mine-laying in the South West Pacific* (cat. no. A 11083/1/373/21A3/21A) and other files relating to the RAAF Catalina mine laying, 1946–7

Theses

Chilstrom, Major J.S., *Mines Away! The Significance of US Army Air Forces Minelaying in World War II*, thesis, Maxwell Air Force Base, AL: Air University USAF, 1992

Cleworth, J.R., *'Beware this Harbor is Mined': Aspects of the History of the Catalina with Special Reference to Its Role as a Minelayer with the RAAF in the Pacific War*, PhD thesis, Sydney: Macquarie University, 2011

Cottle, D., *The Brisbane Line*, thesis, Sydney: Macquarie University, 2002

Published works

Alden, J., 'Results of US Submarine Minelaying Activities During WWII' as reported in *The United States Strategic Bombing Survey (USSBS)—The Offensive Mine-laying Campaign against Japan*, for *Warship International*, vol. 30, no. 1, International Naval Research Organization, 1993

Baldwin, H.W., 'The Greatest Sea Fight: Leyte Gulf', in *Reader's Digest Illustrated Story of World War II*, Adelaide: Griffin Press, 1968

Bateson, C., 'Guadalcanal: First Stop on the Road to Tokyo', in *Reader's Digest Illustrated Story of World War II*, Adelaide: Griffin Press, 1970

Bayfield, P., *The Doug Nolan Story: A Navigator on the Catalinas in WWII*, self-published, 2012

Beevor, A. *The Second World War*, London: Weidenfeld & Nicolson, 2012

'Blockade From the Air', *Wings: The Encyclopedia of Aviation in Weekly Parts*, edited by Anthony Robinson et al. 1977–1980, part 166

Buell, T.B., *Master of Sea Power: A Biography of Fleet Admiral Ernest J. King*, Annapolis, MD: Naval Institute Press, 1980

Charlton, P., *War Against Japan 1941–1942*, Sydney: Time-Life Books, 1988

Cleworth, J.R., *The Fabulous Catalina*, self-published, 2006

Cleworth, J.R., *The Night Shift*, Hill Top: Highland Lodge Farmstay, 2015

Collins, L. & Reed, W., *Plunging Point: Intelligence Failures, Cover-ups and Consequences*, Pymble: HarperCollins Publishers, 2005

Creed, R., *PBY: The Catalina Flying Boat*, Annapolis, MD: Naval Institute Press, 1985

Dull, P.S., *A Battle History of the Imperial Japanese Navy (1941–1945)*, Annapolis, MD: Naval Institute Press, 1978

Encyclopaedia Britannica, Macropaedia, vol. 15, 1982

Encyclopaedia Britannica, vol. 15, 1962

Freeman, B.S.W., *Lake Boga at War*, Swan Hill: Catalina Publications, 1995

Gailey, H.A., *MacArthur Strikes Back: Decision at Buna, New Guinea, 1942–1943*, Novato, CA: Presidio Press, 2000

Gallaway, J., *The Odd Couple: Blamey and MacArthur at War*, St Lucia: University of Queensland Press, 2000

Gaunt, C. & Cleworth J.R., *Cats at War: The Story of RAAF Catalinas in the Asia-Pacific Theatre of War*, self-published, 2000

Gillison, D., *Australia in the War of 1939–1945*, series 3, Air, vol. 1, *Royal Australian Air Force, 1939–1942*, Canberra: Australian War Memorial, 1962

Harris, A.T., *Bomber Offensive*, London: Collins, 1947

Hasluck, P., *The Government and the People, 1939–1941*, Canberra: Australian War Memorial, 1965 (reprint)

Hasluck, P., *The Government and the People, 1942–1945*, Canberra: Australian War Memorial, 1970

Hendrie, A., *Flying Cats: The Catalina Aircraft in World War II*, Shrewsbury: Airlife, 1988

Hinge, A., 'Planting a "War Garden": On Use of Naval Minefields', *Journal of the Australian Naval Institute*, 1994, vol. 20, no. 3, pp. 35–46

Honan, R.F., *That's That: Memoirs of Wartime Service 1939–1945*, self-published, 1989

Horner, D.M., 'Curtin and MacArthur at War', *Wartime*, 1998, no. 2, pp. 34–40

Ishimaru, T., *Japan Must Fight Britain*, trans. G.V. Rayment, London: Hurst & Blackett, 1936

Joint Army–Navy Assessment Committee (JANAC), *Japanese Naval and Merchant Shipping Loss during World War II by All Causes*, Washington, DC: US Government Printing Office, 1947

Kenney, G.C., *General Kenney Reports: A Personal History of the Pacific War*, New York, NY: Duell, Sloan and Pearce, 1949

Knott, R.C., *Black Cat Raiders of WWII*, Annapolis, MD: Naval Institute Press, 1982

Leighton, R.M. & Coakley, R.W., *Global Logistics and Strategy: 1940–1943, The US Army in World War II*, Washington, DC: Office of the Chief of Military History (United States Army), 1955

Manchester, W., *American Caesar: Douglas MacArthur 1880–1964*, Boston, MA: Little, Brown and Company, 1978

McCarthy, D., *Australia in the War of 1939–1945*, series 1, Army, vol. 5, *South-West Pacific Area—First Year: Kokoda to Wau*, Canberra: Australian War Memorial, 1959

McQueen, H., 'Power in the Pacific', *The Independent Monthly*, November 1991.

Mellor, D.P., *Australia in the War of 1939–1945*, series 4, Civil, vol. 5, *The Role of Science and Industry*, Canberra: Australian War Memorial, 1958

Miller, A.R., *Minelaying Operations of the RAAF, 22 April 1943 to 30 April 1944*, Report Nos BR.2 and BR.8, OR Section HQ RAAF Command, Allied Air Forces, SWPA, 1945

Mine Warfare Reports, US 7th Fleet, 1943–1945

Minty, A.E., *Black Cats*, Point Cook: RAAF Museum, 2001

Morison, S.E., *History of United States Naval Operations in World War II*, Boston, MA: Little, Brown and Company, 1947–62

Odgers, G., *Australia in the War of 1939–1945*, series 3, Air, vol. 2, *Air War Against Japan, 1943–1945*, Canberra: Australian War Memorial, 1957

Odgers, G., *Air Force Australia*, Brookvale: National Book Distributors, 1993

Page, T., Pettee, G.S. & Wallace, W.A., 'Ellis A. Johnson, 1906–1973', *Operations Research*, 1974, vol. 22, no. 6, pp. 1141–55

Potter, E.B., *Nimitz*, Annapolis, MD: Naval Institute Press, 1976

Potter, E.B., *Bull Halsey*, Annapolis, MD: Naval Institute Press, 1985

Prados, J., *Combined Fleet Decoded: The Secret History of American Intelligence and the Japanese Navy in World War II*, Annapolis, MD: Naval Institute Press, 1995

Sallagar, F.M., *Lessons from an Aerial Mining Campaign (Operation 'Starvation')*, Santa Monica, CA: Rand, 1974

Saward, D., *'Bomber' Harris: The Authorised Biography*, London: Cassell, 1984

Scott, E., *Australia During the War*, vol. XI, Sydney: Angus & Robertson, 1943

Stanley, P., 'The Invasion That Wasn't', *Wartime*, 2002, no. 19, pp. 6–8

Sunderman, J.F., *World War II in the Air: The Pacific*. New York, NY: Watts, 1962

United States Army Air Force (USAAF), *Mission Accomplished*, National Archives (USA), 1946

United States Strategic Bombing Survey, The (*USSBS*)*—The Offensive Mine-laying Campaign against Japan*, Washington, DC: US Government Printing Office, 1946

US Technical Mission to Japan, *Ships and Related Targets—Japanese Minesweeping Gear and Equipment: Intelligence Targets Japan*, Washington, DC: Office of the Director of National Intelligence (DNI), 4 September 1945

Vincent, D., *Catalina Chronicle: A History of RAAF Operations*, Adelaide: The Catalina National Committee, 1981

Wigmore, L., *Australia in the War of 1939–1945*, series 1, Army, vol. 4, *The Japanese Thrust*, Canberra: Australian War Memorial, 1957

Websites

All websites accessed between September 2017 and January 2019

Air Force Association—raafa.org.au

Australian Dictionary of Biography—adb.anu.edu.au
Australian War Memorial—awm.gov.au
Aviation History Online Museum, The—aviation-history.com
Black Cats—daveswarbirds.com/blackcat
Catalina Flying Memorial—catalinaflying.org.au
Dark History—ghb67.wordpress.com
Extracts and Summaries of the *USSBS* 15 August 1945—usaaf.net/surveys/pto/pbs1.htm
History Channel—history.com
History on the Net—historyonthenet.com
History Place, The—historyplace.com
HistoryNet—historynet.com
Iwo Jima—iwojima.com
Kokoda Historical—kokodahistorical.com.au
Military History Encyclopedia on the Web—historyofwar.org
Military History Visualized (YouTube channel)—youtube.com/channel/UCK09g6gYGMvU-0x1VCF1hgA
Rathmines Catalina Memorial Park Association—rathmines-catalina.com
Trove—trove.nla.gov.au
U.S. Army Center of Military History—history.army.mil
Warfare History Network—warfarehistorynetwork.com
Wikipedia—en.wikipedia.org
World War II Database—ww2db.com

Other

Black Knights, documentary produced by Jeremy Linton Mann, Wingco Pictures
Letter from Herb Booker to Jeff Booker, 3 March 2002
Letters from Reg Cleworth to his family, March 1943 to February 1945

INDEX